Von Ripper's Odyssey

Sian Mackay spent several years in Egypt and the USA before returning to her native Scotland, where she worked as a free-lance journalist with *The Glasgow Herald* and *Times Educational Supplement*, founded Moubray House Publishing and wrote several highly praised non-fiction books. Later, she divided her time between Scotland and Spain, where she contributed to English-language publications and began to write fiction. The genre of her most recent books has been biography. She lives and works in Edinburgh.

Also by Sian Mackay

FICTION
The House on the Chine: Robert Louis Stevenson at Skerryvore
Rafael's Wings
The Verdict of the Double-Six and other short stories

NON-FICTION (as Sheila Mackay)
Early Scottish Gardens: A Writer's Odyssey
Behind the Façade: Four Centuries of Scottish Interiors
Mountain Music: Mallorca
Lindisfarne Landscapes
The Forth Bridge: A Picture History

VON RIPPER'S ODYSSEY

War, Resistance, Art and Love

SIAN MACKAY

Sancho
Press

First published in 2016 by:
Thistle Publishing, London

This edition published in 2017 by:
Sancho Press, Edinburgh

Cover image: *Salzkammergut-Landschaft* (1951) by Rudolph von Ripper

Supported by grants from the Scottish Arts Council and Yaddo, USA.

We have art in order not to die from the truth
Friedrich Nietzsche

Histories never die but go on living in their consequences
Henry James

CONTENTS

PROLOGUE

O ne day towards the end of the twentieth century, a
telephone call at my Palma apartment would alter the
course of the years to come. An acquaintance was on the
line inviting me to take a look at a file containing letters and
photographs from the 1950s. At the time, I was researching
the lives of prominent Europeans who had been visitors
or exiles to the Spanish island of Mallorca. Georges Sand,
Frederic Chopin, the Austrian Archduke Louis Salvador and
Robert Graves were names on my list, and, as my informant
knew, I was always on the lookout for others.

She lived in a town on the foothills of the Sierra de
Tramuntana where I found her house set in a garden of fig,
pomegranate and olive trees at the top of a steep incline.
It was autumn in Mallorca, the ravishing time. The file lay
on the garden table, and I curbed my impatience to open it
whilst she brought out lunch and poured the wine. It was a
dog-eared blue cardboard file with elastic closures such as
you could buy in any island stationery shop at the time. By
way of distracting myself, I remarked on the bees swooning
on the purple fruits of the snaking fig tree overhead, and I
admired away to the east the distant opaline view of the bay
of Pollensa.

'I found the file over there,' she said, 'at an uninhabited
villa in Pollensa.'

We chatted until lunch was over and at last she opened the file. Carefully she set aside a sheaf of letters some written in an old German script, mysterious and flimsy on airmail paper, others in English. Then we sat side-by-side looking at photographs, mostly black and white, which spanned decades. Who were these people in the photographs, severe looking military men from another era, groups of smiling women wearing dirndls, on holiday perhaps, in the Alps? Who was the sophisticated couple, the suave man with the taller, beautifully groomed woman at his side? There they were again dressed to the nines at a 'swanky' evening party suggesting Hollywood movies of the 1950s.

What had my hostess been doing at an uninhabited villa, I wondered? And how did she discover the file?

'A few year ago I was scouting on behalf of a Scottish artist who intended to run painting holidays here in Mallorca,' she said. 'We were searching for a villa big enough to sleep a group, with at least one large room for a studio. Our budget was tight. We weren't looking for the cream of the crop, and one day I heard of an uninhabited villa near Pollensa that was up for rent.'

'If it had been uninhabited for some time, the rent might be lower?' I said.

'That's what we hoped, and I went to see it. Its spacious, light interior immediately struck me as the perfect base we'd been looking for and, although no one had lived there for a long time, a fresh lick of paint would soon revive it. I wandered into the garden where a small changing pavilion stood beside the swimming pool, covered with green algae and peppered with pine cones from the wood beyond it. The pool, too, could easily be cleaned up, I thought. The door to the pavilion was unlocked and I stepped into a time warp: dinner suits and evening gowns from a bygone age hung from a rail, party clothes mildewed and frayed with age. I couldn't believe my eyes, and my sense that I had entered a fairy story increased when a large spider ran across the bench and disappeared under the hems of the dresses. It was as if the spider had arrived to draw my attention to the pile of warped books lying there and, concealed among them, this blue file.

'Realising that the pavilion would have to be cleared of the clothes and books as a condition of my associates renting the villa, I opened the file. And, standing in that silent pavilion, I had a hunch that its contents might be important. Back home that evening, I couldn't get the mouldering clothes, the spider and the images I'd seen in the photographs out of my mind.

'The upshot was that my colleague was keen to rent the villa and I went back a second time. The estate agent agreed that Ca'n Cueg – 'The House of the Frogs' – needed some improvements. Apart from the occasional rental, it had been uninhabited for half-a-century, and, when he told me he'd send someone to bin the contents of the pavilion before we moved in, I made up my mind to rescue the file. I've looked through it many times since then, and discovered that it must have been abandoned along with the clothes in the pavilion when the villa was sold in the 1960s.'

'Abandoned by the previous owners?'

'Yes, they were Baron and Baroness Rudolph von Ripper, the couple in the photographs who bought Ca'n Cueg in the early 1950s. He was an Austrian artist, and although I'm not up on twentieth-century art, I took a couple of photographs of two strange murals inside the house.' She passed them to me, and the Modernist-style murals suggested that Rudolph von Ripper was far more than the lotus-eating socialite photographed at lavish parties. He was an accomplished artist.

The story haunted me, and I longed to know more. As I would discover, the blue file was too slim to tell the whole story of this Austrian aristocrat's life, but its contents hooked me in and I went on to track down further sources in Germany, Austria and the USA. Month after month, year after year, the wonder grew as I pieced together von Ripper's heroism in war and resistance, art and love. Rudolph 'Rip' von Ripper (1905–1960) was a soldier as well as an artist, acclaimed in Europe and America for both these roles during the first half of the twentieth century.

Throughout his life, he was a fierce opponent of tyranny in all its forms. I followed in his footsteps to the Oranienburg-Sachsenhausen concentration camp where he was tortured on account of his powerfully anti-fascist art, deemed 'degenerate' by the Third Reich. He recorded his terrible experiences with searing eloquence in his masterwork, a portfolio of Surrealist prints entitled *Écraser l'Infâme* ('To Crush Tyranny'). In flight from the Gestapo, Rip fled to America in 1938 where Picasso's New York dealer arranged exhibitions of his work. Guggenheim fellowships followed and *Time* magazine made him the toast of the town when its January 1939 cover was illustrated with one of the prints.

Clue by clue, I became immersed in his life and art. Baron Rudolph von Ripper lived – and loved – with brio throughout the great and tragic eras of a lifetime that spanned both world wars and he befriended many of its luminaries including Klaus Mann, Salvador Dalí, Ernest Hemingway, André Malraux and Benjamin Britten. I read newspaper articles about 'the Soldier with an Easel', and books by his friends in high places describing von Ripper's heroism. He became an American citizen and a highly decorated military hero of the Second World War when his astonishing feats included the capture of Hitler's favourite commando, Otto Skorzeny, in the Austrian Alps.

'The bravest man I ever saw,' said a top general. 'The kind they write books about,' wrote Ernie Pyle, the American war correspondent. Why then had history forgotten this heroic war artist?

Post-war, Rip became a CIA agent and lived with his second wife, Evelyn 'Avi' Leege, at Ca'n Cueg, their dream home in Mallorca. In the 1950s the island was being promoted internationally as a honeymooners' paradise. But Mallorca was also a safe haven for agents, spies and former Nazis and Rip realised the truth of his friend Gertrude Stein's remark, 'Mallorca is Paradise, if you can stand it,' when Otto Skorzeny moved into a villa nearby.

Rudolph von Ripper's Homeric odyssey makes thrilling reading, but in the course of writing this book my most cherished hope has been to restore his astonishing art to the twentieth-century canon.

Edinburgh 2016

INFERNO
1905–1938

CHAPTER ONE
THE STARTING PISTOL

In a crowded third-class railway carriage, a sixteen-year-old Austrian nobleman sits sketching the life around him: widows cradling infants, lovers, wounded soldiers and down-and-outs like himself. He has chosen a corner seat, a little apart from the others. No one would take him for an aristocrat in his latest disguise of peasant shirt, tweed waistcoat, moleskin trousers and heavy boots. A dark cotton cap conceals his need of the haircut he'll get when he earns some cash (he has heard that a coalmine near Duisburg is hiring men). No one takes a second glance at the youth whose large head is bent over his sketchpad, and who now and then looks up to capture through his good eye the faces that fascinate him most. The carriage rattles and the wheels on the tracks beat out a metallic accompaniment to Rudolf von Ripper's journey from Berlin. His knapsack contains cheese, bread, apples, basic drawing materials, his shaving kit, two books (Dante's *Divine Comedy* in Italian and a volume of Rimbaud's poems in French) and the few family photographs he succeeded in snatching prior to his hasty departure from Austria. When night falls and the carriage darkens, one by one his fellow passengers doze off, and, by the light of his torch Rudolf studies the photographs intently, as if they hold clues to his unknowable future. All that has befallen him since he left home (in a shameful rage) merges with his uneasy dreams.

There is a photograph of himself as a boy in his sailor suit, squinting into sharp sunlight that casts his shadow on the ground and on the whitewashed wall behind him. His stiff-backed Prussian father, Major General Eduard Maria Ritter von Ripper, is buttoned into his military greatcoat, and his sisters, Clara and Valerie, wear fur collars and muffs with their thick winter coats. And he thinks it curious, given his present predicament, that even then, when he must have been around nine years old, he chose to stand a little apart from his family, hands stuffed into his pockets. No one smiles. It is winter at Lemberg on the eve of the Great War. He remembers his father instructing them to look straight at the camera and not to move a muscle before the click of its shutter.

In another less formal photograph, he's wearing summer shorts and an oversized black beret that suggests the artist he longs to be. This time he's beaming into the camera, linking arms with his sisters and their friends, forgetting for a few moments the waves of ambivalences and contradictions that disturb his privileged existence. This scene might have been captured at Lemberg (now Lviv, Ukraine), Goerz (now Gorizia, Italy) or Klausenberg (now Cluj-Napoca, Romania.) No information is written on the back of the photograph. It was so long ago he can't remember where it was taken. Certainly, it must have been somewhere in the Crown lands, as the far-flung regions and principalities of the Austria-Hungary empire where his family had residences were called before the First World War.

Rudolf Karl Hugo von Ripper had been born on 29 January 1905 at Klausenberg, the provincial capital of the

Austria-Hungary Empire. On the night of his birth, Gustav Mahler's prophetic song cycle *Kindertotenlieder* ('Songs on the Death of Children') was performed for the first time in Vienna. The boy was practically a prince, with blue-blooded Catholic parents from the highest echelons of imperial society: Claire, Countess von Salis-Samaden, a Central European aristocrat, and Baron Eduard von Ripper, aide-de-camp to the previous Hapsburg emperor, Charles I. On account of Rudolf's father's high rank and responsibilities, the family frequently travelled vast distances to one or other of their imperial residences, and the child attended several Jesuit schools. These upheavals were both exciting and confusing to a privileged boy born in the Crown lands who had many strange provinces, customs, languages and climates to conjure with, and a complex history to grasp.

The dual Austria-Hungary Empire in which Rudolf was raised evolved after the *Ausgleich* or 'Compromise' of 1867 transformed the former Austrian and Hapsburg monarchies into a double-headed hybrid ruled over by Emperor Franz Joseph I. It incorporated many countries and ethnic groups: Czechs, Slovaks, Ukrainians, Slovenes, Poles, Croats, Serbs, Romanians and Italians, whose peoples collectively spoke at least eleven languages. When Rudolf was born, Franz Joseph was seventy-five years old and had ruled over these peoples for almost forty years. Would the sun never set upon the Empire his subjects wondered? Their eerie restlessness induced in them a collective sense of impending doom that preyed upon their stagnant country and crept into the avant-garde art and literature of the time. In *The Radetzky March* the novelist Joseph Roth (1894–1939) describes the pre-war Crown lands as tedious backwaters far removed from Vienna, stage sets for lonely young officers trapped in crumbling army barracks and mirthless small town bureaucrats whose lives sift away like sand in an hourglass. General von Ripper had charge of 'crumbling army barracks' near the Russian front, and, dressed in the uniform of a boy soldier, his only son, Rudolf, often accompanied him on tours of inspection.

In common with other aristocratic children, servants, nursemaids and tutors attended Rudolf and his sisters, and despite the boy's facial imperfections – a large head, a weak sideways-looking eye, buckteeth and lisping speech – his indomitable spirit charmed everyone. He was affectionately known as 'Rip'. The love that surrounded him was not in doubt but the divergent aims and influences of his heredity were hard for the youngster to reconcile. Even as Baron Eduard was schooling his son for the highest military office, his mother, 'Mutti', was nudging him down artistic paths and had him tutored in drawing and painting from the age of three. Stealthily, as he lived through each stage of child-hood, twin embryonic personas vied within his young soul. Sometimes when he visited military barracks with his father, he ardently wished to impress everyone he met with the notion that he would become a great soldier like his fore-bears. At other times, encouraged by his mother to capture scenes of the country life surrounding their estates, when Rip sat sketching or painting in the tranquillity of the studio or out in the landscape, he felt passionately drawn to art.

Despite the disruptions to family life, the family's frequent removals from place to place, Rip learned to ride, fence and handle a pistol under the watchful eye of his father. Rip's father was a man to be reckoned with; not a cruel man, but an autocrat devoted to his family at the same time as he wielded power in the imperial army. There were shoots on the family estates: wild boar, partridge, pheasant and everything else deemed suitable for the table.

Great weight was given to learning in Austrian aristocratic circles and, whether they found themselves in Klausenburg, Lemberg, Goerz or Salzburg, the von Ripper children's education continued under the Jesuits. They learned to speak several languages, to dance, practise music and art, and to read Goethe, Schiller and Dante as well as Greek, Russian, French and British classics in translation. Most of these leather-bound works could be found on the shelves of their father's extensive library: vermillion, brown, navy-blue and green leather bindings with gold tooling, each colour denoting the section of the library the books belonged to. There, young Rip was at liberty to absorb illustrations of the art of Renaissance Italy and the Dutch Masters. In this hushed place he could hunker down on a vast Oriental carpet representing a garden of earthly delights: pomegranates, orange and cypress trees, gazelles, and strange geometric formations that begged to be copied into his sketch books.

Rudolf von Ripper would have been familiar with a handsome seven-volume set titled *Die Balearen* (*The Balearic Islands*) in the 'Anthropology' section of the library. Perhaps his parents even put this lavish creation of the Archduke Louis Salvador (1847–1915) into his hands. After all, as courtiers, the Baron and Countess were near contemporaries of the Archduke whose escapades they had followed with a mixture of disapproval and admiration. Louis Salvador had been a controversial figure at court since, despite the fact that he was second in line to succeed Emperor Franz Joseph, he had abandoned his glittering Hapsburg inheritance in favour of the primitive island of Mallorca. *Die Balearen* was his labour of love, his homage to the Balearic Islands: several volumes published in Leipzig between 1869 and 1884 and bound in navy-blue leather tooled with gold.

This masterpiece of anthropology, geography and art was illustrated with Louis Salvador's own accomplished drawings of the islands Mallorca, Menorca, Ibiza and Formentera. Islands scarcely bigger than dots on the spinning globe on Rip's father's library desk, dots in the Mediterranean Sea, roughly halfway between Barcelona and North Africa.

The boy absorbed feisty images from *Die Balearen* to mingle with his dreams: strange rock formations, caves, mountain villages, olive groves and sea inlets haunted by pirates. He learned how to pronounce the name Mallorca, the largest of the Balearic Islands – 'Ma-yorka' – and that it meant 'great whale'. He longed to explore this magical island, and, like Louis Salvador, one day he would. But first, he had to live through his troubled childhood and the ensuing years when he, like the Archduke, would become a wanderer.

General von Ripper and his family were often summoned to Vienna to participate in affairs of state. Stefan Zweig's novella *Fantastic Night* unfolds there on the eve of the First World War when 'the mellow and sensuous city of Vienna … excels like no other in bringing leisurely strolls, idle observation and the cultivation of elegance to a peak of positively artistic perfection, a purpose in life of itself …'

The capital of the Austria-Hungary Empire was a startling contrast to the Crown lands at the beginning of the twentieth-century, and there Rudolf von Ripper encountered another of his personas: not his soldier self and not the artist, but the stiffly dressed courtier to whom others were obliged to show obeisance. He was still too young and too protected to realise that, even as Emperor Franz Joseph showed himself daily in his state coach travelling between his Schönbrunn and Hofburg Palaces, radical intellectuals were plotting to put an end to the old man's monotonous reign. In the minds of the geniuses – and evil genies – scheming in the salons and coffee houses of Vienna in the first fourteen years of the twentieth century, a shockingly new, modern world was being invented. Later, Rudolf von Ripper would piece together their faces in an astonishing jigsaw puzzle depicting the *weltanschauung* of the times. Joseph Stalin was in Vienna writing a communist pamphlet; Leon Trotsky had crossed the Russian border near Lemberg and travelled on to Vienna where he had been living for seven years; Adolph Hitler (1889–1945) a bearded, long-haired down-and-out, was living in seedy hostels and hawking recherché watercolours on the streets of the capital. People noticed him wearing a rubberized yellow cycling cape without a vest underneath, sweating in the summer heat and stinking horribly. The mentally disturbed would-be artist haunted the city like a ghost, excluded from the company of Vienna's respected writers and artists whose names and achievements would shape the twentieth century: Rilke, Kafka, Roth, Musil, Zweig, Mahler, Schoenberg, Webern, Berg, Schiele, Klimt, Kokoschka and Wittgenstein.

In this extraordinary era, within apartments overlooking a leafy Viennese courtyard, Sigmund Freud was probing the human subconscious. The Austrian doctor had realised that the suppressed neuroses embodied in his patients mirrored the starchy, pompous regime that ruled them. Stefan Zweig (1881–1942) belonged to a wealthy Viennese-Jewish family and he, too, described in his novels the sexual mores pullulating behind the façade of the fashionable society he knew so well. Zweig's characters are out of touch with reality, trapped in the neuroses Freud wrote about. The protagonist of *Fantastic Night* is a cryptically named Baron von R..., a wealthy aristocrat who wears faultlessly correct suits of

English tailoring and a pearl in his cravat. Is it mere coincidence that Zweig's fictional soldier Baron von R... bears uncanny similarities, not only in his abbreviated name, to Rudolf's father, Baron von Ripper? He was 'a figure in high society ... acquainted with the most distinguished figures of a city with a population of millions,' – yet who has lost the ability to feel human emotions – 'a cogwheel performing its silent function in the great machine that coldly drives its pistons, circling vainly round itself.' Baron R... realises that he must embrace 'low-life', 'the dregs of humanity' in Vienna in order to rediscover his own humanity before returning to his military base in the Crown Lands. At Rawaruska near Lemberg, he dies fighting with a regiment of Austrian dragoons in 1914, the year that changed everything.

Rip had turned nine that hot summer when the Schönbrunn and Hofburg Palaces were veiled as if with the sleep of the old emperor who ruled them with his shaky hand. As was traditional, the military might of the empire had been given leave to bring in the harvests and, in the far-flung backwaters a day's train journey from Vienna, the von Ripper family would have been on holiday. Liberated from the classroom on the morning of 28 June, Rip was free to run wild through the fields and woods of the family estate and to help the soldiers and country folk to bring in the harvest.

On that same June morning, the elderly Archduke Louis Salvador was asleep in a hotel room in Trieste whilst his cousin, the heir apparent, Franz Ferdinand, and Sophie his wife, were on a duty visit to Sarajevo, the capital of Bosnia and Herzegovina. (In all probability, Louis Salvador had not given his cousin's itinerary second thought, as many others had: why on earth had Ferdinand been sent to direct the manoeuvres of the Austrian Army Corps stationed in the province on a Balkan national holiday? By anyone's reckoning, that was a supremely insensitive and ill-judged move.) The day was sunny and the royal car open-topped as it processed through central Sarajevo. Even after a grenade attack on the motorcade the warning was ignored, and the chauffeur went on to take a wrong turning into a street with no exit. Just as he was backing out of Francis Joseph Strasse, a nineteen-year-old student, Gavrilo Prinzip, stepped up to the car and raised a handgun to shoot Franz Ferdinand in the throat and Sophie in the abdomen.

Louis Salvador woke from his uneasy sleep towards lunchtime as the unwilling heir presumptive to Emperor Franz Joseph, and far away the Crown lands young Rudolf von Ripper froze like a hare in a stubble field sensing the presence of hunters.

He sped back to the manor house where his father took Rip aside to explain why Austria must avenge the double murder. It is unlikely, though, that the Baron spelled out to his son the fact that, while the 1878 Treaty of Berlin had authorised Austria-Hungary to hold and occupy the two provinces of Bosnia and Herzegovina, in 1908 Vienna had tyrannically and illegally annexed them into the empire. This was the gripe of Prinzip and the Serbian Black Hand Nationalists who had condoned the assassinations. As it was, like most Europeans, Rip soon became familiar with a photograph rapidly circulating via the international press showing angry anarchists hanging back and imperial guards seizing Prinzip. He would have seen another photograph, too, of Franz Ferdinand's blood-stained tunic holed with bullets. The tunic had been stripped off the regal body and transferred with the trousers and feathered bush hat by rail to Vienna.

General von Ripper set out for the capital where thousands queued to see Ferdinand's gruesome tunic, trousers and hat, displayed in a black-framed reliquary. Now the empire was truly doomed, and the citizens' baroque display of grief was more to do with their fears for the future of the Empire than for this death. After all, few people had really known or cared about the ineffectual Franz Ferdinand. As soon as Rip's father departed, a hush descended on the von Ripper estates and throughout Europe. The powers of the Empire, and of Germany, France, Russia and Great Britain went behind closed doors to deliberate how to respond to the crisis. God forbid that the upstart Prinzip's shot had been the starting pistol for a European war. How would Austria-Hungary respond? Would Russia support her friends in the Balkans?

'Above the ebullient glasses from which we drank, invisible Death was already crossing his bony hand,' observed novelist Joseph Roth.

For almost a month, harvesting continued as if nothing had happened. To young Rudolf, the hiatus must have felt doom laden. No drama in his life so far remotely matched this, the central drama of his childhood, a drama in which the father he looked up to with a mixture of love and awe had abandoned his family to defend the Empire. It was as if the father had been summoned to Mount Olympus, leaving the son to conjure up shadowy Black Hand gang members hiding out in the fields and woods of the family estate.

The lull seemed endless before all Europe swung into action. With the crucial support of Germany, Austria-Hungary waged war on Serbia. Newspaper boys ran through city streets crying *War Declared!* At the end of July, Russia went into full mobilization in support of the Serbs, and the following day Germany declared war on Russia. In August a reluctant Britain entered the fray for similar reasons as it had fought Napoleon and would soon fight Hitler. A driving aim of its foreign policy was to maintain the balance of power in Europe and, crucially, to keep the Belgian coast out of hostile hands daring to contemplate a naval attack on the British coast. David Lloyd George, the British Chancellor of the Exchequer, expressed the dismay of most Europeans when he wrote, 'I felt like a man standing on a planet that had been suddenly wrenched from its orbit by a demoniacal hand, and was spinning wildly into the unknown.'

Newspapers delivered to the von Ripper household chronicled the ongoing disaster with images taken in Serbia, Bosnia and Albania: thousands of displaced individuals and families attempting to escape the carnage by oxcart along dusty country roads, or on foot, dragging bundles, even a half-dead horse, through drifting snow. In his novel *The Eyewitness*, Ernst Weiss wrote 'at one blow there was no longer a Europe. Boundaries were sealed, and blood flowed all over in the North, in the East, in the South, in the West.' General von Ripper set off to direct troop manoeuvres at the Russian front, and Rudolf von Ripper's childhood was irrevocably shattered.

The life-loving, mischievous boy became rebellious and angry. Time after time he ran away from home and had to be fetched back in a temper. He ran away from the Borromäum, a privileged private secondary school of the Archdiocese of Salzburg. No doubt Mutti empathized with her son's torment over the safety of his father who faced grave danger at the front, nevertheless she presided over her children with a firm hand. Doubtless, the Countess longed to turn back the clock to the previous summer when her son had run free in the fields and woods of the Crown lands. As it was, the family had to make do with occasional reappearances of the careworn General when he returned home on short leaves.

It was an era so bewildering that, at the same time as the flower of the empire's manhood was being annihilated on the battlefields of Eastern Europe, in Vienna and Salzburg society balls and café-life continued much as usual, even after the death of Emperor Franz Joseph in 1916. Young as he was, society's pretence that nothing was amiss impacted profoundly on Rudolf von Ripper's sensibility. Again and again, in his future artwork he would portray society dames dressed to the nines and partying amidst the horrors of battlefields and prison camps. The cover illustration of his masterwork *Écraser l'Infâme* ('To Crush Tyranny', editioned in 1938) would be illustrated with an image of the agony of Christ above whose tormented face and crown of thorns fools partner crinolined women in a frenzied dance. Franz Lehar's box office hit of the day *The Merry Widow* (1907) might have been Rip's deeply ironic choice for the music they dance to: *Vienna, city of dreams and sparkling wine* ... As if waltzing could reinstate the old order.

Another drawing from *Écraser l'Infâme*, 'The Human Heart', depicts a child of the times tugging at the cloak of a big shot wearing imperial garb, powdered wig and bicorn hat. Rip, the artist, identifies with the child who is desperate to elicit a human response from this chilling figure, a thinly disguised agent of death, whose skeleton is visible beneath his cloak, whose face is hidden behind a sardonical mask and whose heart is but a surreal decoration pinned onto his cloak. In a background vignette, reminiscent of Masaccio's Adam and Eve in 'Expulsion from Paradise', Rudolf von Ripper depicts an agonised, naked couple wandering in search of the spiritual nourishment the innocent child fails to find. Horses and a sailing ship fleeing the scene antici-pate the mass exodus of terrified citizens from Nazi held territories during the 1930s.

After General von Ripper's death from cancer and wounds sustained at the Russian front in 1918, Rudolf succeeded him as Baron von Ripper. 1918 was a momentous year of deaths and geopolitical finales: Gavrilo Prinzip died of bone tuberculosis in the Theresienstadt casemates where he had been incarcerated since his sentence; the artists, Gustav Klimt and Egon Schiele, died in the influenza pandemic that ravaged Europe and much of the world; the Wilhelmine period of German history ended with the abdication of Kaiser Wilhelm II, after Austria-Hungary had been defeated in the final battle of the war in Italy and the Weimar Republic wriggled into being. Rudolf von Ripper had been raised to personify old Austria, yet, by the age of thirteen he had lived through the demise of the Empire, a transition so violent that its repercussions would shape the entire course of his life.

Meanwhile, in the vacuum at the end of the war, the young Baron identified with the role his father had played as head of the household. His inbred sense of *noblesse oblige* and teenaged machismo encouraged him to declare his intention to rule the roost from now on. But the highly educated, resolute Countess wouldn't hear of it – he was far too young, she said – and, humiliated and rebuffed, Rip struggled to resolve his confusion. He loved his mother and would come to understand her resistance, but he felt so unsure of his role in his father's absence that he ran away to try out a tame version of soldiering. He had heard that he might put on Austrian uniform and join a mounted patrol guarding an ammunition store at the Schloss Mirabel in Salzburg. For several weeks his recently widowed mother had no idea where he was until, quite by chance, on a duty visit to the castle she encountered her son in an office corridor. Surely there were tears on both sides at their reunion. Mutti had a photograph taken of Rip mounted on a white pony and wearing Austrian uniform for the first – and last – time, and persuaded him to return home.

Perhaps Rudolf von Ripper might assert his authority over the family now? But no, it was back to dull instruction by his Jesuit tutors, and drawing and painting lessons with Artistin Behrens and Elfriede Mayr, artists steeped in German Expressionism. Confused by the Janus of imperialism and subservience and all the other discords of his life, the teenager contemplated running away again but his mother intervened, boarded him at a monastery and urged him to consider becoming a priest. The daily rhythms of religious life soon bored him, and boredom was intolerable to the boy from the tedious backwaters of the Crown lands. Rudolf von Ripper was intelligent and he was tuned into the *zeitgeist*. What was he to do now that the war had limited his options? It was no longer possible to pursue the military career his father had trained him for, fighting with an elite unit in Germany or Austria. Sometimes when he looked into the mirror of his soul, glimpses of his artist self gave him hope. Perhaps he might find consolation in art? Not the outworn art of Behrens and Mayr, but the art of the new world he intended to discover in Germany. He understood that the world he had been born into had vanished forever, except in the minds of the nostalgic older generation, and novelists.

The former empire was now a republic; the victors had carved up Austria-Hungary, re-established countries and enlarged and diminished others – and the economy was in ruins. Between fifteen and eighteen million souls were dead on both sides, thousands more were war wounded, there were unnumbered psychiatric casualties and thousands of half-starved widows and orphans. Two years after the Treaty of Versailles had been signed in the Hall of Mirrors (1919), sixteen-year-old Rip left his desecrated homeland.

His hunger for adventure and autonomy led him to Innsbruck where he hitched a ride across the border into Germany with a travelling theatre troupe. They progressed from town to town in brightly painted horse drawn wagons, stopping for a few nights here and there to set up their Spiegel tent at country fairs. Constructed from wood, mirrors, canvas and stained glass, with booths lined in velvet and brocade, the tent was a magical container for the young aristocrat's dreams. Rudolf von Ripper's defection set the stage for the rest of his life. It was, as he put it, 'the beginning of a turbulent existence with many painful, but few dull moments.'

CHAPTER TWO
EVERYTHING MAGICALLY
ATTRACTS

Rip left the theatre troupe when it arrived in the German city of Thuringia where a job at a sawmill saved him from the streets. He was too proud – and too shamefaced by his defection – to ask his mother for money. Besides, he was enjoying his adventures, and when a circus came to town he jumped on the bandwagon, unable to resist the allure of a vibrant world filled with movement, colour and fun. The teenaged baron was adept as a chameleon at transforming himself to fit any circumstance, and he happily reinvented himself as a member of the circus. He worked as a barker and, disguised as a clown, discovered a talent for comedy in the ring. Eagerly he learned new tricks, such as grinding a drinking glass with his teeth and swallowing it, a party trick he would perform for eager audiences in years to come. Rip progressed northwards with the circus in the direction of Berlin. With his sketchbook always to hand he drew the characters and dramas of the circus and all went well until he fell in love. The object of his affection was a pretty acrobat, the mistress of one of the toughest troupers in the Big Top who discovered Rip's flirtation and threw him out.

It was a chastening experience, and, alone again, Rudolf von Ripper arrived in Berlin where he rented a furnished room in a working class area. He was one among thousands of refugees flocking to the capital of Prussia from devastated far-flung provinces and cities in the vacuum after the war. Displaced from the suffocating conventions and deprivations of provincial life the émigrés gawped, as Rip must have done, at the spectacle of automobiles, elevated railways and neon lights, and brilliant shows of wealth and invention that were on display in emporia such as Wertheim's Department Store. Foreigners, too, had been drawn to Berlin, Ernest Hemingway among them, who was recovering from war wounds sustained in Italy in 1918 and writing *A Farewell to Arms*. Fictional characters that would fire twentieth century imaginations were born in the pages of books written in Berlin by Thomas Wolfe, Stephen Spender, Christopher Isherwood, Vladimir Nabokov and all the others.

Nothing could frustrate the young baron's thirst to gain knowledge of the world and the people who lived in it. He had the confidence to open any door he chose, and his cultural interests propelled him towards the bars and studios of the city's artists and foreign colony. He became acquainted with Ernest Hemingway who would become a lifelong friend and drinking companion after he re-encountered the American during the Spanish Civil War. Klaus Mann (1906–1949) and Erich Mühsam (1878–1934) frequented Berlin and would become significant players in Rip's life. Mühsam had been educated at the same Katherineum School in Lübeck as Klaus's father, Thomas Mann, and his uncle, Heinrich Mann. In the 1920s, they belonged to a group of radical German writers that included Wilhelm Herzog, Frank Wedekind and Lion Feuchtwanger. Erich Mühsam was the son of Siegfried Mühsam, a conservatively Jewish and uncompromisingly

Prussian pharmacist in the town of Lübeck, whose inhumane strictness behind the closed doors of the family home bred in young Erich a hatred of authority. Heinrich Mann had opposed the First World War (even as his brother Thomas was sending off newspaper articles defending it) and his novels fuelled Erich Mühsam's path to prominence as an anarchist poet, essayist and playwright. In 1918, Heinrich Mann's novel *Der Untertan* (*The Man of Straw*) had struck a chord with bewildered readers desperate to understand the grim recent past and sold an astonishing 80,000 copies the week it was published. The novel portrays the life of Diederich Hessling, a nationalist and fanatical admirer of Kaiser Wilhelm II who is unthinkingly obedient to authority and maintains a rigid dedication to the goals of the German state. After Heinrich Mann's *Macht und Mensch* (*Power and People*) appeared the following year, Müsham was inspired to organise anti-fascist demonstrations that resulted in his imprisonment as an activist. Albert Einstein and Kurt Tucholsky, one of the most important journalists of the Weimar Republic, were among the intellectuals and artists who campaigned for Mühsam's release.

Meanwhile Adolph Hitler had put aside his paints, slunk out of his men's hostel in Vienna and joined the German Worker's Party, the short-lived predecessor of the National Socialist German Workers' Party, or Nazi party. In the economic downturn of the 1920s, ideologies, parties and factions scrambled for supremacy in speeches and mass demonstrations that were swiftly followed by arrests and assassinations by the *Sturmabteilung*, or SA. The SA's dark origins were rooted in the specialized assault troops Imperial Germany had employed during the First World War. It functioned as the paramilitary wing of the National Socialist Party, and played a key role in Adolph Hitler's astonishing rise to power. Its militiamen wore grey jackets, brown shirts (a bulk purchase from the German Army that had been intended for soldiers in Africa), swastika armbands, ski-caps, knee breeches, thick woollen socks and combat boots. Accompanied by bands of musicians and carrying swastika flags, they goose-stepped in jackboots with ominous intent through the streets of Berlin. The spectacle impacted on Rudolf von Ripper who watched the parades and heard the speeches with foreboding and disbelief. More than any other item in Hitler's bag of tricks, his skill as an orator would sweep him power as leader of the Nazi Party. At last, the outcast had hit on a way to draw attention to himself. At the end of marches Hitler (who had designed the swastika emblem) bellowed out aggressive speeches, cunningly crafted to encourage acts of violence against left-wing political opponents.

For all his savoir-faire Rip was a mere fledgling, flitting between the interstices of his nomadic existence and celebrating the fact that youth alone had saved him from annihilation on the battlefronts of the recent war. He had come to understand that Gavrilo Prinzip's action had been prompted by a just cause. Prinzip had been a freedom fighter resisting the tyrannical take-over of his country and Rudolf von Ripper vowed that, whenever he encountered circumstances that merited just action, he would do the same. In the years between the assassination of Franz Ferdinand and his own flight into freedom with the circus he had shaped his credo: he hated tyranny even more than war. And there was no mistaking the tyrant in Adolph Hitler, surrounded by his tin soldiers.

Amidst such dramas, Rip's worldview was enlarged by glimpses of human struggle and valour on Berlin's pavements. At street corners, the tattered destitute and war

21

maimed stood side by side selling shoelaces, matches, a pile of cucumbers, shoes they could not afford to mend, anything they could dig up to assist their survival. Here, among the dregs of the city, mixing with soldiers, servant girls and down-and-outs, like Stefan Zweig's fictional Baron von R… Rip's hot young blood was 'seething in this swirling, hot and human mass … everything vulgar, common and plebeian magically attracted.' Far from the gaze of Mutti and his traumatised homeland he embraced his rite de passage into manhood. Like Franz Kafka before him, he would have investigated the red-light district where 'whole networks of streets were opened up under the auspices of prostitution,' as the German-Jewish writer and philosopher, Walter Benjamin (1892–1940) observed in *A Berlin Chronicle*.

Aware that his generation was remaking the world a fairer and freer place to prevent the horrors of war from happening again – surely Adolph Hitler was a mere fly-by-night? – Rip lived life to the full. He savoured his association with the avant-garde artists and intellectuals of Düsseldorf, Bonn and Berlin. In the atmosphere of post-war Berlin, art had to be both radical and political and a young, idealistic artist could only go left of the Weimar government. Although Rip was poverty stricken, he was determined to train as an artist, and, when he heard that a Rhineland coalmine near the esteemed Düsseldorf art school was hiring men, he jumped on a train with hope in his heart. At the Duisburg mine he laboured as a carpenter's apprentice and spent his wages on art materials with an eye to enrolling at Düsseldorf Academy of Arts. The stairway of the main entrance was engraved with words Rudolf von Ripper liked the sound of: *Für unsere Studenten nur das Beste* ('For our Students only the Best'.)

At the Duisburg mine life was raw as the pages of Emile Zola's novel, *Germinal*, and Rip's drawings, tinged with subterranean coal-blackness, were strong enough to gain him admission to the Academy. When, in his euphoria, he painted pink nipples on the busts of the statues in the Main Hall, he won the devotion of his fellow students with backslaps and rounds of beer. He befriended the First World War artist, Otto Dix, who was also training there. The mine at night, the Academy by day – this became Rip's routine until his drawings impressed a wealthy patron who commissioned him to produce wallpaper designs. With money in his pocket Rudolf von Ripper was able to say goodbye to his coalmine friends and embark on the first crucial phase of his artistic development. To the scenes he had mentally stored of the demise of the Empire, he added eyewitness images of the marginalized lives of the theatre troupe and the circus people, as well as the poverty and misery of the working people of Berlin. All he had experienced since he left Austria would be processed in extraordinary detail later, but his immediate focus was to acquire the technical skills he needed to shape his language as an artist.

It was a revolutionary time for all the arts. In an inspired riposte to German Expressionism (a genre soon to be approved by the Nazi Party) the architect, Walter Gropius, had founded Bauhaus Schools in Weimar and Dessau with the idea of creating a 'total art' through which all the arts, including architecture, would eventually be brought together. Bauhaus style became one of the most influential currents in German Modernism and profoundly influenced developments in art, architecture, graphic design, interior design, industrial design and typography. Artists calling themselves Dadaists attacked the Expressionists' ineffectual political compromises in response to the war. So did the *Neue Sachlichkeit* (New Objectivity) painters in Germany in the 1920s whose leader, the Surrealist Giorgio de Chirico, Rudolf von Ripper would pay homage to in his future work. Films coming out of the German studios, notably UFA Berlin, contained important implications for painting that were underlined by Lazlo Moholy-Nagy in his book on documentary film making: *Painting, Photography, Film* (1925). These films energized the artists of Rudolf von Ripper's generation with their distortions and enlargements of reality, close-ups, slow motion, superimpositions, fades and dissolves. The techniques of what became known as film noir gradually slipped into Rip's work and shaped his language as an artist during the next decade when he frequented both Berlin and Paris and became familiar with the work of every important artist in both cities.

Meanwhile, sexual gratification was easy to find at art school – but Rip was a sensitive as well as a sensuous young man, searching for a deeper experience. With uncharacteristic reticence, he never revealed more than scant details of a passionate affair he had at this time that impacted upon him with the *Sturm und Drang* of a Brechtian drama. Just as he had been forced to flee the circus after his ill-judged attentions to the pretty acrobat, this time 'a romantic attachment to a worldly-wise Fraulein who did me wrong' as he put it, led to his swift departure from Berlin. Had he made her pregnant? Did she, like the circus acrobat, have a minder who chased him off the scene? *Oh, the shark had pretty teeth, dear* … the details are never likely to be known, but the episode is telling. Rudolf von Ripper was an adventurer, not only in life but also in love.

Countess von Salis-Samaden longed for her son's return to Salzburg and forgave him his defection two years earlier. He was young and, beneath his impatience and angry outbursts, she knew his 'loving heart [was] filled with good intentions', as she wrote later. When he visited her in 1923, she tried to persuade him to stay in Austria. Rip was eighteen-years-old, he had come of age and now he could rightfully claim his position as head of the family and its concerns. But the moment had passed. His training at Düsseldorf and all his other experiences had turned the rebellious teenager into a serious artist. He was ambitious to make his mark, and that wasn't likely to happen in Austria. In the aftermath of the First World War the Austrian art world had fallen into decline. Hardship was widespread among artists, and although some of the avant-garde still exhibited in Germany and Switzerland, Austrian artists had to struggle to maintain contact with prominent figures of the European avant-garde who had supported the annual Vienna Secession and whose first president in 1897 had been Gustav Klimt.

Rip had his sights set on Paris, the cultural capital of Europe, and, as had happened in Berlin, his talent and pedigree opened the doors of the *haute-monde* as well as the ateliers of Montparnasse. Paris was awash with European aristocrats such as the Duke of Verdura, a jewellery designer who arrived with an introduction to Coco Chanel from her friend Cole Porter whose upbeat American songs were the hits of the era. Like Baron von Ripper, Verdura (the novelist Giuseppe Lampedusa's cousin) was a witty, multi-lingual, titled and single aristocrat who found himself in great demand at salons and dinners. He staged artistic costume balls that became all the rage and his unique sense of style, a playful blend of pageantry and nonconformity, was reflected in his jewellery designs. He captured perfectly the capricious spirit of the times in Chanel's Maltese cross bracelets that became the 'must have' accessory of society women on both sides of the Atlantic. Traditional jewellery design had been in transition in the 1920s when costume jewellery was invented, and anyone spending time with the dream team of Chanel and Verdura would have picked up a great deal about the business. The Catalan artist, Salvador Dalí, paced around them like Felix the Cat. Although some designs of the era still reflected the frigid beauty of a geometrical theorem, 'the great white silence' of diamonds, pearls and platinum was gradually being shattered by touches of colour. While stones such as emeralds, sapphires and rubies were still in demand, semi-precious stones were no longer scorned and were gaining favour with high society women. Avant-garde artists including Picasso, Matisse and Degas added jewellery to their portfolios, and Dalí would soon get in on the act with Surrealist Objects studded with gems which Verdura and Rip were summoned to guard during a spree in Rome in the 1950s when Rip himself had become a jewellery designer.

Everywhere he went Baron von Ripper encountered Salvador Dalí who was hell bent on celebrity and would flit in and out of his future life. In the cafés of Montparnasse – La Rotonde, Le Sélect and Le Dôme were favourites – Spanish artists mingled with émigrés from all over Europe. Many were fans of Cubism, but another Catalan artist, Joan Miró, had embraced Surrealism, a radical approach to art that had become even more entrenched in Paris than Berlin. Surrealist art and writing featured the element of surprise, unexpected juxtapositions and non-sequiturs. The poverty stricken Miró had dispensed with his realistic style after he arrived in Paris in 1924, and was painting under the influence of hallucinations brought on both by hunger and his intensive reading of the new Surrealist poetry. That year, Rudolf von Ripper is likely to have seen Miró's exhibition at Galerie Pierre as well as a collective exhibition, *La Peinture Surréaliste*. Rip was drawn to Surrealism. He admired its advocacy of moral rigour and integrity, and, in particular, its advocacy of a proletarian revolution to counter the growing threat of fascism in Europe. He met the luminaries of the movement, notably the acclaimed Surrealist writer, René Crevel, and its most important patrons, Vicomte Charles de Noailles and his wife, Marie-Laure. He befriended the writer and aspiring politician, André Malraux. The most passionate adherents of Surrealism regarded their work, first and foremost, as an expression of their philosophy. Its leader, André Breton, insisted that Surrealism was a revolutionary movement and although Rip was attracted to its ideology, he held back. For him, to embrace any particular artistic or political stance was effectively to wear a straitjacket.

The carefree lifestyle Rip adopted in Paris soon impoverished him, and, after his refusal to return to Austria, he could hardly ask Mutti to fund the next phase of his life. He must earn his living, and he travelled to Lyon hoping to find work as a silkscreen printer. In this he was unsuccessful, but one day he happened to see a recruitment poster for the French Foreign Legion. The FFL offered soldiers who no longer had a country to fight for with a glamorous option, or so Rip perceived it at the time. He had survived many dangers on the road to freedom, so why should he hesitate now? Perhaps when he looked into the mirror of his soul he came face to face with his long neglected soldier-self, craving action and adventure? He seized the opportunity to earn money – and also to fulfil some of his father's ambitions for him – by enlisting for a five-year tour of duty under the 'declared identity' or pseudonym that was a requirement of the FFL.

In sawmill, circus and coalmine Rudolf von Ripper had proved himself a consummate master of disguise. It was no mean feat to learn the Legion's credo by heart and to goose-step at eighty-eight paces per minute, but the Baron's swift mastery soon earned him his next costume, the FFL's distinctive white kepi and shirt with red epaulettes. Sent to join a Cavalry Regiment in Sousse, Tunisia, the beauty of the desert and its changing moods at different times of the day and night immediately enchanted him. In moments stolen from his duties he portrayed in confident, boldly outlined drawings the desert towns and natives wearing the burnoose. During engagements ghostly memories of his father encouraged him on. Between battles he became bored and depressed and had to face the truth that long periods of waiting for action were part of a soldier's life. When action eventually came in a battle against the Druze in Lebanon, a Riff bullet punctured Rip's left lung and another shattered his knee. His injuries were severe, but whilst he was convalescing, out of the shadow of his suffering he hit on a way to reconcile his artist and soldier selves. Propped up in his hospital bed he sketched the contorted faces of comrades he had witnessed dying in the desert from wounds or asp bites. The drawings were therapeutic and also marked a significant turning point in his artistic life: Rudolf von Ripper realised he had the makings of a war artist.

As Ernest Pyle, the legendary American war correspondent would observe when they became friends during the Second World War, 'you don't think of an artist as being tough or worldly … [Yet] all his life has been a fluctuation between these violent extremes of salon intellectualism and the hard, steady reality of personal participation in war.'

Artistic accomplishments were of no interest to the Legion and after Rip was well enough to return to his Tunisian base camp at Sidi-el-Hani he chafed against its restrictions. He had served for almost two years and the prospect of several more years devoid of art or women to love seemed intolerable to the passionate legionnaire who wrote to his mother a barely disguised plea, 'there is no money here; a little money is freedom; talent is liberty; and liberty is the greatest wealth there is.' He also wrote to a relative, Elizabeth Plantagenet, who responded by sending him two thousand Swiss francs, enough money to enable him to jump the picket fence. On leave with a two-day pass, he bought civilian clothes in a market, binned his FFL gear and concealed himself in a public park while he assessed his best chance of escape. Despite his careful precautions, he ran into an unpopular sergeant from his squadron, and, after a moment of mutual shock, Rip evaded his pursuer by jumping onto a train to Sidi Bou Said in northern Tunisia. From there he drove to Algiers, boarded a Dutch ship bound north and spent the summer in Salzburg.

Whilst it was gratifying to learn that one of his paintings had been accepted for the 1925 New Objectivity Exhibition in Mannheim, Rudolf von Ripper was far from ready to settle down. When he returned to Berlin, Klaus Mann and his sister, Erika, were planning to set off around the world and he decided to go with them in search of artistic inspiration. Fascinated by new techniques for documentary film making, the Chinese civil war struck him as a gripping subject for a new venture. They set off by boat to Djibouti, Indochina and Bali, from where the Manns travelled to America and Rip went on to Shanghai. Artist, soldier and adventurer, he anticipated the thrilling prospect of arriving in one of the most cosmopolitan cities in the world. Shaven heads were fast replacing the pigtails the Chinese called queues and, apart from the very old, women no longer bound their feet. Tower blocks were altering the downtown skyline, some of them upmarket hotels to service the international community. The Shanghai nightlife was second to no other capital in the world, where jazz bands played for an exotic and sophisticated clientele of round- and slit-eyed dancers. During the day white-suited entrepreneurial Europeans and Americans cooked up their schemes on the Bund and opium was freely available.

Rip had just enough money to buy his next outfit, a white sharkskin suit and panama hat. He needed dollars to finance his documentary films, and kitted out *de rigueur* he found work as a runner for an American from Minnesota who was procuring arms and ammunition for Chiang Ki Shek's nationalists as well as the communists in the civil war. It was a dangerous mission, but ever since he had fled his Austrian homeland at the age of fifteen, Rip had lived on the edge. This was his nature, supported by his talent for adapting to the most unlikely circumstances. Edges were places where a boy might become a man, and a man might become far more than he had ever been. He combined his risky day job with studies of Chinese art that would influence his future work, particularly as a Second World War artist when he sketched stark military scenes beneath skies fiery as a dragon's breath. He threw himself into Shanghai life and planned the films he would shoot to capture the incredible mêlée of human life and struggle in China

Chiang Kai Shek had risen to power, a shrewd, focused soldier struggling to unify the communists and the nationalists and bring the civil war to an end. This was the perfect subject for Rip's exploration of film noir techniques: the air acrid with the smell of opium and gunpowder, and the blood of martyrs staining the streets of the Pudong. And, what a contrast the dark-clothed, warring native population made to the elegant capitalists living entirely different lives in the smart new suburbs. He threw himself into the adventure of it all before fate intervened. Rip turned up for work only to find his American boss's body shot through with bullets. His mettle was further tested when he received an alarming tip-off – his own name was edging to the top of a list of foreigners heading for the same fate – and with slant-eyed hellhounds snapping at his heels he caught the next train out.

When he returned to Germany Rudolf von Ripper was twenty-one, ardently devoted to adventure and culture, yet frustrated that his spell in Shanghai had not borne artistic fruit. He felt like a man without a purpose or a home. At the same time as he was struggling to regain his foothold as an artist, he felt bewildered by the chaos of the Weimar Republic. The population of Berlin had soared to four million and the masses continued to arrive from all corners of the former empire. Swept up on a tide from which it was impossible to turn back many fell ill, most remained unemployed and malnutrition was rife. In an attempt to rescue people from despair, welfare organisations set up soup kitchens. Outraged by the social injustice, poverty, squalor and sickness of a country edging towards a political abyss, the German Communist Party (KPD) strove to offer financial, legal and practical assistance to the poor. Many sought comfort in the narcotic atmosphere of their street-corner bar. Men and women returned to the same bar, night after night, to share stories of political intrigue, inhumane events and suppositions. These bars were the bases from which anti-fascists organised hideouts, vantage points, blockades and demonstrations, and Rudolf von Ripper joined them. It was said that a man called Hitler arrived in a bar one night and found his way blocked by the chair of Erich Müsham.

Müsham had become a frequent contributor to the major left-wing weekly *Die Weltbühne*, whose pacifist editor-in chief, Carl von Ossietzky, offered a platform to outstanding German writers who opposed the regime.

Rip witnessed 'misfits' and Jews being arrested and chased off the street. Jews were the minority group singled out and blamed for the country's ills, mocked and scape-goated in posters, art, cartoons and film. They were cruelly caricatured in the right wing press as hook-nosed misers, stealing money from the 'honest Aryan' German workers. Deeply affected by these cruel manifestations of fascism, every mark Rip now made – on paper or canvas – became an expression of his ferocious opposition to the regime which he, in turn, savagely caricaturized. He was a Resistance artist, fighting tyranny in black and white: a graphic artist in drawing, etching and lithography, illustrating left wing and underground publications aimed at warning the world about the rising threat of fascism. He found work as an illustrator for the Jewish owned *Ullstein Verlag* newspapers and periodicals. Having survived the First World War, the publishing company had built new headquarters named Ullsteinhaus in Berlin's Tempelhof district in the 1920s. It was the largest printing and editorial company in Europe, publishing newspapers, magazines and books. Increasingly, the Ullstein group employed successful writers as editors and proof readers, Berthold Brecht among them.

At the same time, Rip continued to practise drawing in the style of the old masters. *Die Hände Des Künstlers* (1927) echoed Albrecht Dürer's 'Praying Hands' and, his own hands, the hands of his artist-self, needed prayer that year. Like Klaus Mann, who had been a drama critic for a Berlin newspaper in 1925, Rip was struggling to tame his worsening and expensive drug addiction. He had become a user of hashish and opium during his forays into Africa, the Middle East and China, and his cabinet of drugs is likely to have included morphine, cocaine, Veronal and ether, as Klaus's did. In the 1920s the personal use of narcotics, easily obtained through pharmacies, was not yet illegal. Drug taking was seen to be cool by their generation of artists, and particularly by the adherents of Dadaism and Surrealism. Like them, Rip had become fascinated by the legend of the French poet Arthur Rimbaud (1854–1891) who wrote poetry under the influence of drugs. Rimbaud's credo had become Rip's own, and his poetry sowed seeds in his mind: he would preface his masterwork to come, *Écraser l'Infâme*, with Rimbaud's 'Introduction' to his hashish-induced poem, *Une Saison en Enfer* ('A Season in Hell', 1873): *Jadis, si je me souviens bien* ... Rimbaud records in his poem the failure of the experiment he had hoped would turn him into the seer he longed to be. Instead it almost drove him mad: *The poet makes himself a seer by a long, prodigious, and rational disordering of all the senses ... He reaches the unknown; and even if, crazed, he ends up by losing the understanding of his visions, at least he has seen them!*

Rudolf von Ripper was admitted to hospital soon after Christmas, in pain from his lung injury in the battle with the Druze. Increasingly frustrated by the lack of recognition he craved as an artist and unable to control his drugs habit, he attempted to end his life on New Year's Day, 1928. Catholicism forbade suicide and deemed it a sin, but the devout Countess Claire's love for her son overrode such tenets of her faith, and she brought him to Austria to convalesce. During that spring and summer, Rip painted *Selbstportrait* ('Self Portrait'). In this painting, there are no references to the soldier-adventurer of the French Foreign Legion and China. Instead, Mutti's rather sheepish-looking prodigal son looks out of the canvas, catching the viewer's eye as he recovers from his dance with death. He holds the tools of his trade, a palette and brush, and wears an artist's smock. 'He is medium tall, slightly stooped, and one eye has a cast that makes it appear to be looking beyond you. His face is long and thin, and his teeth are prominent,' a journalist wrote of him later. But these imperfections are nowhere to been seen in 'Self Portrait'. Gone is the cast from his eye; his full lips, closed mouth and chiselled jaw conceal any hint of buckteeth. If he had been high-minded and rather full of himself on his journey thus far, now he recognized his need to change, and who better to guide him towards the spiritual dimension of life than the pagan Virgil, disguised as a curious yet comforting amalgam of Mutti and Art.

Jadis, si je me souviens bien, ma vie était
un festin où s'ouvraient tous les cœurs,
où tous les vins coulaient.
Un soir, j'ai assis la Beauté sur mes genoux.
Et je l'ai trouvée amère.
Et je l'ai injuriée.

Once, if my memory serves me well, my life was
a banquet which opened all hearts,
where every wine flowed.
One evening I sat Beauty on my knees,
And I thought her bitter,
And I wounded her.

CHAPTER THREE
MERRY-GO-ROUND

After dark, Berlin buzzed with cafés and glitzy night-
clubs. On Kurfürstenstrasse, foxy women in cheap
finery slunk under lamplight intent on survival. At the
ornate TicTacToe club on Lehniner Platz rotating mirror
balls sparkled on the dancers below: groomed men in
dinner suits, women in short silk dresses trailing translucent scarves and feather boas. Fuelled by manhattans or
mojitos, between cabaret performances they danced
foxtrots, tangos and the Charleston. From gigantic hoard-
ings plastered with American-style advertising on the
corner of the Leipzig and Potsdamer plazas, Berliners were
urged to *Smoke Makedon cigarettes*, see *Elizabeth of England*
at the German Theatre, *The Fairy* at the Kommode and
the movie *Flute Concert of Sans-Souci*. Suggestively dressed
in her famous banana costume, Josephine Baker, 'the
Black Pearl', was Queen of Berlin's club land. The Austrian
architect, Adolf Loos, designed for Baker a house in black
and white 'of a barely concealed sexuality'. She is 'the
most sensational woman anyone ever saw,' enthused
Ernest Hemingway who understood that Baker's raw
sensuality reflected Germany's current love affair with all
things American.

Berlin's most successful Modernist architect, Erich Mendelsohn (1887–1952), had been commissioned to design a building epitomizing 'the brilliant surge of energy that has jolted Germany out of cultural stagnation'. Freshly cut garden flowers decorated his table; a wooden Buddha on his desk encouraged his deep contemplation of the task in hand. Mendelsohn was at the zenith of his powers, feted by the Weimar Republic and lauded by fellow architects for the pioneering commercial and industrial buildings he had designed in the 1920s. With assured grace, his pen performed an arabesque across a blank page of his sketchpad, then another and another, until, at last, he hit on a shape for the structure. At the top of the page he wrote 'Columbus Haus'. Both in its style and name, the public would instantly link his new building – and Berlin – with Christopher Columbus and the New World of America whose twentieth-century pizzazz Germans yearned to emulate. He would specify trendy neon lighting.

In the aftermath of his traumatic suicide bid, Rudolf von Ripper rented a waterside studio in Berlin's bohemian Neukölln district that would serve his progress as an artist. Although the future scared him, art had become his strength in times of doubt, his spiritual practise. He aimed to reflect the frantic pace of city and cultural life in realistic paintings, and not to shy away from showing its darker side. After a visit to Rip's studio one grey winter day, Helene von Nostic Wallwitz, a culturally astute aristocrat and close friend of the sculptor, Auguste Rodin, recorded that despite the city's recent innovations Rudolf von Ripper had managed to keep the atmosphere of old Berlin alive. The studio window looking over a harbour filled with colourful boats might have been in Copenhagen or Rotterdam, she wrote. On Rip's easels pictures of revolution, red flags and heated faces, mingled with portraits of intellectuals and workers with screaming, gaping mouths. He adhered to the style of the New Objectivity and chose to depict the seedy side of city life, such as backstreets piled with rubbish, rather than shiny capitalist aspirations. He mingled with artists, musicians and intellectuals at their favourite haunt, the Romanisches Café in Kurfürstendamm, where they attempted to further their careers by rubbing shoulders with influential counterparts. Immersed in high culture as well as current events, here the twenty-three years old artist discovered a milieu to support the reconstruction of his life.

Portrait painting was a well-trodden route to survival for artists in the 1920s. Rudolf von Ripper had already sketched and painted portraits of family and friends, including Otto Dix, whose uncompromising depictions of legless and disfigured veterans, etchings such as *Stormtroops Advancing Under Gas* and his portfolio, *Der Krieg* 1924, would influence his future work. Survivors of the First World War, a common sight on Berlin's streets, were otherwise largely ignored within contemporary German society. Rip's quest for portrait commissions led him to the Berlin door of Carl Sternheim (1878–1942), the celebrated German dramatist and short story writer whose work had satirised the emergent German middle classes during the Wilhelmine period. In 1907 Sternheim had married the writer, Thea Löwenstein, and they had two children. The wealth Thea brought to the union by way of her rich manufacturing family enabled the Sternheims to build the Schloss Bellemaison in Munich. There, Sternheim worked in the company of leading artists including Mechtilde Lichnowsky, Max Reinhardt and Frank Wedekind, and assembled an art collection. In 1908, he had collaborated with Franz Blei to launch the Expressionist literary journal *Hyperion* which published the first eight prose works by Franz Kafka, and in 1915 Sternheim had presented the Fontane Prize to the then largely unknown Kafka. Rudolf von Ripper's close contact with this cultural circle would bring him to a new level of recognition as an artist.

But the portrait he intended to paint of Carl Sternheim was soon set aside after Rudolf von Ripper fell in love with Carl's feisty and capricious daughter, the set-designer Dorothea 'Mopsa' Sternheim (1905–1954). Mopsa was a mirror for Rip, a restless spirit and a political radical who was also addicted to opium. Frances Partridge, the writer and member of the Bloomsbury Group, described Mopsa as 'very attractive – a slight, pretty figure & a thick bob of hair'. Later, the chief foreign correspondent of *The New York Times* Cyrus Sulzberger would describe her as 'erratic and hysterical'. Like the rest of Europe, the Sternheim family had been fascinated by London's 'Ripper case' and their nickname for Rip became 'Jack'. Mopsa and Rip staged sensational drugs and alcohol fuelled parties in their Berlin studio, spent their savings on their exuberant lifestyle, and, whenever the mood struck, they took off for Paris, London, Rome or North Africa.

To the Berlin demimonde, sexual experimentation was as valid as artistic exploration; ménages-à-trois were common and homosexuality accepted. Soon, Rip would embrace both. If he clung to elements of Catholicism instilled in his childhood, like many of his peers he rejected the Catholic view of homosexuality as a 'mortal sin'. Homosexuality was a hot topic of the day: the communist press attacked homosexuality as a 'bourgeois vice', but to the liberated youth of Berlin, particularly those associated with the Bauhaus School, same-sex intimacy was as valid as heterosexual love. On previous trips to Paris, Rip had been captivated by Klaus

Mann's friend, the French Surrealist writer and ardent anti-fascist, René Crevel (1900–1935), 'a witty, angel-faced Orpheus whose hyacinthine hair suggested Classical statuary,' as someone remarked.

The French capital had become a laboratory for international experimental art. Rip embraced Paris once more, this time as a working artist and a connoisseur. The Galerie Surréaliste which had opened in 1926, showed work by Miró, Tanguay, Chirico, Man Ray, Duchamp, Picabia, Picasso, Ernst and others who would influence Rip's work. Surrealism had developed out of the Dadaist movement of the First World War and Paris had become its most important centre. From the 1920s, Surrealism spread swiftly around the globe, influencing the visual arts, literature, film, and music of many countries and languages, as well as political thought and practice, philosophy and social theory. Paris had become a honey-pot for super-rich expatriate Americans who were self-styled patrons of contemporary art, literature and music. Salvador Dalí cultivated one of the foremost hostesses of the American colony, Caresse Crosby, who later invited him to visit her in the USA. At this stage in his life Rudolf von Ripper was more interested in René Crevel than Salvador Dalí.

Crevel was a star in everyone's firmament and may have given Rip his first introduction to the influential Vicomtesse Marie-Laure and her husband Charles de Noailles, who collected his art in the 1930s. Crevel also counted among his American friends Gertrude Stein, the composer Virgil Thomson and the poet Ezra Pound. Stein famously knew everyone who was anyone in Paris, and would tell the world about it in *The Autobiography of Alice B. Toklas* (1933). Toklas and Stein hosted a regular Paris salon attended by expatriate American writers including Ernest Hemingway,

Paul Bowles, Thornton Wilder, Sherwood Anderson, and the avant-garde painters, Picasso, Matisse, and Braque. Warm-hearted Baron Rudolf von Ripper, a respected artist and bon viveur, was a welcome guest wherever he went. He savoured the privilege, began an affair with René Crevel and danced with abandon to the heartbeat of the French capital.

Despite Crevel's success as a published novelist and society darling, at the beginning of his relationship with Rip, he was depressed after ending an affair with the American painter, Eugene McGowan. Humiliating attempts to salve his wounds with handsome gay boxers and bar pick-ups had made Crevel ill and embittered. Rip endorsed the view of Klaus Mann and another friend, Edward Sackville-West, that McGowan was a narcissistic and promiscuous brute whom René was well rid of. 'Eddy' Sackville-West, 5th Baron Sackville (1901–1965), a British music critic and novelist, frequently turned up in Paris. Mopsa and Eddy had met in Germany where the deeply unhappy Eddy had been experimenting with homosexual affairs. At different times, Klaus, Rip and Mopsa all stayed at the Sackville-West family seat, Knole in Kent. Most notable among the Sackville descendants was the writer Vita Sackville-West. Vita's friend and lover, Virginia Woolf, was inspired by Knole's history and the Sackville-West lineage to write the novel *Orlando* (1928).

Crevel's fascination with suicide and homosexuality was rooted in a boyhood that bore similarities to Rip's own, yet was more profoundly troubled. René Crevel's father had been a music publisher as well as a high-ranking French Army officer. When René was fourteen, Monsieur Crevel hung himself in the family's elegant, middle-class Parisian home after he became implicated in a homosexual scandal. In a gesture René described as 'both sadistic and moralistic', his mother displayed her husband's corpse to her children to impress upon them the 'shame and sin' of their father. Thereafter, Madame Crevel subjected them to rigid discipline and withdrew from the outside world until her death in 1926. That year, Crevel developed tuberculosis and was forced to endure agonising hours confined to bed at a Swiss sanatorium in the high reaches of the Alps. After he recovered, he was not an easy bedfellow, nevertheless Mopsa Sternheim eventually joined Crevel and Rip in a ménage-à-trois. With and without René, they stormed the sumptuous fancy dress balls and private parties of the extravagant 'gin-age' that preceded the Wall Street Crash. Crevel fell in love with Mopsa and proposed to her, but it was Rip whom she chose to marry.

A photograph taken on 28 December 1929, their wedding day, shows the happy couple with Mopsa's parents, Carl and Thea Sternheim. They moved into an apartment on Kurfürstenstrasse and from the outset Rip saw eye-to-eye with his father-in-law whose satirical plays and novellas attacked the German bourgeoisie and the proletariat for their submissiveness and ideological blindness to the rising threat of fascism. Everyone was happy with the marriage except Eddy Sackville-West and René Crevel. Eddy and Mopsa had had a close relationship just before she married Rip, and after it he dedicated his novel *Simpson* 'to Mopsa von Ripper: In joyful memory of November 1928 to 1929'. For Crevel the timing of the von Rippers' marriage was devastating, he was recovering from the surgical removal of infected ribs and part of his lungs that year. His disease and the intensity of his suffering drew heavily on the newlyweds' compassion, and Crevel increasingly turned to Salvador and Gala Dalí for support.

Vicomte Charles de Noailles had funded Luis Buñuel and Salvador Dalí's innovative film *L'Age D'or* as a birthday present for his wife. One of the first sound films to be made in France, it tells the story of a couple's attempts to consummate their erotic relationship while the bourgeois values and sexual mores of family, church, and society thwart them at every turn. The film's first screening at the Cinéma du Panthéon was a highlight of the 1930 winter season, and it is likely that Rudolf and Mopsa von Ripper were among the audience. The Surrealists turned out in force along with *la crème-de-la-crème* of Parisian society, including Cocteau, Gertrude Stein, Nancy Cunard, Picasso, André Gide, André Malraux, Darius Milhaud, Giacometti and Fernand Léger.

By the summer of 1931, a 'blissfully happy' Crevel was travelling south to Port Lligat in Cataluña with the Dalís, who had been converting a fisherman's shack on the beach into a home. Crevel described it as 'comfortable in the doll's house line'. He found the nearby town of Cadaqués 'incredibly backward' on account of its poverty and illiteracy and he and Dalí gave a lecture on Surrealism at a specially convened meeting of the Workers' and Peasants' Front in Barcelona. In Port Lligat, Crevel worked on an essay about Dalí, wrote letters to Marie-Laure de Noailles, frolicked with Gala in the garden and marvelled at Dalí's inspiration, the mica-schist metamorphoses of Cape Creus. The elegantly dressed trio was photographed strolling down Barcelona's Las Ramblas, on their way to visit buildings by Gaudí and other Art Nouveau architects.

A few years later, when Rudolf von Ripper was working on the drawings that would comprise *Écraser l'Infâme*, he took inspiration from the so-called Golden Age. 'Merry-go-Round' sums up the privileged, intellectual and decadent life he had known in the French capital. The merry-go-round might have been based on the 'timelessly squawking, constantly rocking carousel' he had ridden on as a boy in the Prater of Vienna. Stefan Zweig recalled in *Fantastic Night*, 'the thumping polka, the dragging waltz, horses heads of painted wood going round in their crazy circle.' The drawing also hints at the travelling theatre troupe that had taken the teenaged Rip over the Austrian border into Germany and his subsequent spell with the circus. It suggests, too, Catholic processions in which the identities of the bearers shouldering swaying *tableaux vivants* depicting the life of Christ are concealed under dark curtains. Only their bare feet are visible, the feet of the proletariat, the true bearers of society's merry-go-round upon which privileged naked figures cavort behind half-open curtains.

One of three self-portraits within the drawing shows Rip making love to Mopsa on the back of a fairground horse; a second self-portrait shows him riding a horse alone. Nearby, René Crevel rides a fantastic cockerel that suggests the betrayal of Christ. Crevel wears a clown's cap, his comedic-tragic face reminiscent of Marcel Marceau as he cavorts with the ambiguously sexual Sackville-West. An aloof, moustachioed Dalí-like figure observes the scene, half-hidden behind the curtain. In the third self-portrait, Rip lies prostrate on the ground, playing a harmonica in a desperate attempt to keep the merry-go-round turning. But he knows it is a futile attempt. Everywhere in Europe the Golden Age is doomed.

Rip and Mopsa rented out their Kurfürstenstrasse home to an arty American couple and spent the spring and summer of 1930 in Salzburg before embarking on an extended trip to Spanish and French Morocco. Rip knew the territory well from his days in the French Foreign Legion, and his return to the area with his sophisticated bride brings to mind the arty, intellectual, sexually frustrated characters, Port and Kit Moresby, in Paul Bowles's novel *The Sheltering Sky*. Indeed, the von Rippers' journey might have coincided with Bowles's first visit to French Morocco in 1931, before the author returned to settle there. That spring, no doubt with a good supply of drugs in their luggage, the von Rippers travelled back through Paris and Zurich to Berlin for Rip's first solo exhibition of thirty-five oil paintings, watercolours and drawings at the Porza-Versicherung gallery. The Porza community had been founded in 1927 to represent an informal international group of prominent socialist intellectuals and artists. The exhibition put Rip on Berlin's artistic map, but the overtly anti-fascist nature of his work also made him a target of the fascist *Sturmabteilung*.

In December 1932, Rip and Mopsa had a quarrel whose nature was never stated and they separated. It was a grievous blow to them both. There had been love between them as well as periods of tremendous stress related to the political situation and their drugs habit. Increasingly unstable, Mopsa went to Crevel in Paris while Rip sought refuge with Eddy Sackville-West in London. There, he established solidarity with the British-based German Resistance, a beleaguered group of several hundred artists and writers, many of them so destitute they were forced to beg for food and money from refugee-relief organisations and the Quaker movement. Nicknamed the 'Emigrandezza', they were educated political opponents of the Nazi regime, and not all of them were Jewish. The mass emigration of Jewish refugees would come later. Life in London was tough for the émigrés: their British visas stipulated 'no political activities of any kind' and had to be renewed every three months. The dramatist Ernst Toller was in London, as was his mistress Dora Fabian who worked tirelessly on the Nobel Peace Prize campaign to free Carl von Ossietzky and other political prisoners arrested by the Third Reich. Like Rudolf von Ripper, the Resistance's main focus was to assist the underground in Germany and to alert the rest of the world to Hitler's brutality and his plans for war.

It was difficult for the London Germans to obtain news about what was happening at home. Their mail was censored, and new refugee arrivals like Rudolf von Ripper were invaluable sources of information. Even in Britain, 'Emigrandezza' members of the SPD (German Socialist Party), the KPD (German Communist Party) and smaller left-wing parties squabbled about their differences, although everyone knew that solidarity between the SPD and the KPD was the only hope, and it was a slim one, of ousting Hitler in the forthcoming Reichstag election. Hitler had already been elected Chancellor of Germany and had dictated that the *Sturmabteilung* would oversee security at party meetings. The Weimar Republic had been converted into the Third Reich, a single-party dictatorship based on the totalitarian and autocratic ideology of Nazism, whose aim was to establish a 'New Order' of absolute Nazi German hegemony in continental Europe. Rip designed an election poster for the SPD which appeared on Berlin billboards alongside placards signed by Albert Einstein, Heinrich Mann and the artist Käthe Kollwitz, urging the SPD and the KPD to form a united front against fascism.

Rip had provided the Resistance with valuable data on the excesses of the Nazis, written articles warning of the coming Holocaust, and designed the poster for the SPD. But it wasn't enough. He was twenty-seven years old and he yearned for action. Often, he must have listened in to BBC World Service reports: *It has become a familiar sight.*

Thousands of Berliners turn out to cheer and wave during Adolph Hitler's staged performances, backed by parades of hundreds of jackbooted stormtroopers. In aggressive speeches the German Chancellor repeatedly attacks restrictions imposed on Germany by the Treaty of Versailles, promotes Pan-Germanism, anti-Semitism, anti-communism, and foreign and domestic policies aimed at seizing Lebensraum or 'living space' for the Germanic peoples. On 30th January, a triumphant torchlight procession of stormtroopers invaded the Berlin district of Charlottenburg to arrest anti-Nazi protesters ...

Imagining the fate of friends who had fallen into Nazi hands was unbearable. And, as his future drawings reveal, Rudolf von Rippers imagination was filled with all the depictions of Hell he had ever seen, from Hieronymus Bosch to illustrations of Dante's *Inferno*. Rip, the man of action, felt impotent hanging about in London like a fly caught in a web, unable to move in any direction. Then one blessed day, the Resistance came to his rescue with a commission to create political-satirical drawings of the Third Reich from a place of safety.

Why did Rudolf von Ripper choose Mallorca as his safe haven that winter? The fact that Spain was a monarchy as yet untainted by overt fascism must have influenced his decision. He had lived dangerously, resisting tyranny wherever he found it – he needed the fire of passionate opposition in order to create – yet, at the same time, he longed for peace. Some of his Düsseldorf Academy contacts who had spent time painting in Mallorca in 1931 are likely to have come back raving about the island's beauty. Rip might also have heard about the tranquil island inhabited by gentle hospitable people from the Catalan artists in Paris, Miró, Picasso and Dalí. *Winter in Mallorca*, George Sand's account of her visit to Mallorca with Frederic Chopin, was a European classic Rip might well have read. But perhaps the greatest influence on his choice of Mallorca was the Archduke Louis Salvador's Mallorca volume of *Die Balearen* that had stirred Rip's boyhood imagination.

The death of Archduke Louis Salvador at Brandeis Castle in 1915 had spared the old man from ever having to wear the mantle of Emperor. Rudolf von Ripper had been child at the time, but now, as a man, he could strongly identify with aspects of Louis Salvador's earlier life. They were both aristocrats who fled their native Austria as teenagers and they both aspired to be artists. Louis Salvador had been more than ready to flee the stultifying Hapsburg court in search of a new invented life and Rip had similarly fled his desecrated homeland.

Louis Salvador's first glimpse of Mallorca had been in September 1865, standing at the ship's rail of the steamboat *Jaime II* after a summer expedition to the neighbouring island of Ibiza. He was nineteen years old and accompanied by Eugenie Sforza di Montignoso his guardian, valet and travelling companion. And although in his odyssey so far, Rip hadn't actually changed his name, the Archduke, too, had been a master of disguise. The day Louis Salvador arrived in Mallorca his calling card bore the alias, Ludwig, Graf von Neudorf. *Neuen dorf*: New village, a name that reflected Louis Salvador's desperation to find a place where he would be left in peace. After that first visit, the young Archduke returned two years later to make Mallorca his home. This time he was in flight from a tragedy Rip had heard spoken about in lowered voices during his childhood. Louis Salvador had been a student at Prague University in 1867 when his beautiful fiancée, Archduchess Matilde, was at Weilburg dressing for a fiesta. Her father, Archduke

Albert, was smoking a cigar beside the fire in his library, waiting for their guests to arrive. When Matilde appeared to show him her fabulous gauze ballgown, the alcohol her lady-in-waiting had used to dress her hair ignited and her dress went up in flames. With horrific speed Matilde became a human torch. It was whispered that, after the blaze died down, her ashes contained the gemstones of her jewellery: a golden sapphire 'bib' necklace encrusted with diamonds, perhaps, as favoured by fashionable Hapsburg women of the time. There was sympathy for the Archduke's bereavement, yet courtly eyebrows were raised after he 'went native' on a primitive Mediterranean island.

Like Byron's romantic hero, Don Juan, the ceaselessly changing seas upon which Louis Salvador now sailed mirrored his mental turmoil. His generation was the first to experience speed in transport. Speed and the wide-open spaces of seas and skies were balms to his soul after a lifetime confined at the Hapsburg court, and locomotion applied to sailing ships became the young aristocrat's passion. The name of his next vessel, *Nixe I*, meant a siren, a sea-creature, a sexless *femme fatale*. Matilde reincarnated, perhaps, as *objet d'art*. But in Mallorca, it was his homosexuality that the Archduke chose to celebrate, particularly in his love affair with Vyborni, a 'beautiful boy' who had been a fellow student at Prague University. Louis Salvador became one of the first northern Europeans to settle in Mallorca, and one of its first environmentalists. The island acted as an exotic umbrella, shielding from Hapsburg eyes the affairs, friendships, conspiracies and further tragedies that would mark his life.

CHAPTER FOUR
LET'S PLAY WITH FIRE

The pale fugitive was up before dawn and when the blaring horns of the trans-Mediterranean ferry announced its approach to the harbour of Palma de Mallorca, Rudolf von Ripper was at the prow to savour his first glimpse of the island. He was experiencing the archetypical arrival of visitors by way of the sea, long before the advent of tourist flights in the 1950s. Perhaps Louis Salvador's words struck a chord with Rip: 'I have always been a nomad without fixed residence ... I circle the seas, driven first of all by my affections, a circumstance which has turned me into a wanderer, so to speak, on the fringes of humanity.' After all, Rip had been a nomad ever since he left his homeland as a teenager. His travel itinerary of the past decade had been impressive: Austria, Germany, France, Switzerland, Morocco, Lebanon, China, England and now he could add Spain to the list.

As the sun rose and coloured the world with hues beyond the imagination of most northern Europeans, Mallorca resembled a jewel, Rip might have thought, set in a dream-filled sea. The ferry drew closer and sunlit buildings appeared along the front, then the Moorish palace and the Gothic cathedral and, beyond the city walls, dinky white windmills peppered the countryside. This island, halfway between Barcelona and the sensuous North African coast, promised the welcome return of the young radical's taste for life, if not love of a woman. It's easy to imagine him shouldering his rucksack, gripping the handle of his suitcase and hastening down the gangplank, ready to explore the Archduke's island: eerie haunts of smugglers and pirates and eagles and vultures soaring above ancient olive groves straight out of Ovid's *Metamorphoses.*

Hotels were as few as tourists at the time and in the capital, Palma de Mallorca, Rip would have had the choice of one of the cheap *hostals* such as Hostal Borne or the Modernist Gran Hotel at the other end of the scale. Worn down by his travails with Mopsa and the menace of fascism at home, perhaps he allowed himself the consolations of a Spanish courtesan whilst he lingered in the dusty ancient city. As he would have discovered, Palma is a trove of architectural treasures spanning the Roman, Arab and Catholic invasions of the island. Wandering the shady labyrinthine streets that lead inexorably to Palma Cathedral, a *Baedeker* guide might have informed him that after the thirteenth century conquest of Mallorca by King Jaume I it had taken three hundred years to construct the cathedral from stone shipped over from Perpignan. It would have described the extraordinary, embellished buildings of the recently constructed Catalan Modernist School, and the Gothic churches that had gone up in every *barrío* after the Conquest, alongside mansions originally built for the conquistadors. Abandoned now, the gates of their Italianate courtyards were firmly closed under wide overhanging pantiled roofs and sculpted façades. Before the publication of the Spanish *Baedeker* in 1897, Louis Salvador's *Die Balearen* had been the foremost guide to island, attracting a steady stream of well-heeled visitors, including the Archduke's mother, the Grand Duchess of Tuscany, and Sisi, the estranged wife of Emperor Franz Joseph. To cater for this new income stream, early expansion of the still primitive island included the construction of hotels and two railway lines: from Palma to the mountain town of Soller and to Inca on the Plain of Mallorca.

The island's legendary beauty was fast becoming a magnet for European and South American artists too, who had established the *Escuela Pollença* (Pollensa School) in the northwest of the island. Rudolf von Ripper's itinerary on his first visit to Mallorca has not been recorded but it is likely that he chose Pollensa as his place of safety and that he rented a room in the rickety Hostal Miramar overlooking the bay, since the hostal was the precursor of the hotel Rip stayed in on his third visit to the island in 1952 when he purchased the villa, Ca'n Cueg.

The view from the port's Pine Walk was glorious: fishermen hunkered on the harbour wall mending bright blue nets, elegant schooners at anchor and, away to the north, the Pollensa valley luxuriant with almond orchards in delicate blossom, date palms and ogee-shaped cypresses. Above the valley the Sierra de Tramuntana reared, snow capped in February during Rip's visit. Absorbing this fecund landscape, Rip must have felt as if he had arrived from the dark side of the moon. Here, in the year of 1933, in this idyll that had been granted to him, he would learn a new language of art and of life. Here in this haven of peace and beauty, his battered twenty-eight-year old soul would measure all his fights and flights, his bungled suicide bid and attempts at love. And although the commission the Resistance had entrusted him with was never far from his mind, he would spend a day or two finding his bearings.

From the town of Pollensa, a country road leads for twenty-two kilometres to the thirteen-century monastery of Lluch, set high in the Sierra. His Catholic upbringing, his love of mountains and their wildlife and his interest in architecture would have attracted Rip to make a pilgrimage to this heartland of the Catalan world. Up there, the paths of carbon makers and hunters crisscross the silver meseta of the Sierra de Tramuntana where holm oak woods thrive above clumps of cistus and heather. Like any young wayfarer of his day, he would have taken his field glasses along to savour the flights of Mallorca's indigenous Black vulture and Eagle owls with piercing orange eyes and jagged brows. Visitors could stay overnight in one of the monks' cells and, if they arrived in time, they could hear the afternoon practise of *Els Blauets*, the blue-coated boys' choir established at the monastery since 1531. On his way back to town, Rip might have noticed a stone bridge leading over a *torrente*, rushing with snow melt off the sierra. If he crossed it he would have found himself in a small pinewood and been fascinated by the white house beyond, different from any other Mallorcan house he had seen. Mies van der Rohe, his Bauhaus architect colleague, might have designed this cuboid villa. If he enquired about the house, he would have been told that its name was Ca'n Cueg, the House of the Frogs.

A hangout of the Pollensa artists was a rustic beach café, Bar Juma, where their paintings were displayed. The café acted as a club where the artists gathered to discuss their work and drink morning *carajillos*, coffees laced with brandy. They wore collarless shirts of striped Mallorcan cotton, dark loose trousers, espadrilles and sombreros, gear readily available at the local market, and Rip who had worn many costumes in his life as aristocrat, clown, bohemian, gunrunner and legionnaire, must have thought this one took some beating. Several artists gathered each morning: Spaniards and South Americans mostly, and an

Austrian artist trained in Munich, Jean Egger (1897–1934). Sometimes they brought sketches to the bar of paintings they were working on for the comments of others.

Most of them would have struck the sophisticated Rudolf von Ripper as lotus-eaters producing out-dated art. Their obsession was to paint the ravishing Mallorcan landscape and textures in blaring colours that to the eyes of an artist trained in France and Germany sullied rather than reflected the island's beauty. Egger was an exception whose canvases, created with a subdued palette and subtle use of abstraction, would not have disgraced a Paris gallery. Egger's art could never be called 'degenerate'. German doctors had advised the tubercular artist to spend time in Mallorca, and, since his arrival in the spring of 1932, Egger had been busy constructing a studio on a finca he bought at L'Hort in the *barrío* of Ternelles, where some of the other artists had settled. Dionís Bennàssar (1904–1967) was prominent among the Mallorcan painters, and must have been fighting in Morocco at the same time as Rip. In the Rif War as a 'Spanish Legionnaire', Bennàssar had lost the use of his right arm and a War Invalids' pension now allowed him devote himself to painting. Another artist, the Argentinian Tito Cittadini (1886–1960), had been seduced by Anglada Camarasa's descriptions of the island when they met in Paris in 1910. The Catalan painter Camarasa (1871–1959) was regarded as the father of the Pollensa School and may have been instrumental in organising several visits Joan Miró made to Jean Egger's studio.

It was too risky to divulge the true nature of the work Rip had come here to do, and it must have been a relief to him that politics was off the agenda of the artist colony. On the other hand, he was forced to carry around the sunlit streets of the port the terrible dark secret he could not share, unless he trusted Jean Egger. Did they discuss BBC World Service reports that the Reichstag building had gone up in flames and that a Dutchman called Marinus van der Lubbe has been accused of setting the fire as a cry to rally the German workers against fascist rule? Perhaps they stuck to discussing Cubism and Surrealist art, since Rip had to tread carefully. Egger was Aryan and Austrian like himself, but he might well have been an informer. It was interesting that Egger had changed his name from Hans to Jean; another expatriate Austrian adopting a different name for a reinvented life like the Archduke. The Third Reich had spies based far beyond Germany as Rip knew only too well from the experiences of comrades in the London-based German Resistance.

Rip began confiding to his sketchpad his increasing angst about the sadism of the Third Reich. The front-page of a recent copy of the Swiss newspaper *Neue Zürcher Zeitung* would have fuelled his passion: *The new Reichstag Fire Decree suspends basic rights and permits detention without trial. The activities of the German Communist Party are being suppressed and around four thousand of its members have been arrested ...* Graphic drawings filled his sketchpad: images of modern warfare, tanks and bomber planes, gigantic insects and Boschian monsters symbolizing gas and biological weapons, innocent citizens – labourers, intellectuals, men, women and children – being driven down the sloping surface of the earth into the abyss. Eventually *Horsemen of the Apocalypse* would take shape as an elaborate sketch informed by Holbein's series of woodcuts, *Dance of Death*, and Durer's *Four Riders*, depicting conquest, war, famine and death. Rudolf von Ripper's work blistered with his outrage at the Third Reich's suspension of human rights and the recent arrests of innocent civilians. The seemingly unstoppable reach of Nazi tyranny even into the private realm was intolerable.

That year Tito Cittadini immortalized Bar Juma in a painting, *Bar Scene 1933*, complete with soda syphon, fisherman, waitress, two artists in sombreros and a view of the beach. The existence of the Pollensa School had been a factor in the decision of the Argentinian architect and art lover, Adán Diehl, to build in 1929 'the finest hotel on the Mediterranean': Hotel Formentor. Diehl's hidden agenda was to encourage his wealthy guests to collect local art. He took a percentage on sales and helped the artists to thrive. The picturesque eight-kilometre route by taxi from Pollensa to the Formentor Peninsula passes a mirador on spectacular cliffs three hundred feet above the sea where rare Elenora falcons swoop almost at eye level. The island of Menorca is visible on the eastern horizon, and the pastel strands of Alcùdia to the south. Salt-loving plants huddle in crevasses round the lighthouse at the edge of the promontory known as 'the meeting place of the two winds' on account of the vicious winds that converge there. Diehl, however, situated his luxurious Hotel Formentor above a ravishing, sheltered bay of apricot sand, turquoise sea and pine trees. It was a place that Rip would return to, both in his memory and in reality, for the rest of his life.

Surely it was on this visit to Mallorca that Rudolf von Ripper began to dream of living in Mallorca and setting aside his pencils and black ink to paint, paint, paint in glorious colour. If only there had not been an evil brute set loose in Europe whom he must vanquish! Ever after this first visit he would refer to the island as his 'haven of peace and beauty', but, now, on hearing that the Nazi party had won more votes than the SPD and the KPD put together in the March elections, and that Adolph Hitler was now the self-styled *Führer und Reichskanzler* of Germany, he realised he must go home. The *Sturmabteilung* was systematically removing Jewish architects, lawyers and doctors from public office. Communists, socialists, so-called misfits such as homosexuals and artists were being arrested and tortured in ever-greater numbers.

Rip travelled back to Paris where he was reconciled with Mopsa. Far from safe themselves even in Paris, drugs and alcohol helped the couple to pull together, assisting comrades they considered to be in even greater danger than themselves to escape to neutral countries. Whereas in the 1920s drug taking had been a matter of personal choice, by the 1930s it had become a criminal act. Drug taking had become illegal in most countries of the world and criminal syndicates had seized a huge percentage of the previously legitimate market. The von Rippers had no choice but to supply their needs via the black market.

Gathering valuable information from refugees arriving in France and passing it on to the Resistance in London and Amsterdam put them in great danger. Rip's and Mopsa's lives were intensely stressful. Dissident and artist friends, some of Jewish origin, told stories of being chased off the streets by fascist thugs, robbed of their homes and denied the chance to earn a living. The architect, Erich Mendelsohn and his family had fled to London. Others didn't leave in time. Erich Müsham had just made arrangements for his pets to be cared for and had bought his train tickets when he was arrested in Charlottenburg. Friends disappeared, phones were tapped and apartments put under surveillance. Heinrich Mann had been expelled from the Academy of the Arts and Ernst Toller from the German chapter of PEN. The Berlin Bauhaus School had been closed down and staff and students who had not fled the country had been arrested. Carl von Ossietzky, one of few public figures who dared to speak out against Nazi militarism, had tragically underestimated the speed with which the Nazis would round-up 'enemies of the state' and had been arrested immediately after the Reichstag fire. Hundreds of targeted artists, writers and musicians left for Britain and America in the nick of time. Rip had watched the erosion of civil society over the past years with incredulity. Now he was horrified, and not for the first time he displayed his 'preference in most situations for the underdog' that would inform his actions throughout the darkest years of the coming war.

After the Reichstag fire the Nazi party let their monster loose. In Berlin, SS Colonel Rudolph Diels (1900–57), chief of the new Prussian state police department 1A (soon to be renamed the Gestapo) who had interrogated Marinus van der Lubbe, wrote in his journal: *Every SA (Sturmabteilung) man is 'on the heels of the enemy,' each knows what he has to do. The Sturm is cleaning up the districts. They know not only where their enemies live, they have also long ago discovered their hideouts and meeting places. The gay victors roar along the Kurfürstendamm and the Linden in elegant automobiles. Manufacturers or shopkeepers have presented them with these cars or put them at their disposal in order to assure themselves protection. The cars of Jews and demo-crats are simply confiscated ... the 'bunkers' in the Hedemann and Voss Strasse have become hellish torture chambers. The SS Columbia prison, the worst of these torture chambers, has been established.*

The Sturm knew not only where their enemies lived ... After Rudolf von Ripper's 1931 Porza exhibition he had been listed as 'an enemy of the state' and it wasn't long before he heard that Gestapo agents had raided his Kurfürstenstrasse studio. They found nothing incriminating but left a warning: return to Germany and risk the consequences. Oblivious Berliners shopped for novelty goods in the latest American store to hit town, F. W. Woolworth's, even as the SS interrogated and tortured victims in prisons throughout central Berlin. Under the leadership of Heinrich Himmler, the SS (*Schutzstaffel* – 'defence corps') had swiftly become one of the largest and most powerful organizations in the Third Reich. After the March elections its *Schutzhaft* (protective custody program) swung into action in cooperation with the SA to make the first arrests of officials and members of the Communist party. By the end of April twenty-five thousand people had been seized in Prussia (ten thousand of them Berliners) and held in the prisons and first concentration camps at Oranienburg and Dachau. They were obliged to wear triangular pieces of material: red for political prisoners, purple for Jehovah's Witnesses, black for anti-socials, green for criminals, pink for homosexuals, blue for immigrants. Jews displayed two yellow triangles to represent the Star of David.

Stormtroopers marched through the city streets enforcing the boycott of Jewish businesses whose bank accounts were frozen. Jewish shops were marked with yellow stars. Sleepers who awakened to the predatory monster in their midst trembled and swallowed pills to get them through the days and nights: Luminaletten, Adaline, Veranol, Phanodorm. They put their affairs in order as best they could, packed ubiquitous brown suitcases that had formerly been packed for holidays. Mass exodus ensued. Half a million traumatised Germans left their homeland during the next decade. Hundreds of refugees crossed the borders into Switzerland, France, Denmark, Sweden and Norway. Others made for the edges of Europe. They arrived hungry and haggard at ports on the coasts of Holland, Portugal, Spain and the South of France: entrepôts for far longer sea journeys to North and South America, Australia and across the English Channel to London.

On 9 May, a Teutonic fire ceremony worthy of an operatic scene by Wagner was the Nazi party's further response to the Reichstag fire. Rudolf von Ripper's friends Klaus Mann and Heinrich Mann headed a long list of authors issued to fascist student groups by the SS that morning. The following evening on the Opernplatz near the university, bands played patriotic songs and uniformed Nazis arrived in force, – SA, SS and Hitler Youth – to light a bonfire. The books of over a hundred authors were passed along a chain of hands and tossed into the flames to the rant of Goebbels and his cohorts. Each writer was denounced with a 'fire speech': *In the fight against decadence and moral decay! In the fight for discipline and common decency with the family! I submit the work of ... to the fire.* Thirty German universities participated in similar portentous events throughout May and June. The works of Berthold Brecht, Albert Einstein, Ernest Hemingway, James Joyce, Erich Müsham, Joseph Roth, Carl Sternheim, Ernst Toller and Stefan Zweig were among books labelled 'dangerous', marked with a cross and locked away in 'poison cabinets' in city and university libraries. Shopkeepers who displayed banned books were charged with high treason.

Rudolf von Ripper sought respite that summer among the lakes and mountains of his Salzkammergut homeland, working as an artist for the Salzburg Festival and visiting his family. In *Portrait der Mutter Des Künstlers* (Portrait of the Artist's Mother, 1933) he acknowledged Countess von Salis-Samaden's role in his artistic development. Ever since his suicide attempt, Mutti had been his unfailing emotional and financial lifeline, a woman able to express warmth and love, unusual attributes in her repressed generation. In her son's portrait, her face is assured yet *Gemütlich.* Gone are any traces of the pretensions of the Austria-Hungary imperial court, yet, unlike her brother, Rip's uncle, who was a Nazi sympathizer, she remains a staunch Austrian patriot. The Countess wears comfortable clothes with a scarf draped casually around her neck as she sits knitting. A ball of wool lies on her lap. Rip was well versed in ancient mythology: his painting was a tribute to Mutti, an ageing Ariadne guiding him through life's labyrinths. Soon he would need her more than ever.

In the autumn he was back living on the edge. The Paris-based Resistance had produced a political pamphlet known as the Brown Book (*Braunbuch* or *Livre Brun*) portraying the burning of the Reichstag and Nazi brutalities. Goethe was a favoured author of the Third Reich and the pamphlet was camouflaged between illustrated covers purporting to be an edition of Goethe's *Hermann und Dorothea*. Surely this anti-Nazi propaganda would penetrate the psyches of every sane German who read it? Rip put on the clothing of choice for young intellectuals – dark polo-necked sweater, corduroy trousers, tweed jacket – boarded a train in Paris and smuggled copies of the Brown Book into Berlin. Surely Rudolf von Ripper's Austrian citizenship would render him immune to danger? But *the Sturm had long ago discovered his hideouts and meeting places* ... Although the American couple had vacated his apartment, it was too risky to stay there and Rip booked into a Kurfürstendamm hotel. In mid-October 1933, Gestapo agents raided the apartment again. This time they found a coded message referring to 'shipments of cement to Switzerland', which the SS interpreted as a list of names in Rudolf von Ripper's network. It was all they needed to put an end to what was regarded as the upstart's degenerate and treasonous art. On Kurfürstendammstrasse, which Rip knew so well he could call it home, he stood on the brink of a deep abyss.

With their powers to track down anybody, anywhere, easy as pie, two Gestapo agents in homburgs and raincoats seized him outside his hotel on 19 December. They manhandled him up to his room to pick up items he would need for the journey through hell that awaited him: a shaver, a mirror, a shirt and a pair of pyjamas. They bundled him onto the backseat of a Black Maria. It sped through rain-spattered, neon-lit streets to the former Museum of Decorative Arts in Prinz Albrecht Strasse, which the Nazis had commandeered as the SS Columbia prison, or Columbia-Haus (not to be confused with Erich Mendelsohn's building, Columbus Haus). Thanks to the painstaking research of Dr Winfried Mayer and to Rudolf von Ripper's later accounts, the stark details of his gruesome incarceration at the Columbia prison and at KV Oranienburg can be told.

Rudolf von Ripper was brought before five Gestapo agents on the orders of SS Colonel Diels, whom he had met socially at Prussian gatherings. What a decent guy Diels had been, before his chilling rise to power. During an aggressive interrogation aimed at infiltrating his network, Rip fired back by demanding to know what happened to a letter he had written to the Austrian legation asking for protection. He had heard nothing. Had the letter been delivered? Their response was to lock him overnight in a grim basement cell and next morning two brown-shirted stormtroopers arrived to beat him up. The last thing Rip remembered before he passed out was the raised arm and clenched fist of one of the thugs reflected in the glass of a framed picture of Hitler hanging on the wall. Still unconscious with a fractured cranium, he was thrown into a basement cell beside other abused prisoners.

When he eventually regained consciousness he was almost paralysed, spitting blood and in agonising pain. 'That wasn't the first or the last time they beat me up and collected a few of my teeth, but I didn't squeal,' he wrote later. 'My heart was filled with undying hatred for the Third Reich and all it stands for.'

Rip's injuries were so severe that the prison doctor transferred him to the custody of the police department at the State Hospital. During his three-week stay there, the SS repeatedly interrogated him and threatened that he would be charged with 'propaganda, treason and espionage' and beaten fifty times a day after his release from hospital unless he signed a confession. The doctor urged Rip to confess if he wanted to save his life, but he persisted in repeating that, as a foreign national, he was being held illegally. Still recovering from his head injury, he was returned to the grim SS Columbia prison in Tempelhof, to be subjected to further torture and humiliation. He would bear the scar of his fractured skull for the rest of his life.

His cramped cell contained a low wooden frame with a straw mattress and two old blankets with a barred window above it. Perhaps here, in his suffering, his memories of Mallorca's beauty gave him hope: one day he would return there after this monstrous regiment of Nazis had been slain. As it was, the guards constantly spied on the prisoners through a peephole, and flung open the door every two hours, when the prisoner immediately had to stand to attention at the back wall and recite his cell number and prisoner number. This pitiful ritual had been explained when Rip first arrived at Columbia-Haus, as he wrote later. 'Got it?' the guard demanded, and when Rip said, 'Yes,' he slapped his face several times then added, 'Show respect when you talk to me, you dog!' Every two hours a new guard entered his cell shouting, 'Bastard,' and he was beaten again. 'And so it went – every two hours a different guard, and every two hours repeated blows.' Even during the night prisoners were under constant observation. 'The electric light was kept on, and we had to be constantly ready to stand to attention for the message. It was almost impossible to get any sleep.'

Throughout the building defenceless prisoners were subjected to the arbitrary abuse of the security guards on a regular basis. Premeditated attacks took place in the corridors and on the stairs where they were posted. Frequently, at a shrill whistle blast and roared command the prisoners had to run through the long corridors from the ground floor to the top floor of the building. An official of the Young German Communist Party later testified, 'On each landing were the SS beasts, armed with rubber truncheons, whips, stool legs and bullwhips.' The prisoners were beaten on their heads and bodies as they ran past. 'Anyone who fell down from exhaustion or the impact was beaten until he got up and continued to run. Some lay senseless. This insane attack lasted about an hour. It seemed to last forever before the prisoners were pushed back into their cells.'

In January 1934 Rudolf von Ripper spent his twenty-ninth birthday at the Tempelhof hellhole. That month he was tested almost beyond the limits of his endurance when one morning he was taken to the basement and ordered to make a full confession. He replied that he had nothing to confess and was struck fifty times with a bullwhip then returned to his cell. 'They drew a line with chalk on the floor and I had to stand to attention without moving my feet from the line. I stood in this position for twenty-seven hours – it was January, and the window was open. Twice I lost consciousness and collapsed – I was doused with water until I revived and was ordered to continue to stand on that line.'

Rip had witnessed the arrival of four German Communist Party officials at Columbia-Haus. One of them, John Scheer, had a neighbouring cell, and Rip wrote that due to the terrible abuse he had suffered, Scheer's condition was so bad he could not have walked ten meters. In February he heard footsteps in the corridor and a voice shouting, 'Get up and get ready to leave,' outside Scheer's cell. Rip could hear the engine of a vehicle in the courtyard and he saw through his cell window Scheer and three other prisoners, including the former head of International Red Aid, being taken away. Later it was announced over the loudspeaker that the four men had been shot for attempting to escape.

'Not a day passed without shocks,' Rudolf von Ripper wrote later. 'One day the door of my cell opened and two SS men entered. You'd better confess everything, they said, and I answered, I have nothing to confess.' The chief inter-rogator said he'd have to report that Rip had lost control under pressure and that he had had to shoot him to protect himself. 'Think about it, I'll be back in three minutes.' When he returned, asking, 'Have you thought it over?' Rip was silent. 'Turn and face the wall!' the man roared. He took aim then said Rip wasn't worth wasting a shot on and Rip realised he wouldn't risk using a firearm when the shots would be overheard in the adjacent cells. 'But the next day I was taken down into a room in the basement where I had never been before. It was dimly lit and I was ordered to stand in a corner. There was a table with a stack of paper, pen and ink, and the wall was peppered with countless bullet holes and covered with brown splashes. I felt completely paralysed.' The SS duty man said the paper and ink was there so he could confess in writing, but Rip repeated again that he had nothing to confess. 'Stand against the wall,' came the command. 'I stood facing the wall, staring at the bullet holes and the splattered mortar. Behind me someone shouted, 'Ready, fire!' and there was a two-minute slam as bullets and chunks of mortar flew around my head. A sudden agonizing spasm seemed to rend my heart, and I collapsed. From a distance I heard loud whinnying laughter as I lost consciousness. For three days I couldn't get up and my heart felt violently clenched.'

On another occasion, desperate for a cigarette, Rip attempted to bribe the guards. They seized him and forced his mouth open. 'Since you like to play with fire, let's play with fire,' one mocked as he stuffed lit cigarettes into Rip's mouth. The burning was so unbearable that tears streamed down his cheeks. One of the guards urinated into a jug while the other held Rip squirming on the ground under his jackboot, and they poured the contents down his throat.

Was ist deine leidendste Erfahrung?
Ist dir Trinken bitter, werde Wein ...

What is the deepest loss you have suffered?
If drinking is bitter, change yourself to wine ...

Rudolf von Ripper was among a group of prisoners brought before the Chief of the Secret State Police, Hermann Goering, at Prinz Albrecht Strasse. During his interrogation, Rip doggedly insisted that he had nothing to confess. After an exasperated Goering shouted, 'Well and good, but war is war. You are old enough to know what you do.' When Rip insinuated that the Nazi regime's treatment of prisoners constituted a war crime, Goering replied, 'Be assured, you are appropriately treated,' hurriedly left with his entourage, and Rip was ejected from the room 'with kicks and punches'.

His failure to provide the SS with a confession left it without grounds for prosecution. Might they be wasting their time with Rudolf von Ripper when, after all, cells were constantly needed for the interrogation and torture of hundreds of incoming prisoners? Besides, there were the forthcoming Olympics to consider and an incident involving a foreign national would not be wise. Rudolf von Ripper was a damned nuisance but SS Diels was already plotting to turn him into a useful citizen. He had something special in mind for the young upstart and had him transported by train twenty-five miles north of Berlin, to the first Nazi concentration camp at Oranienburg.

CHAPTER FIVE
HITLER PLAYS THE
HYMN OF HATE

In the seventeenth century the Electress Louise Henriette of Orange-Nassau commissioned Mark Brandenburg to build the first Baroque castle at Oranienburg beside the River Havel. Pleasure gardens were laid out in the Dutch style, complete with an orangery. It would be a prosperous place since the river, three canals and two lakes supplied the new town with ample water for the brewing of beer. In March 1933, a brewery within sight of the Brandenburg castle on Berliner Strasse was taken over by the local SA and refitted as a concentration camp under the command of SS Rudolph Diels.

Soon after the National Socialists seized power, KV Oranienburg became a key site in the persecution of the opposition: a chilling, small-scale experimental camp serving Berlin before the construction of the System of Terror under the Inspectorate of Concentration Camps between 1938 and 1945. Another building on the outskirts of Oranienburg housed the administrative headquarters of the entire concentration camp system during the Third Reich. The men who sat behind desks in this leafy suburb determined conditions of imprisonment, coordinated forced labour and planned the organized mass murder of millions of human beings.

A photograph, probably taken by a prisoner at Oranienburg who escaped and fled abroad, reveals the shocked pallor of a line-up of shuffling prisoners dressed in humiliating striped pyjamas. Seized from homes and loved ones, the cultural elite of Berlin have fallen victim to the monster in a nightmare of mythological portent. Anaesthetised by dread, they are force-marched round and round the yard at Oranienburg by jackbooted thugs. This is their punishment for producing art and polemic warning the world to wake up to the coming Holocaust. On 17 March 1934, Rudolf von Ripper found himself here among Bauhaus professors and students, artists and intellectuals who had been accused of high treason.

The citizens of Oranienburg were permitted to see only what the Nazis wanted them to see. When they dared to look behind the high iron gates to the brewery, they saw folk like themselves stripped of their identities, their heads shaven, their heartbreak palpable. Day after day, over one hundred prisoners in boots and overalls were herded into a wagon train and taken up to 12 kilometres from the camp to level hills and lay rail tracks. Rudolf von Ripper was one of them. Each prisoner received coffee and a daily dose of lard coated bread as a meagre lunch. Day after day, when the townsfolk witnessed detainees being marched through the town to forced labour on behalf of the council, they looked away, kept their heads down and their thoughts to themselves. When might their turn come to find themselves on the other side of that gate? In the subterranean darkness of the cellars the SS experimented on their prey. Some of the first Nazi torture devices were put into practice at KV Oranienburg, including the odious standing cells, cells so narrow that men and women were forced to stand up day and night. Spaces designed to drive them mad before their inevitable, agonising, protracted death.

In diesem Wetter, in diesem Graus,
nie hätt ich gelassen die Kinder hinaus,
ich sorgte sie stürben morgen,
das ist nun nicht zu besorgen.

In this weather, in this horror,
I would never have let the children go out,
I was worried they might die the next day,
Now that is not something to worry about.

Having endured other detention camps, Carl von Ossietzky arrived at Oranienburg in 1934, where one of his former publishing colleagues was forced to flay him. Erich Müsham came too, having been tortured at the notorious Moabit prison on Lehrter Strasse and at KV Sonnenburg. His teeth had been knocked out, his glasses smashed and his head branded with a swastika. He had been forced to dig his own grave and to endure a mock execution before he was transferred to KV Oranienburg. There, sadistic torturers systematically broke his bones. For days he was left in the cellars, slumped on a sack of straw, almost blind and in agony from a blister bulging out of his ear canal. Thomas Mann, who had escaped to France, wrote that he felt sick at the thought of what Müsham and others suffered at the hands of the Nazis. In Paris, his friend Harry Kessler noted, *they are mentally tortured and thrashed three times a day, morning, noon, and night. But what gets the victims down more than anything ... is that they are forced to watch the ill usage of their fellows. That induces complete breakdown.*

Rudolf von Ripper witnessed the ill usage of his fellows and made sketches on scraps of paper that would later inspire one of his most accomplished drawings, *Defence of Culture: And the Walls Live.* In the cellars at Oranienburg, guards augmented the prisoners' suffering by spying on them day and night through grilles in the cell doors. In his drawing, Rip strips away the doors and walls of the cells to reveal the victims as Dante-esque souls in torment, elongated figures transparently naked, crying out to the heavens for a merciful release or hunkering in helpless despair. One victim hangs suspended and immobile in a standing cell, all self-possession lost. Two vulgar, grinning guards supervise the scene. It's all in a day's work for brutal fascists serving the Führer.

A former prisoner, Gerhart Segers, described in his eye-witness account, *Oranienburg 1933*, the obstacle course located in the back yard of the camp. Prisoners already suffering from malnutrition and torture were forced to jump through rods, climb a three meter high saddle horse, jump a wide ditch, then crawl like snakes about ten meters through a thin frame and finally walk a plank suspended over a pit. One day when forced into the obstacle course, five prisoners, Rip amongst them, started singing a traditional workers' song the Nazis had borrowed as a standard band tune. 'The men were driven back to their cells and then dragged out for roll call,' Segers wrote. 'No one wanted to say who had sung. The commander stood before them and shouted, "We are the masters of Germany now." A small voice from the ranks of the prisoners asked, "For how long?" As a punishment, the prisoners were herded with rifle butts into a grotesque forced sport, through a maze of obstacles and mines which the SA guards had originally built for their own exercises.'

Visitors, occasionally permitted access to the ground level of the former brewery on Sundays by appointment, had no idea that the floor they stood upon was all that separated them from the Dante-like inferno the SS had constructed below. The Third Reich's publicity machine swung into action, cunningly concealing its sinister duplicity by promoting KV Oranienburg as a centre for the re-education of opponents of the Nazi party. Propaganda films shot on the ground floor showed young men like Rip wearing dark sweaters and corduroys and supposedly creating arts and crafts. This select group had been directed to take part in a 'community education' programme and, despite his dire circumstances, Rudolf von Ripper came up with an idea to utilize his comedic and theatrical talents. He wrote a script and developed a set for an approved drama called *Visit German Castles!* Prisoners who had been active in Communist amateur dramatic groups played the principal roles. In the script, a travel agent recommends a chaperoned American tourist to visit sites with names ending in 'burg', including Oranienburg, a scenario that allowed numerous ironical allusions and had the prisoners as well as the guards in the audience roaring with laughter. But another literary endeavour was a step too far and resulted in Rip being sent to the standing cells that were the gruesome invention of the camp commandant. There were two at Oranienburg. Gerhart Segers, wrote that the standing cells were 'a kind of upright stone coffin, a room with a floor area of 60 to 80 centimetres.'

To distance himself from the horror perhaps, when Rudolf von Ripper recorded his experience later he wrote in the third person, 'the door closes right in front of his face, he cannot even stand, and after a while he collapses with his knees against the door and his back against the wall.

Four and a half days later, when the door was opened again, he fell out with swollen limbs, completely unable to move.'

SS Diels censored all letters making it impossible for Rip to write to his mother or Mopsa about the grim reality of Oranienburg or about how they might obtain his release. It was only after Rip had been held for seven months that Mutti, Mopsa and René Crevel discovered his whereabouts and sought the intervention of the French Embassy in Berlin. But before that, Fate in the form of Art was preparing to come to his rescue.

SS Diels had noticed Rip sketching fellow inmates and ordered him to paint a large oil portrait of Adolph Hitler. He was marched under guard to an art store in town to get the materials, no expense spared. In this borrowed time, Rip's wounded heart filled with hope and he lingered over this most odious of portrait commissions. Brushstroke by brushstroke he shaped an image of the 'silly little monkey' disguised as the Führer and, stealthily, with the conniv-ance of a comrade, he planned his escape. A friend of his comrade's wife would visit Rip and sign in as his fiancée, under the pretence that Rip was in the process of divorcing Mopsa Sternheim. Early in April, before the visit, Rip mixed paint identical to the colour of the enamel mugs visitors and inmates drank from and painted a scrap of paper with it. On the other side he wrote a message to the anti-Nazi Austrian Chancellor, Engelbert Dollfuss, via the Embassy in Berlin, informing him of his desperate plight. He fixed the message to the mug he prepared for his 'fiancée's' visit and when he poured out her coffee he said loudly enough for the guard to hear, 'Darling, your mug's dirty, you'd better wipe it.' The woman went to the communal sink, wiped the mug with her handkerchief and removed the concealed message. She returned the handkerchief to her pocket and

Rip refilled her mug. This courageous woman, whose name is not recorded, succeeded in getting the message to the Austrian legation.

About two weeks later, Rip was in the courtyard when he noticed a car with diplomatic plates and the Austrian flag parked at the gate and a legation secretary in conversation with the camp commandant. But, however much he longed for his immediate release, it did not happen. Several weeks of negotiations between the Austrian legation and the Prussian Prime Minister ensued before a message was at last sent from Oranienburg to Columbia-Haus requesting delivery of Rudolf von Ripper's effects: '1 shaver, 1 mirror, 1 shirt and 1 pyjamas to be washed.' On 2 May 1934, Rip confirmed their receipt and signed an affidavit to the effect that no coercion had been exerted upon him and that he would never turn against the new state and its institutions in speech or writing. He was freed on 11 May 1934 with a warning to leave Nazi-occupied territories immediately.

Rudolph Diels's furious parting shot would haunt Rip for the rest of his life: 'When you get to Austria, or wherever you go, remember that the arm of the Gestapo can reach across our borders, wherever it is desired. Take my advice. Keep your mouth shut.'

Austrian Nazi rebels murdered Engelbert Dollfuss on 25 July 1934 and that same month the SS murdered Erich Müsham shortly before KV Oranienburg was closed on the orders of Heinrich Himmler. More than three thousand people had been imprisoned and tortured there in the fifteen months of its operation. *If you hear that I committed suicide,* Müsham had told a fellow prisoner, *you must not*

believe it. The notorious Theodore Eicke who killed the SA chief Ernst Röhm in the Night of the Long Knives was one of Müsham's murderers. As commander of the Deathhead Division of the Waffen-SS and later commander of Dachau concentration camp, Eicke was feared as an evil brute even within SS ranks. After being awarded the Nobel Peace Prize, Carl von Ossietzky died in 1936 from tuberculosis and the effects of the brutality he had suffered in Nazi concentration camps including Oranienburg.

Today, all that remains of KV Oranienburg on Berliner Strasse is an ancient brick wall encrusted with weeds and ivy. The bricks are alizarin, the colour of dried blood. On the other side of the wall, a Lidl supermarket and busy car parking lot buzz with activity. A simple plaque set in stone near a bench acknowledges the existence of the camp and commemorates the death of Erich Müsham. Across the street, the windows of a typical Eastern Bloc housing estate eye the scene, but no one wants to sit on the bench and remember *that's where the SS once perpetrated its monstrous deeds.*

Deeply moved by the horrific torture his friend endured before his sadistic murder, Rudolf von Ripper resurrected Erich Müsham (and touchingly restored to him his spectacles) in his ironically titled drawing *Le déjeuner sur l'herbe* (also known as *Le Picnic*) which suggests the influence of Claude Monet's painting of the same name and Édouard Manet's *Le Petit Déjeuner*. A group of six concentration camp prisoners takes the permitted coffee break in a sunlit forest clearing, their naked bodies emphasizing their vulnerability even as menacing forces stealthily surround them: the shadow of a helmeted stormtrooper with a bayonet, a wagon train rumbling through the birch trees. In this brief respite from the gruelling labour of laying railway lines and levelling ground, their downcast eyes and emaciated bodies emphasise their exhaustion and despair. The figure on the left, wearing glasses and reading a book, resembles Erich Müsham; the man with strong features on his left resembles Carl von Ossietzky.

Situated on the outskirts of Oranienburg, the vast Sachsenhausen Concentration Camp, less than two miles away, replaced KV Oranienburg in 1934. Heinrich Himmler had expansion in mind: Sachsenhausen was to be the model for the network of concentration camps that would soon spread throughout Germany, Austria and Poland: Auschwitz-Birkenau, Bergen-Belsen, Jasenovac, Treblinka and all the others. The Nazis' declared intention was to give 'architectural expression to the Nazi world view and symbolize the subjugation of prisoners to the absolute power of the SS'.

A grim drive leads to the site of KV Sachsenhausen-Oranienburg where appalled twenty-first century visitors trail, struggling to imagine its unholy chambers and empty huts overflowing with human beings like themselves. Afterwards, they might find some solace in the exhibition at the visitor centre where words, photographs and objects record many of the victims of Oranienburg and Sachsenhausen, Erich Müsham and Rudolf von Ripper among them. Rip's exhibits include a photograph taken on the day of his wedding to Mopsa Sternheim and a copy of the Brown Book.

On the day of his release from Oranienburg, Rudolf von Ripper took a train from Berlin to Amsterdam where, despite his traumatised state, he found sufficient strength to relate his experiences to the Resistance. His life would never again be free from Nazi interference, but in the here and now, in relative safety, he reviewed his options. Where to go next? Germany had been barred to him, Austria was a hive for Gestapo agents, and he was a wanted man in Paris. The truth was that even this most fearless of men needed care and protection, and he travelled to Brussels where his father-in-law, Carl Sternheim, was living in exile. Mopsa joined him and they made a pact not to fight with each other. After hearing about the horror 'Jack' had been through, over the next few weeks Mopsa encouraged him to write newspaper articles about his brutal treatment at Columbia-Haus and the Nazi terror he had witnessed at Oranienburg. These articles, which appeared under a fictitious name in the Dutch newspaper *Het Volk, Paris Midi* and the *Manchester Guardian,* provided the European Resistance with invaluable information and helped to spread the truth about Nazi brutality. They also enraged the Third Reich.

Mopsa was able to give Rip news from Paris. It was a vain and volatile time. That the self-aggrandizing Dalí was as hell-bent on becoming an international celebrity as Hitler was on conquering Europe must have sickened Rip, as it did many others in their circle. Indeed, Dalí's refusal to declare himself an anti-fascist had led the Surrealists to label him an anti-humanitarian reactionary and he had narrowly escaped expulsion when the Surrealists' leader, André Breton, attempted to oust him from the movement. In 1934 a fascist attempt organised by private militias to overthrow the 1932 leftist coalition government erupted in the Paris Riots. It triggered the creation of organizations aimed at countering the rise of fascism in France, and the Surrealists committed themselves even more ardently to anti-fascist political action. In June René Crevel had been a key organizer of the Paris Congress of Writers in Defence of Culture at which Heinrich Mann (now living in exile in the south of France) and Ernst Toller were key speakers. On the night of the Congress Crevel's pain had become so excruciating he gassed himself in his apartment. There was news, too, of Klaus Mann who was undergoing rehabilitation for drug addiction at the Siesta Sanatorium in Budapest and would soon leave for America. In a letter to another friend, Klaus had written that being cured of his addiction was 'like being exiled from artificial paradise'.

Therapeutic as writing articles for the European press undoubtedly was, Rip's recovery from the serious physical and psychological consequences of his abuse would take time – and a change of scene. He decided to quit the mine-field of Europe and return to Mallorca where he had been enchanted the previous year. It was an inspired decision, but first, true to form, he was ready to embrace another risk in his one-man fight against tyranny, and he agreed to stage an exhibition at Paris's Galerie des Quatre Chemins. Even if he had been in good health, it would have been foolish to turn up in the French capital. Sure enough, German agents were right on his tail. Hadn't SS Diels warned him about the long arm of the Gestapo that could reach across borders? He arrived in Paris to the news that he had been denounced to the French Government as a deserter from the Foreign Legion, and he evaded arrest only through André Malraux's intervention. Exhibiting anti-Nazi drawings in Paris had been a risk too far and the experience brought Rip to his senses. He had exited the Nazi inferno by a hair's breadth, and now his first priority must be the recovery of his health and sanity in his 'haven of peace and beauty'. It would be two years before the Third Reich and Italy's Mussolini stirred up the havoc of the Spanish Civil War and threatened his Mallorcan paradise.

Apart from the fact that Rudolf von Ripper stayed in Palma and Pollensa during his second visit to the island, his exact itinerary remains a mystery. During his year in Mallorca he created many of the drawings for his master-work, *Écraser l'Infâme*. Pollensa was the artistic heartland of Mallorca in the 1930s, visited by luminaries including Juan Miró, and given Rip's propensity to seek out places of artistic activity, and the fact that he chose to reside in Pollensa in the 1950s, I place him there in the imaginative reconstruction that follows.

Throughout his confinement in the inferno, Rudolf von Ripper had become adept at concealing his suffering beneath a debonair exterior, but it would have been a hard and lonely act to keep up in the company of the irrepressible Pollensa painters. The tranquil old men who congregated in the bars to play chess or dominoes were all the company he needed; they welcomed him and they didn't ask questions. Rip, the self-confessed 'lonely traveller' needed to retreat and, when he felt well enough, to mine the gold hidden in the grim shadows of all he had experienced and transform it into art. He had little money to rent a place to live and work but his needs were simple. In those days, *casetas* or cottages, such as Jean Egger had constructed, came cheap: typically one or two rooms, with a primitive bathroom and kitchen decorated with Mallorcan tiles, and set in small gardens filled with flowers and birdsong that might have reminded Rip of cloisters.

He would have heard that Jean Egger had been forced to return to Germany for urgent medical treatment in October 1934 and had died a few days later. Perhaps Rip walked out to the Ternelles barrío to revisit Egger's studio, L'Hort, and stand in silence for a few moments on the terrace strewn with wildflowers, recalling their brief encounter two years previously. At least Egger had been saved the living hell of the Holocaust.

Rip's interest in all forms of arts and crafts would have taken him to island studios to see their unique designs of tiles, wrought iron, pottery, glass, tapestry and fabrics produced to a high standard. As part of his mission to recover his health, he would have been drawn into the countryside to walk in the foothills of the Sierra de Tramuntana until his strength ran out. Did he revisit the fascinating villa, Ca'n Cueg, and admire features he had not previously noticed: the arched Moorish aqueduct forming one of the boundaries of the property, and the open view to Puig Tomir, one of the highest peaks of the Sierra de Tramuntana? On his last visit, had he heard that Willy Messerschmidt had something to do with the house and that he had been questioned by the Gestapo and denounced as a traitor for selling planes to Romania? And that with the swift intervention of his buddies in the Nazi hierarchy, Hess and Goering, Messerschmidt was back in business, fulfilling Third Reich contracts for his Luftwaffe bomber planes?

An olive grove had been recently pollarded near Ca'n Cueg's aqueduct. Silver grey branches lay spread on the ground, and poultry pecked in a small enclosure beside a traditional cottage tucked away in a corner of the garden. Perhaps a caretaker lived there, tended the land and fed the hens. Ca'n Cueg's perfect design and proportions would have struck the young aesthete as the perfect place to settle down. Rip was almost thirty years old and surely it was time to start a family, but that wasn't going to happen with Mopsa who visited him that year in Mallorca, trailing her old resentments.

Then, as now, tourists visiting Pollensa were drawn to climb the chief attraction of the town, the Calvary. This would have been a good way for Rudolf von Ripper to test his fitness: if he could make it to the top, he could count himself on the road to recovery. Typically, visitors climb the three hundred and sixty-five steep steps of the Calvary counting each step as they go, admiring the delightful small houses flanking the way and the curving cypresses planted at regular intervals. As if in a perspective drawing, the steps grow narrower as they rise and steps that were constructed of sturdy stone at the start of the climb gradually turn to pebbledash. The best way to ascend is to climb one hundred steps then pause to rest and admire a bird's-eye-view of the town below: its lush, wide valley and the mountains soaring above the aquarelle bay of Puerto Pollensa. The surrounding countryside is enchanting in springtime, with fields of different shades of green, from lime to lovat, under hundreds of blossoming fruit trees. Stone dykes meander across the distant canvas of the view, delineating charming fincas scattered here and there, with their citrus and almond orchards. Rip would have climbed another hundred steps, bent a little to the left on account of his damaged lung. His skull would have throbbed along the line of the healing fracture, but his aches and pains would not have deterred his determination to reach the summit of the hill and sit awhile in the tranquillity of its chapel.

But the oratory of the Church of the Calvary turns out to be a morbid place displaying woeful paintings of the trials of Jesus, a plain altar of greyish marble faced with a carved wooden panel showing the Stages of the Cross and wooden benches. After the thirteenth century Catalan conquest of Mallorca, the Knights Templar who owned this site built a gallows on it. Convicted criminals were forced to climb the three hundred and sixty-five steps knowing they were about to die a horrible death at the summit. Most of their victims were island Jews and Arabs persecuted by the Knights Templar.

I imagine the sun breaking through the clouds and a light wind rustling branches of holm oak and wild olive trees and Rip leaving the oratory to sit on a bench in the courtyard, pondering the banal images in the oratory, images that failed miserably to bring home to the viewer the true extent of Christ's suffering. Perhaps he thought about the victims of the Knights Templar and of the Third Reich, and, given one of the most powerful images Rudolf von Ripper was about to create that year in Mallorca, perhaps it was after his visit to the Calvary that he remembered the torture of one historical victim in particular, Saint Catherine.

Catherine had been born into fifth-century Alexandria, where she converted pagan philosophers and the wife of the Roman Emperor Maximus. The enraged emperor condemned Catherine to death on a breaking wheel. Later called a Catherine Wheel, this torture device, a large wagon wheel, was used until early modern times for public execution by cudgelling victims to death. Rip was familiar with illustrations of the wheel. The condemned were lashed to it and beaten through the gaps in the radial spokes with an iron cudgel or a club until their limbs broke. According to legend, when the wheel broke into pieces after Catherine touched it, she was given a more merciful death by beheading. Angels carried her body to Mount Sinai, where the sixth-century Emperor Justinian established St Catherine's Monastery, a repository of early Christian art, architecture and illuminated manuscripts, a place of pilgrimage in the Egyptian desert.

His admiration of the French writer and philosopher, Voltaire, would have reminded Rip of another breaking wheel, too. In 1762 Voltaire had championed the cause of Jean Calas, a Protestant Huguenot shopkeeper living in Toulouse whom the Catholic hierarchy accused of murdering his son. Calas was tortured to death on a breaking wheel. Voltaire worked for three years to have the verdict against Calas overturned and the case made him famous throughout Europe as a champion of human rights. The image of the breaking wheel resonated to the extent that Rip would portray the wheel and the tyrant, Adolph Hitler, in a dramatically different guise from the idealized portrait Diels had ordered him to paint at KV Oranienburg.

The day came when he felt fit enough to start work in earnest on a series of surreal black and white drawings inspired by the experiences of his developing artist-self from childhood in the Austria-Hungary Empire to the present. Every line and nuance of his work had been hard won and he would title the series *Écraser l'Infâme*. He depicted the sadism of the Third Reich by borrowing techniques of film noir: dark spaces shafted with light and creepy shadows suggesting apocalyptic threat. He would expose by means of caricature the vulgarities and brutalities of the new ruling classes in fascist countries. His mind was stored with a vast trove of art history to inform his work: German and Flemish graphics of the fifteenth and sixteenth centuries, the medieval and contemporary art of the École de Paris, Surrealism, and his favourite Mexican muralists, Rivera and Orozco.

As he worked, the spirit of Voltaire accompanied him, Virgil to his Dante. Voltaire had become famous in his lifetime for his wit and his championing of civil liberties, including freedom of religion and freedom of expression, free trade and the separation of church and state. Like Voltaire, Rip's passionate mission had become the denunciation of cruelty and oppression in all its forms. Voltaire's catchphrase *il faut écraser l'infâme* (tyranny must be crushed) had been his blatant indictment of the Catholic church and all it stood for. Voltaire had been a prolific letter-writer as an old man, when he signed all his letters with the phrase. By borrowing *Écraser l'Infâme* as the title of his own Surrealist indictment of tyranny, Rip emphasised his identification with the outstanding figure of the French Enlightenment. Just as Voltaire fled into exile in his youth to escape the Bastille of a repressive French regime, Rip had been forced to flee the Third Reich. Like Voltaire, Rip's enforced exile would set the stage for the remainder of his life.

The theatrical setting Rudolf von Ripper chose for his uncompromising drawing, *Hitler Plays the Hymn of Hate*, is a desecrated Gothic church where a Lutheran pastor gives his blessing behind a breaking wheel. (The drawing's original title was 'Les Chrétiens allemandes'.) SS Goering stands on scales of justice weighed down by the knowledge that he, not Marinus van der Lubbe, had laid the Reichstag fire. Pro-Nazi European royalty and heads of state encourage Adolph Hitler in his sinister game whilst ignorant society women amuse themselves on a merry-go-round. When Hitler plays the organ the wheel turns, torturing the naked human beings who hang there in their death throes. Soon *Time* magazine would draw the attention of thousands of Americans to Rudolf von Ripper's compelling image: print number 10 in the series he would edition in Paris in 1938, *Hitler Plays the Hymn of Hate*.

CHAPTER SIX
¡ARRIBA ESPAÑA!

I n October 1935 a signature appeared in Eddy Sackville-West's visitors' book at Knole, 'Mopsa Sternheim von Ripper'. She had come to England to see her husband's exhibition, 'Kaleidoscope: Fourteen Surrealist Drawings by Rudolf von Ripper', on show for the first time at London's prestigious Arthur Tooth & Sons gallery. 'These weird and terrifying drawings, done in unique, semi-surrealist form, created a stir in art circles,' noted a journalist from *Collier's* magazine. The introduction to Rimbaud's *A Season in Hell* prefaced the drawings, some of which von Ripper had worked on in Mallorca and would soon be incorporated into his portfolio of seventeen prints, *Écraser l'Infâme* (1938). The exhibition was well reviewed in the British press – 'extraordinary pictures', 'technically excellent', 'worth seeing' – and the artist was deemed a 'Symbolist draftsman of undoubted technical achievement'. The drawings drew the attention of the British art historian Anthony Blunt (later exposed as a Soviet agent) who, despite reservations about their 'nightmarish character', found them 'intensely moving'. Mopsa wrote to her mother, 'Jack's exhibition is a dream' and that the impressively framed pictures looked 'terrific'. 'Jack himself is constantly being interviewed and photographed.' Yet, despite the positive reception by press and public, recognition in the form of hard cash was not forthcoming. As Mopsa lamented to her mother, this was very bitter for her husband, since paying for the frames and other costs of the exhibition had run up 'quite a lot of debt'.

The Tooth Gallery images of Nazi brutality included *Hitler Plays the Hymn of Hate* and incensed the Third Reich. The German Foreign Minister, Konstantin Freiherr, was sent to the British Foreign Office to protest that the work was 'an insult to a friendly state' and to demand the closure of the exhibition. Rip received a confidential summons from 'a very important personage' at the Foreign Office who asked not to be named but who wanted to meet the artist 'to share a moment of private pleasure' (the 'personage' was almost certainly Winston Churchill). He told Rip that he had taken delight in refusing the Nazis' demand to close the exhibition on the basis that the Tooth Gallery was a private enterprise that could not be interfered with under the laws of a free country. It was a drop in an immeasurably large ocean, but Rip must have been gratified by the British response.

The exhibition undoubtedly increased public awareness of Nazi tyranny and brutality. It also helped to awaken British audiences to Surrealism. The International Surrealist Exhibition at the New Burlington Galleries in July the following year attracted an average of one thousand people a day. Two thousand guests attended the opening by André Breton. Ever the showman, Salvador Dalí sensationally wore a deep-sea diving suit whilst delivering a lecture and almost suffocated under the helmet. The poet David Gascoyne found a spanner and released him before he passed out. Dalí returned to Paris to exhibit his 'Surrealist Objects' for the first time.

The following spring Rudolf von Ripper took the 'Kaleidoscope' artwork and other drawings to be photographed in preparation for publishing an artist's book or portfolio. After the financial failure of the Tooth Gallery exhibition, he intended to recoup his outlay by selling the work as a printed edition. But the venture was dogged by misfortune. When he returned to collect the artwork, the photographer confessed that it was nowhere to be found. The drawings had simply vanished. Had the German authorities *stolen* the artwork from the photographer's studio with the aim of suppressing it once and for all? In interviews later, Rip stood by the story of theft, but Mopsa's journal entry on 15 April 1936 reveals her fears over her husband's continuing addiction to drugs and the bad luck it brought in its wake. That evening, 'he left a roll of drawings, the work of two years, lying in a taxicab,' she wrote. The 'two years' included the year he had spent in Mallorca after his release from KV Oranienburg. Despite 'a feverish search' to retrieve the drawings and the offer of a generous reward for their recovery, they never reappeared. Deeply depressed, Rip retreated to Austria in a determined, but unsuccessful, attempt to break his drug addiction. He prepared for a second exhibition at Galerie des Quatre Chemins, and in the following two years he concentrated on recreating the missing drawings from photographs. But first, he had a just war to attend to.

Near Granada in August 1936, fascist Nationalists murdered the poet Federico García Lorca. The Spanish Civil War was underway. Hitler and Mussolini sent troops to the aid of General Franco and the Loyalists began recruiting in Paris. Rudolf von Ripper's bellicose instincts surfaced and he seized the opportunity to mount a direct riposte to

European fascism. He travelled to Spain that autumn to defend the Second Spanish Republic against the threat of totalitarianism.

Would-be members of the International Brigade, military units made up of volunteers from several European countries and America, touched base at Madrid. His depression allayed by his reinvention as a soldier and adventurer, Rip relished the scene and as usual he found his way to the heart of the action. The bars around the Plaza de la Puerta del Sol buzzed with networks of reporters, dissidents, spies and resistance fighters, including Rip's old drinking buddy, Ernest Hemingway, and Klaus and Erika Mann. Rudolf von Ripper is 'as much at home discussing philosophy or political idealism as he is in describing the best way to take cover from a machine gun,' observed Ernest Pyle, the American war correspondent. Rip volunteered as an aerial machine-gunner in the Spanish Republican Army and for seven weeks fought fascism from a Russian Chatto twin-engine bomber.

Ernest Hemingway shared Rip's commitment to combatting tyranny wherever he found it. He wanted to see how the lines of social demarcation were being drawn in Spain 'on the basis of humanity'. Hemingway was in Spain as an anti-war correspondent fired by his desire to keep the United States out of involvement in the future conflict he predicted would come. Spain, he believed, was 'a dress rehearsal for the inevitable European War'. His base was Madrid, but his stated intention was to visit all the nearby towns to find out what the war had done to the 'little people': waiters, cab drivers, cobblers, and shoeshine boys. After that survey, he would tour the front lines to 'see what the boys are doing with the new toys they've been given since the last war.' He paused in Madrid long enough to register at the censor's office at the International Telephone and Telegraph

Company (*Telefónica*) and to start an affair with another American correspondent, Martha Gellhorn. In Madrid, he met 'a stiff-backed, Prussian-looking' German communist named Hans Kahle, who had fought at the Western Front in the First World War. Kahle had fled Nazi Germany and reached Spain in time to hold command of the Eleventh International Brigade under General José Miaja during the defence of Madrid.

Hemingway was a frequent visitor to Kahle's Brigade composed of German communists and veterans of the First World War who all had military training. Rudolf von Ripper never gave a detailed account of his experiences in the International Brigade, but he is likely to have joined Hans Kahle's unit. From a Russian bomber plane, Rip participated in the defence of Madrid that continued throughout April. The city's Gran Via was so often strewn with broken glass that Hemingway remarked it was as if a hailstorm happened every day. The senseless shelling of the civilian population went on, day after day. The air was gritty with granite dust and the Gran Via holed with jagged craters. Conditions were grim both for the civilian population and the briga-diers and, although food was brought in from Valencia, it was inadequately stored and in short supply. Rip's eyewit-ness experiences of 'atrocities no less formidable than in the early years of Hitler's reign', provided the inspiration for another drawing entitled *Arriba España!*

Rudolf von Ripper 'seems to have been born without the normal sense of fear that inhibits most of mankind,' as Ernest Pyle observed. Fearlessness had become a central aspect of his adult personality, instilled by his early military training, his passionate opposition to fascism and the use of narcotics to enhance his mettle in tight corners. The fact that he smug-gled drugs into and out of Spain would tell against Rip in years to come. Many young men of von Ripper's generation resorted to drugs to ease their torment when Europe's cruel and oppressive regimes made them wonder if they had been born at the wrong time. After Rip was shot down over Madrid with twenty-one shrapnel fragments lodged in his legs and back, according to Fritz Molden in his memoir *Exploding Star* he was taken prisoner by the Falangists and sent to hospital. Some shrapnel fragments, too deeply embedded to be extracted by doctors, remained in his body for the rest of his life. He was eventually evacuated to France whilst his *amigo* Hemingway stayed on to create a documentary film entitled *Spain in Flames*. Hemingway shot sequences during the siege of the Alcázar of Toledo, the Loyalist triumph in the Guadarrama Mountains in January 1937, the destruction of defenceless towns by Fascist warplanes and the evacuation of the children of Madrid during Franco's relentless artillery bombardment of the city centre.

Rudolf von Ripper retreated once more to Salzburg to work on the drawings he still hoped to exhibit at the Galerie des Quatre Chemins. According to Countess von Salis-Samaden, when her son returned to Paris on the eve of his vernissage, the artwork vanished. Mutti wrote in a letter (1960) that Gestapo agents raided Rip's hotel room and stole the drawings whilst he was out. Either her account became conflated with the episode when the photographer 'lost' Rip's drawings two years earlier, or the Gestapo thieved his 'degenerate art' on two occasions. This much is certain: yet again, Rip had put himself in grave danger, and, on 20 February 1937 the Gestapo succeeded in having him arrested and imprisoned as a French Foreign Legion deserter. At first he was held in the Cherche-Midi military prison, then, probably because he was still suffering from shrapnel injuries, he was moved to the seventeenth-century monastery housing the Val de Grace Military Hospital. The conditions he faced are not documented, but the experience of imprisonment undoubtedly precipitated another harsh fugue during which he was forced to reappraise his situation.

His involvement in Spain had triggered an ideological turning point in his life. Any lingering faith he had in Marxist communism had been thoroughly shattered by the outcome of the Spanish Civil War and by mounting evidence of Stalinist totalitarianism. And now, where was he to turn? He could no longer expect to survive in Europe. He had been expelled from Germany; Austria was about to be invaded by the Nazis; Paris had become a hive of German undercover agents intent on stimulating counter-espionage and betrayal.

Mopsa von Ripper called on their influential contacts to assist in Rip's release, including the writer Jean Giraudoux, a prominent Jewish lawyer friend, Dr Apfel (later gassed at Auschwitz), and Countess von Salis-Samaden. A case was successfully made stating that Rip had withdrawn from the Legion because his injuries in the battle with the Druze had rendered him unfit for service. The FFL uniforms he had discarded in the park at Sidi-el-Hani a decade earlier had to be paid for before Rip was freed on the first of June, after three months of detention.

He intended to travel to England to improve his precarious financial situation – several portrait commissions awaited him there as a result of his 1935 'Kaleidoscope' exhibition – but to his dismay he was refused an entry permit. It has been suggested that the Foreign Office was aware of von Ripper's drugs smuggling escapades into and from Spain. He had no choice but to retreat to Salzburg, where, in the winter of 1937, he evaded an attempt by Gestapo agents to kidnap him and deliver him to Germany. In dire danger and aware of the Third Reich's intention to annex Austria, with the help of an American benefactor, Cummins Catherwood, Rip prepared to emigrate to the USA. But first he had serious business to attend to. He must secure the permanency of *Écraser l'Infâme*.

Ever since the summer of 1936, Rudolf von Ripper had been learning printmaking techniques, and he had reconstructed some of his lost 'Kaleidoscope' drawings as etchings at the Paris printmaking studios, Le Pressier and Louis Kaldor. The process had been interrupted by his involvement in the Spanish Civil War and by periods of heavy drug addiction and withdrawal. Isolated in Austria, Rip had acquired a printing press, copper plates and tools with financial help from 'an Englishman' (probably Eddy Sackville-West) according to a letter written by Countess von Salis-Samaden. With the degree of urgency his perilous situation demanded, he focused his creative energy on transforming all the drawings that constituted *Écraser l'Infâme* into prints. The portfolio would be a summation of his life.

Mopsa came to the rescue and arrived at the side of her knight errant, Jack. In the spring of 1937 she wrote to her father that she had been 'working endlessly with Ripper on a folder (engravings)'. It was Rip's task to etch the drawings onto copper plates and Mopsa's to ink up the plates and print off artist's proofs. 'I sit all day at the press and do not see any people, but it is a great joy, because each print is exceptionally beautiful,' Mopsa wrote. By the autumn, the couple had produced artist's proofs of sixteen prints as well as the title page and the verses from Rimbaud's *A Season in Hell*. On 1 February 1938 work began at the Le Pressier studio in Paris to print a limited edition of one hundred portfolios of *Écraser l'Infâme* on the finest papers, including

Imperial Japanese, Velin de Rives and Marques de Rives. The typography was printed at the Louis Kaldor studio. Each portfolio was stamped by hand, numbered and signed by the artist: *R.C.VRIPPER.*

In the late thirties, Paris printmaking studios were hives of industry where contemporary artists explored the medium of printmaking. In this, Rudolf von Ripper was in the vanguard along with the elite of Parisian artists. But the production of one hundred portfolios was far above the norm for print runs. Why did he produce so many? He knew he would soon be emigrating to the USA where he would need to supply a new market for his work, and, before his departure, he sold some of the portfolios to recoup his outlay on production. Vicomtesse de Noailles was one of his customers. He planned to leave further portfolios with a friend in a place of safety, probably with an eye to selling them when the coming war was over. Added to these calculations, he was almost certainly among the Paris artists who were selling portfolios to raise money for social causes, notably the Spanish Civil War which had personally affected a number of them. Miró, Picasso, Tanguay and other artists collaborated to create a portfolio of prints at the Paris studio of the English printmaker, Stanley Hayter. *Solidarité et Fraternité* raised funds to support the Republican cause and the relief of distressed Spanish children.

After he had delivered the copper plates of *Écraser l'Infâme* to the safekeeping of a trusted friend, Rudolf von Ripper's work was done. Like Dante during his wanderings and encounters in the Inferno he had looked evil in the face and unmasked it.

In the wake of the Nazi terror, film noir was imported from Germany and ripened in Hollywood. Screenwriters and producers worked at a frantic pace throughout the 1930s to create films in the genre that would satisfy the demand of a huge international audience. Rudolf von Ripper had been well aware of the technique, developed during the 1920s at the German film studio UFA when the threat of fascism was already seeping into every aspect of German culture. Nail-biting plots, romantic intrigue, creepiness, the sense of threat lying round every corner lodged deeply in the collective subconscious and enthralled cinemagoers on both sides of the Atlantic during the years of exodus when refugees crossed from Europe to America in constant procession. In emulation of human fear and paranoia, film noir's expressionist technique carved up the celluloid frame to the point of abstraction; shadows, darkness, and sudden shafts of light suggested apocalyptic threat. Rudolf von Ripper's life bore hallmarks of film noir. He lived on a knife-edge, but he pressed forward.

The darkness inflicted upon Europe by fascism informed film noir's menacing atmosphere. Menace had cloaked Rudolf von Ripper's life before and after his arrest by the Gestapo and would haunt him for years to come. He had combined film noir techniques with Surrealism to great effect in *Écraser l'Infâme*. Now though, he must tread carefully, finish his work and get out before it was too late. The Austrian filmmaker, Billy Wilder, had fled from Berlin to America the week the Reichstag burned. Fritz Lang fled after Adolph Hitler invited him to become the Nazi regime's filmmaker of choice. Different cloaks from the same Nazi manufacturers weighed on the shoulders of members of the Berlin Bauhaus, on Albert Einstein, Arnold Schönberg, Berthold Brecht, Max Breuer, Walter Gropius and thousands of other refugees who sought refuge in the New World.

The film *Casablanca* opens with an image of planet earth suspended in space followed by a map of Europe and North Africa. A stentorious voiceover describes an archetypical route taken by countless refugees to reach the safety of the New World: Paris to Marseilles by road or train, boat to Oran in Morocco, and overland to Casablanca. The hero of *Casablanca*, Richard Blaine, climbed aboard at Paris's Gare du Nord nursing a damaged heart after Ilsa failed to join him. The fictional Richard Blaine and the real Rudolf von Ripper might be mirrors for one another: urbane men in their mid-thirties, neither conventionally handsome (Bogart, playing Rick, has prominent teeth and a lisp like Rip) but both raffish, worldly wise and with an eye for beautiful women. Fiercely anti-fascist, they had both fought on the loyalist side in the Spanish Civil War and had become disillusioned by Marxist communism.

From Marseilles, Rick sailed across the Mediterranean to Morocco (occupied at the time by the Free French) and travelled on to Oran where hundreds of refugees waited for permits to sail to America. When the Free French Commander asked why he had come to Casablanca, Rick replied: 'To take the waters.'

'Strange to come to the desert where there is no water,' says the commander with a lifted eyebrow.

'I was misinformed,' Rick said, tersely drawing on a cigarette. He halted his journey at Casablanca and, with the faithful Sam, opened the legendary Rick's Bar Americain.

Two weeks before the Nazi annexation of Austria, in October 1938 Rudolf von Ripper boarded the SS Rotterdam bound for New York, a man with a mission whose heart was filled with the goodbyes he had said to family and friends he might never see again.

Rudolf von Ripper with his father and sisters in the Crown lands c.1913

Écraser l'Infâme. 'The Human Heart'

Écraser l'Infâme: 'Horsemen of the Apocalypse'

Écraser l'Infâme: 'Merry Go Round'

Écraser l'Infâme: 'Defense of Culture'

Écraser l'Infâme: 'Le déjeuner sur l'herbe 1933'

Écraser l'Infâme. 'Hitler Plays the Hymn of Hate'

Purgatorio
1939–1951

CHAPTER SEVEN
OVER THE RAINBOW

Soon after the Nazis seized Austria in the *Anschluss*, posters showing Rudolf von Ripper as a 'wanted man' and offering a reward for his capture were widely displayed. Countess von Salis-Samaden wrote later, 'Letters from Rip are missing. I am sure there was a raid on my house, an SS man lived in my house and next to us a man from the Secret Police, we were always well controlled ... I miss letters from the concentration camp Oranienburg and the first letter from Brussels after he was expelled from Germany.' Her son had escaped to America in the nick of time, a refugee rescued from the Holocaust by American benefactors. Rudolf von Ripper was one of the first European artists to be funded by the Catherwood Foundation, which provided him with a studio in Greenwich Village.

When he stood outside the modest two-storey building on Bethune Street in October 1938, he could see the East River under the high, twisting flyover leading to the Brooklyn Bridge. The Statue of Liberty was out of view in the East Bay, but a sliver of its grey water was enough to remind Rip of his first glimpse of that potent symbol. As the SS Rotterdam slipped past the lady with her high-held torch, he had hauled himself to the ship's rails, grey with exhaustion and seasickness to pay her homage. The majority of his fellow passengers were Jewish. In caps, shawls and headscarves they arrived on deck to give thanks for their deliverance from near-certain death in the extermination camps. He stood out among them, an Austrian aristocrat, Aryan, Catholic, and, above all, an artist. Yet he was united with them all. And although he arrived in that crowded boat like any other refugee, down on his luck and traumatised by the Gestapo, his battered old cabin trunk contained treasure in the form of several portfolios of *Écraser l'Infâme*.

Exiles who had safely arrived in Great Britain or the Americas could count themselves lucky. As Rip would soon learn, Mopsa von Ripper had joined the French Resistance with the hazardous task of guiding British airmen shot down over France across the mountains to the Spanish border. In Gibraltar or Lisbon, the airmen boarded feluccas or rendezvoused with bomber planes waiting on the flat plains of the Atlantic coast to ferry them to the safety of England. Even as Erika and Klaus Mann were writing their book about famous German exiles, *Escape to Life*, thousands of refugees from the Hitler and Franco regimes were embarking on perilous journeys to Britain and America. In the early months of 1939, around five hundred thousand Republican refugees fleeing Franco's Spain swarmed over the Pyrenees at Col-des-Balitres, an area known as *La Retirada*, The Retreat. Rudolf von Ripper might well have been among them had he not been wounded out of the International Brigade and lost faith in its intentions. Thousands of civilians, too, were heading for the Pyrenees in flight from the Gestapo. Many would die on the mountains. Disguised as tourists on mountain hikes, they carried their few possessions in rucksacks, just one step ahead of Nazi agents scouring France for Jewish escapees. Hunted and terrified, some of the refugees considered suicide. The German poet Walter Mehring and his wife were determined to end their persecution at the French border town of Cerbère, but the local pharmacies refused to sell them the drug they needed without a prescription. Gustav Mahler's former wife Alma Mahler-Werfel, Fritz Werfel and Heinrich Mann were in the Mehrings' group that set off with a guide from Cerbère to climb almost two thousand feet to the summit of Col-des-Balitres. Gustav Mahler's scores, packed into suitcases, had gone ahead by train under the guardianship of Varian Fry, an agent of the newly formed Emergency Rescue Committee who became known as 'the American Schindler'. Hundreds of anti-Nazi writers, artists and musicians reached safety thanks to Fry.

Over the slippery rocks of steep goat tracks and smugglers' routes the refugees clambered, the thorny bushes of the garrigue tearing at the hems of the women's dresses. Enduring sunburn, sweat and thirst, they climbed to the summit where a second guide waited to take them over the border into Spain. Gestapo agents arrived in Cerbère the day after the Mehrings' group left, a hair's breadth from being sent to the death camps. They escaped, but by the time the writer, Walter Benjamin, arrived at Portbou the Spanish police had received orders to return all refugees to the Gestapo in France. To return was not an option for Benjamin. The day before he crossed the mountains, he had shared half of his stock of fifty morphine tablets with his friend Arthur Koestler. Ill and exhausted after the arduous Pyrenees crossing, Benjamin swallowed fifteen of his remaining pills in his hotel bedroom at Portbou on the night of 25 September 1940. He had an angel in his suitcase: Paul Klee's 'Angelus Novus' which he had bought from the artist two decades earlier in Berlin. It was a treasured possession, akin to a holy icon. The author of *A Berlin Chronicle* was buried at Portbou.

From the outset Rudolf von Ripper found himself embraced into the company of refugee friends in New York. Erika and Klaus Mann had set up home in Manhattan with a group of artists, including Joan Miró, Kurt Weil and Ernst Toller. Peter Pears and Benjamin Britten arrived from England in 1939. 'Many of us young people felt Europe was more or less finished,' said Pears, whose friend Wystan Auden was already in New York with his American lover, Chester Kallman. Auden and Erika Mann had entered a marriage of convenience in 1935 to secure her British citizenship and, although they never lived together, they remained good friends until her death. Britten, Pears and Auden set up a similar ménage to the Manns, sharing their rented apartment in Brooklyn Heights with Paul Bowles and the writer Carson McCullers (in whose footsteps Rip would follow soon to an artists' retreat called Yaddo). These arty, bohemian groups attracted colourful and noisy guests including Rudolf von Ripper, Thomas Mann's younger son Golo, Gypsy Rose Lee and Salvador Dalí. Rip had no choice but to accept the Catalan artist's presence at Brooklyn Heights with his customary good grace, despite Dalí's showdown with the French Surrealists who had labelled him a racist painter, a friend of Franco and an apologist for Hitler. After all, he and Dalí shared the same benefactor: the billionaire tycoon Cummins Catherwood (1910-90) whose fortune derived from a family inheritance accumulated in the munitions industry and from his dealings as a Philadelphia stockbroker.

America loved Dalí; he was an Ad-man's dream. Americans wanted fun, entertainment and 'surrealism', but, as Rip was well aware, surrealism with a small 's' was far removed from the intentions of André Breton's Paris group. In this brave new world, dominated by billboard advertisements and neon lights, American surrealism promoted everything from Ford motorcars to chewing gum, it permeated Hollywood films, and Dalí, with his outrageous waxed moustache and performance art, was delighted to personify the dream.

Rudolf von Ripper's agenda was very different. The pace of New York, the hustle and bustle of its citizens and the astonishing mechanized and electrified phenomena captivated him from the outset. Freed from his tormented relationship with Mopsa and exhausted after years spent resisting fascism, he felt gratified by the New World's warm embrace. Nevertheless he felt deeply frustrated by America's reluctance to join the Allies. As the terror in Europe increased after *Kristallnacht* (November 1938), zealously he seized every opportunity to broadcast the truth about Hitler's dismemberment of Europe and a few weeks after he arrived *Time* magazine provided him with a dream platform. With flagrant irony and despite fierce opposition, *Time* magazine decided to name Adolph Hitler 'Man of the Year, 1938' and to illustrate its January 1939 cover with Rip's work. Print number 10 from *Écraser l'Infâme* was captioned, 'From the unholy organist, a hymn of hate' (the print later known as 'Hitler Plays the Hymn of Hate'). It was the first time the magazine had displayed art in preference to a photograph on its cover and Tom Matthews, *Time*'s art editor, may have been a key to Rip's major coup. Matthews was a close friend of the writer Robert Graves who had recently arrived from his home in Mallorca on a lecture tour in New York and Philadelphia, and Matthews later became godfather to one of Graves's sons. They must have been intrigued by the fact that Rudolf von Ripper had worked on drawings from *Écraser l'Infâme* on 'Robert's island' of Mallorca.

Time based its hard-hitting editorial on an interview with Rudolf von Ripper. 'After months in jail and in a concentration camp, where I myself had been subjected to torture and witnessed, inflicted upon others, those tortures which later led to the systematic liquidation of millions of human beings, I took up my fight again, with pencil and brush. And it seemed to me a single handed fight in those dark years between 1934 and 1939 when ignorance, treachery and fear slowly broke all spirit of resistance against the rising monster.'

The editorial likened von Ripper's work to the artistry and anger that fuelled Francisco Goya's etchings of the Napoleonic War and George Grosz's images of the First World War. 'Not often in history has a regime officially at peace stirred an etcher to the anger and disgust shown in a portfolio to be exhibited early this month at the Baltimore Museum of Art. Entitled *Écraser l'Infâme* these etchings are by a 33-year-old Austrian, Baron Rudolph Charles von Ripper, an 'Aryan' and devout Roman Catholic, who, in the winter of 1933–34 spent three and a half months in a Nazi political prison on a charge of high treason.' The article described Rip as a 'self-taught artist and international wanderer' whose work is 'elaborately Freudian and symbolic, his etchings are related in texture and technique as closely to Goya as to contemporaries Grosz and Max Ernst. Artist von Ripper, an 'Enemy of the State' in Germany, considers his work his answer to a Gestapo-Commissioner who warned him to keep his mouth shut.'

After the magazine hit the newsstands, Rudolf von Ripper became the toast of the town. 'Not only the connoisseurs appreciate his remarkable talent,' wrote Klaus Mann.

'His artistic work is original, even daring, without having that unconvincing touch of snobbery which sometimes spoils our pleasure in "surrealistic" creations'. No doubt Rip celebrated his bull's-eye with several magnums of best champagne shared with his New York friends. His apotheosis made him optimistic. If he could achieve this within a few weeks after his arrival in the United States what more might the New World have in store for him? The influential network Rudolf von Ripper could count on wherever he went swung into action. George Keller's Bignou Gallery dealt in contemporary artists including Picasso, Dufy, Utrillo and Matisse, and it arranged to exhibit Rip's prints at New York's ACA Gallery as well as Baltimore Museum of Art. In addition to the Bethune Street studio, Cummins Catherwood found Rip a cottage, appropriately named Sumatanga ('welcome weary traveller') in the grounds of his Pennsylvanian country estate. Robert Graves was living with the poet Laura Riding in a cottage nearby where Rip is likely to have encountered the couple.

Philadelphia's unofficial yet legendary greeter of celebrities, the socialite Reeves Wetherill, was the congenial host at Wanamaker's Crystal Tea Room in the city and might well have eased Rip's passage into high society. Wetherill was a friend of Cummins Catherwood and both men would visit Rip in Mallorca in later years. In Philadelphia, Robert Carlen observed that Rudolf von Ripper 'was an interesting painter, a very good modern painter'. Carlen sold limited edition prints, 'good colour reproductions from France and Germany' with Monet and Degas the most popular. An artist himself, Carlen had hit on the idea of selling prints when he had been desperate for cash to buy canvas and paints in the 1920s. 'You could sell a plate for $200 to the American Artists Group and they would pull the proofs from them, print them up, then the artist would sign them.' Limited editions were run off to a maximum of 250 prints and Carlen's business took off, selling prints door-to-door in well-off Philadelphian neighbourhoods. He welcomed Rudolf von Ripper into his stable of Carlen Gallery artists and added his prints to his list.

A mile from Saratoga Springs in Upstate New York, a driveway opens between gateposts and crosses a bridge between two ponderous lakes. The road twists round a steeply curving hill with wooded banks on either side and peters out at Yaddo Mansion. When Rip arrived at Yaddo artists' retreat on 28 June 1939, his fame preceded him. The residents at Yaddo were well aware of his *Time* illustration and the magazine's uncompromising editorial. Indeed, Yaddo would claim that Rudolf von Ripper's *Time* coup was instrumental in influencing America to join the Allies in the struggle to end Hitler's mad dream of world hegemony.

Cummins Catherwood's Midas touch had presented Rip with the Bethune Street studio and access to Sumatanga. The fact that Catherwood had a home at Saratoga Springs, near the internationally famous racecourse bordering the Yaddo estate, suggests that he also had a hand in Rip's next metamorphosis. Rip would have been well disposed to the proposal to spend a summer at Yaddo since Carson McCullers and other cultural contacts, notably his Paris *copain*, the musician Virgil Thomson, were enthusiastic Yaddo artists. Indeed, Thomson had been entrusted with the task of recommending suitable artists to the trustees.

For the first time since he had left the Austrian Crown lands, Rudolf von Ripper found himself living in a large manor house on a wooded estate that might well have reminded him of his childhood homes. Yaddo had a fascinating history. In the previous century, when the estate had comprised a farm, gristmill and tavern owned by a Revolutionary War veteran, Jacobus Barhyte, the land was said to be the source of 'mystical creative power'. Barhyte's Tavern had been popular with several well-known writers of the first half of the nineteenth century, including Edgar Allan Poe who is said to have composed 'The Raven' in this landscape. The billionaire philanthropist Spencer Trask and his wife Katrina bought the estate from Barhyte in 1891, and, before tragedy struck, it had been their favourite family home. Trask's shrewd investments included Thomas Edison's revolutionary electric light bulb and, later, the revival in 1896 of the ailing *New York Times*. When the original house burned down one winter, the Trasks replaced it with a new mansion and named it Yaddo: an extraordinary pastiche of architectural styles and reminiscent of an illustration from a story by Hans Andersen. Its interior was kitted out with Jacobean-style furniture, a motley collection of antiques, sculptures, paintings and *objets d'art*, including breast-shaped lamps, floral pendants and stained glass windows commissioned from the studios of Tiffany & Company. An eager stream of artists, composers, statesmen and industrialists arrived to attend the Trasks' house parties. To Katrina Trask, an impassioned patron of the arts, Yaddo was far more than an escape from city life. It was an entrance into a better world, a spiritual as well as a physical kingdom.

The Trasks had already suffered the deaths of two of their children when tragedy struck again. Katrina contracted cholera and, when she was expected to die, her doctors deemed it safe for their two remaining children to come to her bedside to say goodbye. In a terrible twist of fate, Katrina survived and both children died of the disease. She and Spencer were still mourning their loss when Katrina went walking one day in the Yaddo woods when 'an unseen hand seemed laid upon me'. Her vision prompted her to establish a retreat for artists, a Phoenix out of the ashes of their terrible loss, 'a permanent Home to which shall come from time to time ... authors, painters, sculptors, musicians and other artists both men and women, few in number but chosen for their creative gifts and besides and not less for the power and the will and the purpose to make these gifts useful to the world'. A trial summer residency was organised at another Trask property on the shores of nearby Lake George. The project was a success, not least because the artist, Georgia O'Keefe, had been an enthusiastic first resident artist, and in 1926, after Spencer Trask's death, the colony was established at Yaddo.

Yaddo writers and artists were, and are still today, offered unstinting hospitality and studios to work in undisturbed between the hours of nine and four every day. As a painter, Rudolf von Ripper would have been given one of the purpose-built studios in the woods of the estate. After very good dinners in the Jacobean-style dining room of the Mansion he was free to unwind in the Drinks Room with his fellow guests. The novelist and travel writer Eleanor Clark wrote, '[the summer of 1939] was distinguished by the presence of four European refugees from the Nazis: the Austrian novelist Hermann Broch; Dr Martin Gumpert, author of a book about Hahnemann's discovery of homeopathy; a former editor of the *Berliner Staats-Zeitung*, named Richard A. Berman, who before getting out of Germany had spent a year hiding under a bed in a farmhouse and who got to the US via Samoa; and the Austrian artist, better known for etchings than oils, Rudolph von Ripper ... The air was thick with untellable romance, on a scale close to legend, as to both grandeur and tragedy'.

Hermann Broch (1886–1951) was famous for his novel *The Sleepwalkers* (1932). The Nazis had arrested him after the annexation of Austria in 1938. Broch was associated with the Modernists Robert Musil, Rainer Maria Rilke and Elias Canetti and, after a campaign by supporters including James Joyce he had been allowed to emigrate to America. Rudolf von Ripper and Hermann Broch formed a deep friendship at Yaddo where Broch was working on another novel, *The Death of Virgil*, and an essay on mass behaviour, which he never finished. Broch wrote that in America he felt 'deeply uneasy in my shoes walking through the irreality [sic] of a soi-disant peaceful country, i.e. a country which has nothing [more] in mind than to maintain its peaceful habits ... and the shape of things here, this business of business, of competition and of petty ambitions in petty politics, in petty academic intrigues, petty writings, petty pseudo art, petty erotic affairs, etc., etc., all this is only a very low level of reality.'

Broch was the eldest of the Yaddo refugees and Rip was the youngest. Gumpert, who had emigrated to the USA several years earlier, was writing a history of the Red Cross; Berman, entranced by stories he had heard about Robert Louis Stevenson's life in Samoa, was planning to write a book about the Scottish author. Eleanor Clark describes Berman as 'small, somewhat deformed, of sickly pallor and apparently [he] had some kind of hormone deficiency that spared him the need of using a razor.' Years later, Clark summed up von Ripper as 'a baron and erstwhile cavalryman in his mid-thirties, reputed to be the only man ever to succeed in escaping from the French Foreign Legion ... [His] flamboyant dash through life would continue through daring exploits in the American forces in the war we were about to bear the start of, ending ... via the smuggling of something or other in a

Spanish prison'. Eleanor was high on her own long distance romance that year with the Irish poet, Louis MacNeice, and Rip found in her a fellow prankster. Yaddo's director found it necessary to send her a letter of reprimand requesting that she get down to work and curb the late night parties in her room that were disturbing some of her fellow guests.

Rudolf von Ripper posed for the summer 1939 group photograph taken in the ornate Great Hall of Yaddo Mansion. It shows the other refugees lined-up on his left: Hermann Broch, Richard Berman and Martin Gumpert, and the Americans forming rows in front of them, seated on chairs or cross-legged on the carpet. Eleanor Clark is there, and the writer Newton Arvin who 'wore dark suits to breakfast, sat like a furled umbrella, and buttered his toast to the edges'. Rip stares at the camera with fierce intensity from his position next to Katrina Trask's Jacobean-style throne. Appropriately enough, a statue of Athena, Goddess of War, is positioned beside the throne. Both the throne and the statue have remained in exactly the same place for over seventy years. In the twenty-first century, standing on the exact spot where Rip was photographed in 1939, time dissolves. A veil lifts, and he springs to life in the words of the correspondent Ernest Pyle who would follow Rip's exploits during the coming Italian Campaign: 'His knowledge of the English language is profound and his grammar perfect, but he still pronounces his words with a hissing imperfection. He swears lustily in English. He is meticulous in his personal appearance, yet doesn't seem to care whether he sleeps between satin sheets or in the freezing mud of the battlefield.'

Released from the battlefields of Syria, North Africa and Spain and the Nazi concentration camp, Rip must have appreciated the comforts of Yaddo where daily life was filled with privileges he had not known since childhood. Thick white towels and bed linen were changed once a week and after work excellent meals were served at the vast Jacobean dining table. But underneath his bonhomie and party tricks Rip burned with frustration over America's continuing failure to support Europeans who were being 'subjected to the Nazi sword'. The film of *The Wizard of Oz* had just been released. It seemed that all of America was singing its hit song 'Somewhere Over the Rainbow' at the same time as atrocities such as Rip had witnessed and suffered were increasing daily on the other side of the Atlantic. News of the expanding network of Nazi concentration camps spreading across Europe blistered his soul. He had done his best with the *Time* interview but his attempts to convey the full extent of the Third Reich's terror tactics to his new American friends, anti-fascist as most of them were, was akin to describing the dark side of the moon, so he got on with his work, enjoyed the company at Yaddo, and partied.

The Yaddo group regularly tuned into radio reports from the BBC World Service. Exactly two months after Rip's arrival, news came of the Nazi-Soviet pact and the invasion of Finland and Poland. A note in the archive records, 'Yaddo's writers, many of whom are actively involved in anti-fascist politics, are stunned by the August 28th Hitler-Stalin Pact, which crushes hopes that Soviet communism will be a force against fascism.' Then, on 3 September, between crackle and hiss, they heard the voice of Neville Chamberlain announcing that Britain was at war with Germany. Eleanor Clark described Yaddo's literary left 'huddled in shock and dismay around the one large radio upstairs as the world outside Yaddo's gates ... suddenly turned more dangerous and confusing.'

Everyone congregated soberly in the Drinks Room to down a few stiff ones. A planned music festival was cancelled.

Richard Berman, unable to contemplate further his Robert Louis Stevenson story, cabled his friend Winston Churchill to offer unqualified support of Britain's stand against the enemy. On 5 September, Berman took his broken heart upstairs where he collapsed and died in his Yaddo bathtub. As the youngest and healthiest of the refugees, Rip was delegated to travel by train to New York with Berman's coffin and deliver it to an international refugee organization.

On a summer evening in the twenty-first century, the Music Room at Yaddo Mansion is filled with the bittersweet riffs of a Schubert piano sonata. The room resembles a chapel, with long rows of pews, stained glass windows, carved wood panelling and almost-life-size oil portraits of two of the Trask children. An attentive small audience sits dispersed among the pews while a young Russian composer plays the Steinway grand piano that was often played by former artist-in-residence, Leonard Bernstein. The pianist's technique is terrific but, as the work develops, something disturbing floats through the music. In the Russian's interpretation, the form of the sonata holds up well but the running motifs between the planks of the piece sound wayward and almost menacing. After the small silence that follows his last note, the pianist takes off his black-framed spectacles and wipes them on his shirt: 'I won't be playing here again,' he announces pensively. 'There was something in the air, very uncomfortable. I can cope with God on one shoulder and the Devil on the other, but not with whatever was in the room when I was playing just now.'

Yaddo is filled with ghosts, spirits, *duendes*: traces of the visionary Trask founders and their children, traces of all the

Yaddo artists, writers and composers, and of all the work they have created here during eight decades. Perhaps the bittersweet spirit of Rudolf von Ripper had been part of that 'whatever it was' the Russian referred to: morphic resonances, transformed into birdsong in the Yaddo woods by day, and thousands of shimmering fireflies under its dark waving trees on summer nights.

Rip captured Hermann Broch's exquisite sensitivity in an elegant line drawing before he said goodbye to Yaddo on 20 September, sustained by the award of the first of two Guggenheim Fellowships. His entry in the 21st century Yaddo website reads: 'Nobleman, circus clown, soldier and artist, Rudolph Charles Hugo von Ripper (1905–1960), was one of the most remarkable creative spirits ever to pass through [Yaddo] ... It seems he used his time [here] like he used any brief pause in his life, as a moment to catch his breath before launching his next literal or figurative attack ... While his personal heroics were the stuff of legend his art may have been an even greater force in the war. When *Time* magazine named Hitler 'Man of 1938', they chose von Ripper's grim etching 'Hymn of Hate' to illustrate the cover. With its gruesome Goya-esque imagery and bitter critique of the complacency of Europe's leaders it was arguably a crucial first step in turning American opinion towards the war.'

CHAPTER EIGHT
RED BULL

S everal of Rudolf von Ripper's former Bauhaus contacts
including Walter Gropius, Wassily Kandinsky and Marcel
Breuer, had settled in New England. Gropius was designing
houses in the Boston area, Kandinsky held a position at
Harvard School of Architecture, and Breuer was developing
a project at New Canaan, Connecticut, where Rip settled
down in a studio barn to continue his politically inspired
graphic work

The award-winning American poet, Muriel Rukeyser,
might have met Rudolf von Ripper when she was working
as a journalist in Spain during the Civil War. He now set
out to illustrate a volume of her poetry commemorating the
abolitionist John Brown (1800–1859) who believed armed
insurrection was the only way to overthrow slavery. The
verdict of some historians has been that Brown's death by
hanging triggered the American Civil War. Through his art,
Rip tossed Americans a veiled but potent rebuke: had they
forgotten the atrocities of their own Civil War?

When his prints illustrating Rukeyser's emotive poems,
The Soul and Body of John Brown, were exhibited at the
Bignou Gallery in 1944 a reviewer praised von Ripper's
'fine draughtsmanship and the deep emotional grasp of

the subject ... [he] understands the ripple of movement in terms of line, and his beautifully sustained drawing of figure ... is eloquent of the rhythm which pervades all these etchings'. Rip was not the only émigré to reflect in his art a response to America. Benjamin Britten collaborated with Wystan Auden on the operetta *Paul Bunyan* (1941) based on the story of the folkloric American lumberjack. Britten's music incorporated a variety of American styles: folk songs, Blues and hymns. Critics including Virgil Thomson slated the work and one of them found Auden's libretto 'flaccid and spineless'. In a metamorphosis yet to come, Rip would welcome Benjamin Britten to Austria for a performance of his *Michelangelo Sonnets.*

Rudolf von Ripper also revisited his talent for portraiture during his New Canaan period, and achieved another *Time* magazine cover. After Hitler invaded Denmark and Norway in April 1940, *Time* commissioned Rip to come up with a portrait of Nazi General Nikolaus von Falkenhorst, ground commander for the invasion of Norway. It is said that suddenly one day in the previous February Hitler had given Falkenhorst until 5pm to come up with a strategy, and that, having no military maps or charts to hand, the General had planned the operation from a *Baedeker* guide to Norway he happened to pick up at a bookshop en route to his hotel. Rip's drawing on the cover of the 13 May 1940 issue of *Time* was captioned *Falkenhorst – Invader of Norway* and his portrait of Broch appeared in a special issue on Exiled Writers in the *Saturday Review of Literature.* The following year, his portraits of Thomas Mann and the Austrian director and film star of the silent era, Erich von Stroheim, appeared in *Decision,* a magazine edited by Klaus Mann.

Salvador Dalí and Rudolf von Ripper had both shown work at the Bignou Gallery in 1939, and Rip also exhibited at Yale University Library. Dalí the showman had become a huge celebrity in America after he created a pavilion for the New York World's Fair that year. Later, after the Bonwit Teller scandal he was front-page news. The New York department store had commissioned Dalí to design two window displays. When Dalí discovered that one of his displays containing a bathtub had been tampered with, he thrust the tub through the window in a fury and followed himself, under a shower of glass shards. A passing detective immediately arrested him on a charge of malicious mischief and he hit the head-lines again.

On 1 September 1939, the day war had been declared in Europe, Fulco, Duke of Verdura had opened a shop on Fifth Avenue with the financial backing of Vincent Astor and Cole Porter. Verdura was a master jeweller whom Rip had encountered in Paris in the 1920s when Verdura joined Coco Chanel's stable of aristocratic servants and went on to create both costume jewellery and precious jewellery for the House of Chanel. Soon after his Fifth Avenue shop opened for business, Verdura collaborated with Salvador Dalí on a jewellery collection for a 1941 exhibition at a New York art gallery. Cummins Catherwood, one of the first collectors of Dalí's Surrealist jewels, snapped up an astonishing twen-ty-two pieces from the exhibition. In one of his most extraor-dinary guises – as 'Keeper of the Dalí Jewels' – von Ripper would re-encounter Dalí and Verdura. But first, having survived one inferno as an artist at the hands of the Nazis, there was to be a re-visitation of that grimmest of regions. In this inferno, though, he would be fully in command both as an artist and a soldier, hunting Nazis in Europe.

The Japanese attack on Pearl Harbour in December 1941 shocked America into joining the Allies. Rudolf von Ripper had been waiting for this. Here, at last, was his opportunity to avenge the Third Reich's sadism in the death camps, its annexation of his Austrian homeland and seizure of the family property. Around this time, Rip heard that Mopsa had been arrested by the Gestapo in France and severely tortured before being sent to Ravensbrück concentration camp for women, twenty-five miles north of Berlin. Like Klaus Mann, who was serving with the Psychological Warfare Branch of the American Army in Italy, Rip became an American citizen and anglicised his name to Rudolph Carl von Ripper. He set about enlisting.

But would he be accepted? As 'Mr Ripper' was well aware, a foreigner with a bad eye, a suspected heart murmur, a damaged lung and the scars of over twenty wounds was not a promising candidate for military service. The Army doctor who examined him approved 'limited service'. On 5 September 1942 he was sent for 'strange and childish' basic training with the American Army Medical Corps in Texas. 'I worked for OWI [The Office of War Information] designing war posters; but I wanted to fight,' he lamented, then cheered up when he was sent to the Army Art Corps in North Africa: 'Now I can fight *and* paint,' said a jubilant Rip. As Corporal Ripper, an American soldier fluent in German, he was ordered to report to the headquarters of the 34th Infantry Division at Cape Falcon, near Oran, Morocco, where he was attached to the G-2 section responsible for the interrogation of German prisoners of war. He began drawing at once, a humanitarian scene far removed from anything he had experienced at the hands of his Gestapo interrogators at the SS Columbia Prison: a makeshift cell lit by a guttering candle in a bottle where a GI stands arms folded by the curtained exit whilst the German prisoner of war enjoys a billycan of coffee with his note-taking interrogator.

When the War Department discontinued the activities of the Army Art Corps in August 1943, Rip was transferred to the Military Intelligence Service with the red bull insignia of the 34th Division (known as the Red Bulls) sewn onto his uniform. 'The 34th Infantry Division is a National Guard outfit from the Middle-west,' Rip wrote. 'Most of its members come from Iowa, South Dakota, and Minnesota. Knowing little of the United States, having hardly been out of New York, I was deeply impressed by the straightforwardness and the hardiness of these Midwesterners, who were my comrades. Most of them had strong isolationist, anti-militaristic backgrounds and nine out of ten of the men hardly realized what was at stake in the war they fought so bravely and so stubbornly. They had a job to do – and they did the job well. They were truly representative of the US Army, that wondrous thing created almost overnight by a democratic society.'

On 3 September, after General Eisenhower announced the Italian government's agreement to an armistice with the Allies, the German response was ruthlessly to occupy Italy and its fierce resistance took the Allies by surprise when it landed troops at Salerno on 9 September. Rip was there with the Red Bulls, ready to record the stark mayhem in a perspective drawing: battleships on the horizon, landing craft, a platoon marching away from the beach, a group of soldiers brewing up coffee over a makeshift fire. 'It has been my aim to suggest, through my own experiences, a picture of the life in action of the American soldier,' Rip wrote. But he also recorded the similar fate of what Hemingway had referred to as 'the little people' in Spain: a sombre procession of Italian refugees, men, women and children, fleeing down a steep donkey track, balancing their bundled belongings on their heads.

By late September the Germans had withdrawn north-wards to construct the Gustav Line across the boot of Italy, directly in front of the monastery of Monte Cassino, with the intention of staunching the offensive of British, French, Canadian and Polish Allied troops. At the beginning of October, the 34th, 36th and 45th Divisions of the American Army pushed up the west coast of southern Italy to Naples, the most northern city capable of receiving air support from bases in Sicily held by the Allies. The Allies then advanced into the difficult terrain of the Apennine Mountains with crests and peaks rising three thousand feet above ground level. Confronted with a succession of ridges and rivers subject to sudden flooding across their line of advance, the Allied commanders' plans were constantly thwarted. Corporal von Ripper, soon to be promoted to Lieutenant, recorded the journey in startling detail: olive groves, rocky terrain, exhausted men kipping in dugouts, wiremen laying communications lines and concertina wire.

One of the best-known American war correspond-ents in Europe, Ernest Pyle (1900-45) travelled with the troops, sleeping in tents or dugouts, ignoring enemy fire and witnessing engagements with the enemy. On the night of 12 October the Fifth Army attacked across the Volturno River. On the German side, the terrain favoured rearguard defensive tactics during their retreat north. Ernie Pyle was fascinated by Rudolph von Ripper, whose stated aim was 'to take the applesauce out of war' through his drawings. Pyle endorsed his approach; he himself chose to write from the perspective of the common soldier, rather than to recount the movements of armies or the agendas of generals. His 'folksy', syndicated reports on the war in Europe brought him an enthusiastic following in American newspapers and won him the Pulitzer Prize for journalism. 'Lt. Rudolph

Charles von Ripper was one of the most fabulous characters in this theatre of war,' Pyle reported. 'He is the kind they write books about. I happened to meet him a few days after he arrived on this side ... Last fall he was put in a front-line regiment, and in October he was wounded by shell splinters. He doesn't seem to mind being shot at all.'

Thanks to the Mafia, readily available drugs assisted Lt. Ripper's war exploits and eased his painful injuries. Although the war had disrupted European drugs trafficking to the extent that it largely disappeared, according to historian Alfred McCoy, American military planners – and in particular the US Navy which had landed the troops in Sicily – forged a short-term political alliance with the Sicilian Mafia via Lucky Luciano from his prison in New York. Mussolini had struggled to break the Mafia, but it briskly revived under US military occupation and benefitted from links back to the United States with their confreres in organized crime. As the trafficking routes were re-established through the Middle East and Europe to the United States, revived and restored Sicilian and Corsican Mafia syndicates in Southern France became major participants.

Rudolph von Ripper's reliance on drugs by no means diminishes the heroism that was becoming legendary. Pyle was not the only American correspondent to become enthralled by the Austro-American, derring-do lieutenant. Early in 1944, Cyrus Leo Sulzberger (1912–1993) arrived at the Italian front line wearing the ubiquitous attire of a journalist of the Roosevelt era: homburg, trench coat, collar and tie, with horn-rimmed glasses. His elevated way of speaking belied a privileged background: wealthy East Coast family members who owned *The New York Times*, a Harvard University education. Sulzberger was thirty-two and had proved his worth working for the *Pittsburg Press* and the *United Press Agency*. The newspaperman stood out and caused some amusement among the GIs at army headquarters until he reluctantly agreed to change into uniform and began travelling with the troops. Sulzberger was an archetypical newshound with a fine-tuned nose for a good story, and pushing north with the American divisions, he heard other reporters discussing the 'incredible individual Rip', and made a point of befriending him. Sulzberger knew their mutual friend Hemingway; he had the ear of General De Gaulle, Dwight Eisenhower and other high-ranking politicians and leaders of the day, yet he described Lt. Ripper as the toughest man he had ever known, and as loyal as anyone could ever be. They became lifelong friends

'At that time, Ripper's name was almost legendary [among the troops],' Sulzberger wrote in his war memoir *Unconquered Souls*. Both Sulzberger and Pyle (in *Brave Men*) recorded a 'Ripper' anecdote from the trenches that was circulating throughout the entire 5th US Army. Like the two newspaper men, the GIs followed the exploits of Ripper, the strange German in US uniform who frequently disappeared behind the Nazi lines for days, killing silently with his knife, only to creep back to the nearest post of the US Division where he would mischievously steal up to a frightened guard. Each time the guard would shout 'who goes there?' into the darkness, Lt. Ripper would say his name in an exaggerated German accent, and the guard would order the 'goddamned Kraut' to come out of the bushes. At gunpoint, Rip would be led to the battalion where the command post would be telephoned and a strange fellow wearing US uniform but speaking 'like a Teuton' reported. 'Is his name von Ripper by any chance,' would come the reply with an order to 'let the bastard go free and tell him to stop being a nuisance'. Eventually, Rip was forbidden to go out on solo patrols unless he had the Division commander's permission.

The campaign of the American 5th Army slowed to a crawl. After crossing the Volturno the troops had had to struggle for every meter they advanced, knee-deep in mud and under grim weather conditions. It seldom stopped raining and the troops lived in almost unimaginable misery, covering themselves with stones and sleeping in crevices, behind rocks or in caves. Ernie Pyle wrote that it was as if the troops lived in prehistoric times when they would have wielded clubs rather than machine guns. 'There are no words adequate to describe the hardships and privations endured by all who carried the fight to the enemy,' wrote Major General Ryder, commander of the 34th Division. 'It was a heartbreaking period for the men in the front lines ... the hazardous crossing of the Volturno River near Caiazzo and the fierce engagement with the German 3rd Panzer Grenadier Division, the re-crossing of the river, the trek over the mountains to the ferocious fight for Mt. Pantano, 3300 feet of snow covered, precipitous crags. Then came the capture of San Vittore and Cervaro, the crossing of the Rapido River, the final breaking of the German Gustav line and the bitter fight to control Cassino.'

In pencil and ink on his sketchpad Lt. Ripper captured it all: soldiers with pinched faces, waist deep in water, their rifles held above their heads as they cross the Volturno River; the horrifying scene the US infantry stumbled across in the eerie silence of a forest outside the village of Caiazzo: the bodies of five naked teenagers, raped then kicked to death by brutal assailants, their mouths agape in anguish at their terrible fate. In Rip's drawing, 'Distant view of San Vittore, Cervaro and Cassino', soldiers march single-file into a craggy landscape where the campaniles of peaceful agrarian towns they can see down in the valleys tolled the hours before this war. Monte Cassino dominates the three towns from its mountain stronghold, the fortress the Allies breached to break through the Gustav Line.

In addition to recording the Caiazzo forest tragedy in a drawing, in his capacity as an Intelligence Officer Lt. Ripper was detailed to investigate the war crime, as Sulzberger records in his memoir. After interviewing villagers and German prisoners of war, he succeeded in tracking down a German lieutenant and sergeant who surrendered their arms, confessed to the crime under interrogation and were sent to a POW camp. Major General Ryder was so impressed by Rip's conduct that he thanked him in person. His successful investigation and his many other heroic actions during the Italian Campaign attest to his steely-mindedness and professionalism. His capacity to work as an intelligence officer as well as carrying out his own covert assassinations of Germans behind the American lines, while finding time to continually record scenes of war in his art is staggering. Both his soldier self and his artist self were vitally engaged.

Von Ripper's art documents the theatre of war through the eyes of an unsentimental military man, but the poet in him seizes free reign to interpret the natural world. Skies with clouds like angel wings or bursts of fire suggest the influence of Oriental art on his work. His mountains appear magical, like the dwellings of Gods or of saints rather than mortal warmongers. These natural forms of arresting beauty lead the eye above and beyond the diminutive dark figures of soldiers trapped in the landscape, enacting their grim business under celestial horizons that hold out the promise of hope in the face of near despair. Was it this then – this hope, the poetry – that kept Rip going during his murderous missions, bivouacked in foxholes, waiting for the spring?

What you see is what you get, his work seems to say – a sketch of a soldier smoking a pipe in a dugout embedded in thick snow; a self-portrait in the field; a sketch of the severed head of a comrade, flies decorating his face like jewels. His war art is representational. Gone are the knowing references to Bosch, Goya, Grosz and the other artists that had inspired *Écraser l'Infâme*. What you see is what you get, but keep looking. See how the starving, begging children the 34th Division came upon creeping out of doorways at San Vittore embody the inhumanity of war.

'In Rudolph von Rippers work,' Major General Ryder wrote, 'we find a mirror that vividly reflects the various engagements of the early days of the Italian Campaign. He lived continually under the conditions his pictures portray, the mud and muck of the valleys, the snow and sleet of the mountains.' Rip documented in drawings the northeast section of the town of Cassino in flames, medics assisting wounded soldiers, a dawn patrol hunting out the enemy … he was tireless in his pursuit of veracity, as passionate an artist as he was a soldier intent on avenging Europe's monstrous regiment, the Third Reich.

CHAPTER NINE
BETWEEN RADIANCE
AND DARKNESS

Although the Army Arts Corps had been disbanded, Rip persisted in sending artwork to the War Department in Washington because, as he told Ernie Pyle, he wanted it to be published after the war. Pyle continued to record Lt. Ripper's exploits. 'It is hard to reconcile the artist with the soldier in von Ripper, yet he is obviously professional in both. It may be that being a fine soldier makes him a better artist,' Pyle observed. During the horrific struggle to secure Anzio in January 1944, Rip had a 'field day' when 'he went out with his sniper's rifle and claimed seventeen Germans in a single day from a carefully concealed position he had prepared the night before.' Once, leading a night patrol, 'he got four machine-pistol slugs in him. One slug hit his upper lip just where it joins his nose. Another ripped a deep groove in the back of his hand. Another shot an index finger clear off at the first joint. The fourth went through his shoulder.'

Pyle struck up a friendship with Rip after he visited the studio where he was convalescing. 'Right now he has a nice little room on the top floor of an apartment building in

Naples taken over by the Army. Here he works at a huge drawing board, doing watercolours and pen-and-ink sketches of war. He sleeps on a cot in the same room. Around the walls are tacked dozens of his sketches. Von Ripper's dead men look awful, as dead men do. Live soldiers in foxholes have that spooky stare of exhaustion. His landscapes are sad and pitifully torn. His sketches aren't photographic at all. He has given me one of these, labelled 'Self-Portrait in Italy', which shows himself and another wounded man, against a background of wrecked walls and starving children, being led downhill by the bony arms of a chortling skeleton representing ultimate and inevitable death. You get to see things like that when you're a soldier for a long time.'

Before all his bandages were off, Rip was back patrolling again. 'His long experience at warfare has made him as cunning as a fox,' Pyle reported to his avid following of American readers back home. 'You can't conceive of his being rattled in a tight spot and he seems to have been born without the normal sense of fear that inhibits most of mankind. Von Ripper is so calm and so bold in battle that he has become a legend at the front. High officers ask his advice in planning attacks. He will volunteer for anything.' But Rip was human, after all. He made light of his injuries but admitted to Pyle that he was in constant fear of three things: falling into Nazi hands, losing his left eye (his better one) and injuring the right hand he painted with.

When the terrible winter ended in April, Rip must have been jubilant to encounter at Army Headquarters his friend, Klaus Mann, now a Staff Sergeant and translator subordinate to the 5th US Army. The soldier-artist made quite an impression on the writer who described Rip as 'tanned, covered in scars, successful, over-confident, amusing and amazing,' in his journal. Rip and Klaus travelled to Naples in a jeep where 'an impromptu dinner and long evening entertainment' took place in Rip's studio. It must have comforted Klaus, who was suffering from one of his depressions, to spend time with his old friend who was bridge to the past. They agreed to meet whenever they could and on 15 June, after the capture of Rome, Klaus wrote that 'Ripper turned up – more dynamic, self-complacent and amazing than ever – and took me in his car (seized from a Jerry) to Rome'. The studio in Naples, where Klaus was served another impromptu dinner, was one of several retreats Rip used to paint in when he was off duty.

Shortly before the liberation of Rome, in the spring of 1944 Lt. Ripper had assisted the British A-Force 'in one of the most daring and incongruous feats of espionage' of the war. Maxie Parks of the 34th division recorded how, 'Wearing a British duffel coat over his uniform, von Ripper was taken by British submarine to the coast north of Rome. He changed aboard the submarine into a seminary priest's red cassock and was given papers identifying him as a student at the Collegium Germanicum in Rome, the Vatican's German Academy for priests. At the rendezvous point the submarine surfaced and he set out alone in a small rubber dinghy – an American officer of Austrian royal lineage disguised as a German priest on a spying mission for the British!'

Word of Lt. Ripper's heroism reached Major-General William J. Donovan (1883–1959) Chief of the OSS, the wartime Office of Strategic Services. From its inception in 1942 the OSS had been a shadowy force in Europe carrying out military operations deemed beyond the remit of regular troops of the American Army divisions. The divisions were subordinate to Donovan's office, which in turn was directly answerable to the Joint Chiefs of Staff in Washington. The OSS specialised in 'covert operations' behind enemy lines, espionage and sabotage such as blowing up bridges and cutting telephone lines carried out by rigorously trained intelligence officers who gathered information and supported partisan and resistance groups. During the summer of 1944, uniformed officers of the OSS whose sleeve insignias bore an unfamiliar golden spear tip on a black background, increasingly and without explanation became visible to the troops in the headquarters of the American Army. These mysterious men had the power to access secret maps and aerial photographs, rummage in personnel files and question soldiers before leaving as swiftly as they had appeared. Lt. Ripper was to become one of them.

That year Donovan, who had masterminded the creation of the OSS, proposed to President Roosevelt a new peacetime civilian organization which would gather international intelligence by overt and covert means. The seed was sown for the establishment in 1947 of the Central Intelligence Agency, the CIA.

In September 1944 Lt. Ripper was transferred from the 34th Division, not entirely against his will, promoted to Captain and recruited by General Donovan to work for the Secret Intelligence Division of the OSS. Whilst Rip was sorry to leave the Red Bulls who had become like family to him throughout the joys and hardships of the previous year, he relished this new role. Besides, he would not be leaving the Red Bulls forever. The headquarters of the OSS was at Caserta, where Colonel Howard Chapin and his deputy, Lieutenant Commander Alfred Ulmer, planned its operations. Rip had to undergo the obligatory parachute training at the centre near Bari where another captain, Pete Payne, recalled his 'eccentric comrade's masterly first jumps, despite being a bit overweight'.

Fritz Molden (1924–2014) turned up in Bari. The son of upper middle-class Viennese parents, he had become an

Austrian Resistance fighter and had been arrested in 1938 as a member of the Catholic underground resisting the *Anschluss*. He escaped from a penal colony on the Russian front and lived with partisans in the Apennines until he crossed into Switzerland where he served as a liaison officer between the OSS and the Austrian Resistance. Molden received parachute training at the same time as Captain Ripper and he remembered that it was anything but fun. At Bari, twenty-five officers were trained for six days and required to undertake two or three jumps every day. Whilst Rip and Molden were training a tragedy occurred when 'four or five comrades, I think there were five', failed to open their parachutes and were killed instantly. According to Molden, the material used to produce the parachutes in America was substandard, and even knowing how dangerous it was, 'I had to jump'.

As soon as the training was over, Captain Ripper was impatient to see action. 'Never have I seen so many scars on one man's body,' Molden noted and added that von Ripper 'was pleasant enough if he liked you; if he didn't it was better to keep out of his way.' Clearly Rip did like Molden, since they went on to become lifelong friends and agents in the future CIA. Rip was determined to be dropped into Styria in south-east Austria, an area he knew well and where the Germans had dug in. 'It was agreed after some back and forth, that three American Liaison Officers should be sent as a vanguard to Austria, and one each to the Tyrol, Carinthia and Vienna,' wrote Molden. Lt. Fred Mayer was selected for the Tyrol, Captain Ripper for Carinthia (the most southerly Austrian state) and Captain Jack Taylor for Vienna. These three highly trained scouts were commissioned to connect with resistance groups and the underground movement with the help of radio equipment, and to direct the dropping of relief supplies.

'Ripper ... was one of the first to be dropped by parachute into Austria,' Sulzberger noted. 'When he was in Austria working with the underground he was captured by the Gestapo in a routine roundup at a railway station,' he recorded in his memoir, *A Long Row of Candles*. 'He had papers identifying him as his alias, a draughtsman called Karl Ritter, and, of course, he spoke German like a native – but, for a while, he had a cyanide pill in his mouth ready to crush it with his teeth if they discovered his true identity.' Rip confided in Sulzberger that the SS Columbia prison and KV Oranienburg had sprung to mind at that moment and he had been ready to commit suicide, 'because no man who has been tortured once can stand it a second time'. On this occasion he outwitted his captors, then, on a secret mission in Carinthia he ran into a German patrol at Spittal station near the Millstätter See. After an exchange of shots Rip was able to board a moving train and escape into the Lienz Dolomites. From there he made his way through German occupied territory to the Po Valley. He swam across the river and eventually reached the Allied lines south of Bologna where he rejoined the Red Bulls.

'I came back to the 34th in November 1944,' Rip wrote later, 'after the Red Bulls had pushed all the way to Pisa, helped break the Gothic line and were entrenched in the Apennine Mountains, south of Bologna, astride Highway 65. [The Germans constructed the Gothic line along the summits of the Apennines during the fighting retreat of its forces against the Allied Armies.] Bogged down by winter conditions, they were waiting, with the rest of the US Fifth and the British Eighth Army, for spring – spring which would give them the chance again to hit the enemy – and spring which brought the last big push north.'

Captain Ripper was photographed in Italy in 1944. He is thirty-nine years old and, for all his bravura as a Red Bull, it is clear that the war has exhausted him. Gaunt and hunched in the uniform of the 34th Division, his gloved hand rests on his field glasses.

Between the two worlds, he was suspended ... One eye was opened wider than the other. The left eye delved narrowly into the past while the right gazed wide and affrighted into a future of blackness, error and ruin. And he was suspended between radiance and darkness. Between bitter irony and faith. Sharply he turned away.

Rudolph von Ripper kept on sketching, even when he was at the front, and 'when it finally came, the 34th took Bologna and broke into the Po Valley; the Allied Armies routed the Germans who laid down their arms in the first move to final surrender'. To his joy, his final mission was to work once more with the Austrian Resistance in the mountains of his homeland. He knew these mountains well. He was the right man for the job. His 'wanted' image was still plastered on walls and lampposts in Austrian towns and cities. Now he could take his revenge.

As a counterintelligence agent, Captain Ripper was 'one of those officers who ensured that the works of Brueghel, Titian and Rubens [and others] hidden by the Nazis in the salt mine at Bad Aussee were transported to the Kunsthistorisches Museum in Vienna', according to the Austrian art historian Gerhard Habarta. The mountainous area surrounding Bad Aussee, in the Styrian region of the Salzkammergut, was abundant in caves and underground salt mines and tunnels. Ausseerland was well known to Rip – and also to the Nazi hierarchy. During the war the region had attracted many top Nazis who 'Aryanized' and inhabited around thirty country estates they had seized from Jewish families. The Nazi propaganda minister, Joseph Goebbels, spent his holidays on an estate at nearby Grundlsee. From the spring of 1944, in the rough terrain north of Bad Aussee, a hidden refuge named *Igel* (Hedgehog) was inhabited by up to thirty-five Wehrmacht deserters and draft dodgers who were fed by sympathisers from the village. By 1945, the Altaussee region had become a last refuge for high-ranking members of the Nazi party as well as pro-fascist governments that had supported the Nazis in the Balkans. At the end of the war several key individuals responsible for the Holocaust, including Adolf Eichmann, Franz Stangl (commandant of the Sobibor and Treblinka extermination camps) and Anton Burger (commandant of Theresienstadt concentration camp) headed for the area.

As early as 1943, Goebbels had set up a special unit to invent and spread rumours about an *Alpenfestung*, or Alpine Redoubt, in the area. He enlisted the assistance of the intelligence services of the SS and the SD to produce faked blueprints and reports on construction supplies, armament production and troop transfers to the region and he made sure that neutral governments came to hear about the fortress. The Allies were not alone in being duped by Goebbels's scheme. In March 1945 when his hometown had been about to fall into Russian hands, SS *Obersturmbannführer* Otto Skorzeny arrived in Vienna to learn the fate of his family. Skorzeny's nickname was 'Scarface' and his reputation for brutality led to his nickname, 'Hitler's favourite commando'. In July 1943, Hitler had selected Skorzeny to lead the operation to rescue Italian dictator Benito Mussolini, who had been overthrown before the 1943 armistice and imprisoned by the Italian government. After a daring and successful mission, Skorzeny escorted Mussolini to Rome and later to Berlin where he was awarded the Knight's Cross of the Iron Cross. Like other high-ranking Nazi officers, in April 1945 he received Hitler's order from Berlin to base himself at 'the Alpine Redoubt' and to organize its defence against the advancing Allies. As Skorzeny discovered for himself, the existence of the fortress turned out to be a myth. This successful and utter deception of allied military intelligence is considered to be one of the greatest feats of the German *Abwehr* during the Second World War.

Still believing in the reality of the redoubt, the Allies wasted valuable eleventh-hour resources in tracking it down. On 8 May 1945 an advance party of the US Army including Captain Ripper reached the Ausseerland region and the main force of the US Army arrived the following day. They had been duped by Goebbels' ruse, yet there were gains to be made. There was the sensational discovery of the Nazi looted art hidden in the salt mines and top Nazis to capture. SS Ernst Kaltenbrunner, chief of the *Reichssicherheitshauptamt* (Reich Head Office Security) was one who had moved his headquarters from Berlin to the Villa Kerry in Altaussee in late April. Hoping to escape the Allied advance, he fled to nearby Wildensee where he was captured by a US patrol on 12 May. Later a box containing 60 kilos of looted Nazi gold was found near Villa Kerry.

It was as if OSS Captain Ripper had been flushing out pheasants as in days long past on the family estates. In revenge of epic proportions he hunted down six SS generals as well as a host of Nazi officials and Gestapo agents hiding out in mountain cabins under various disguises. In an interview for *Collier's* magazine after the war, Rip recalled, 'only one was rash enough to go for his gun. I beat him to the draw and that Nazi became No. 63 on my list [of dead Nazis]'.

He described his 'biggest moment of all' when he had located the Austrian Waffen SS Colonel Otto Skorzeny hiding in a shepherd's hut. Skorzeny emerged from the woods and surrendered with the prediction that he would be useful to the Americans in the aftermath of the war. On his way to prison, 'Blue-eyed, bullet-headed Dr Scheel [the alias of Otto Skorzeny] ... began whinnying about the good works he had done for the province and how he hoped these things would be taken into account.' Rip told the Collier's journalist that he turned to the scar faced Nazi and said, 'Look at me. Do you recognize me? The name is von Ripper. I used to live here. I did a stretch in one of your concentration camps and I found out what you were like. When you took over here, you posted me as [a] wanted [man]. I couldn't come back. But I swore I'd never stop fighting you until I could come back, and I swore I'd get you. So you can imagine, Herr Docktor, what a satisfaction it is for me to take you, the top Nazi in my home town, back to Salzburg as my prisoner and throw you into jail.'

As Captain Ripper was well aware, Otto Skorzeny was a friend of SS Diels, the commandant at KV Oranienburg who had condoned his torture, warned him about 'the long arm of the Gestapo' in 1934 and hounded him in Austria, Paris and London before he took refuge in the USA. Rip's revenge felt sweet, but it would have bitter consequences less than a decade later when Otto Skorzeny turned up in his beloved Mallorca.

After the war, General Lucian Truscott described Rudolph von Ripper as 'the bravest man I've ever seen'. He had entered the American Army as a non-combatant corporal and was discharged in May 1945 as Captain Ripper. The art he produced during the Second World War is held in the archive at the US Army Military History Centre, Washington D.C. with a list of his military decorations: Silver Star with 1 Oak Leaf Cluster, Legion of Merit, Army Commendation Ribbon, Purple Heart with 1 Oak Leaf Cluster, Distinguished Unit Badge, European African Middle Eastern Campaign Medal with 5 Bronze Battle Stars, World War II Victory Medal, Division Citation (HQ 34th Infantry Division).

Rudolph von Ripper dedicated his war art 'to those who gave their lives, as to all men who died to defeat the forces of hatred and oppression ... not educated for war, as were their opponents, who had years of spiritual, mental and physical preparation to condition them, the American soldier, moulded by the most individualistic concepts of society, gave a magnificent example of devotion, courage and faith, and defeated the better prepared enemy. It was this spirit, supported by the resources of a great country, which destroyed [Hitler's] monstrous endeavour to enslave mankind.'

Chapter Ten
One of the Boys

The monster of fascism had been slain, Otto Skorzeny secured behind bars, and Captain Ripper discharged with full military honours. In Austria a war-weary yet triumphant Rip packed his kitbag and headed for Paris where Marie-Laure, Vicomtesse de Noailles, was hosting a glittering mid-summer party to celebrate the Liberation. As Rip discovered, a few of the old crowd had managed to survive in Paris during the occupation, but many more had emigrated. His Spanish Civil War compadre, Ernest Hemingway, was in town and new faces enlivened the scene, notably Simon de Beauvoir and Jean Paul Sartre, who had written three novels during the war. Cyrus Sulzberger records that he was delighted to bump into von Ripper at the party.

Back in Civvy Street, dressed in hand-tailored clothes, champagne flute in hand, Rip was Baron von Ripper once more, a debonair aristocrat radiating pleasure and erudition as he toured the Vicomtess's splendid baroque apartments. Hanging on the walls was what Sulzberger described as 'a fantastic painting collection; a hodge-podge mixture where you can see a Bérard hanging next to a Rubens, a Dalí beside a Goya, a Burne-Jones and a Picasso.' And among these great works hung 'a collection of Rip's etchings', *Écraser l'Infâme*.

Surely here, revisiting this autobiographical labyrinth that drew deeply on all he had experienced since childhood in the backwaters of the Austria-Hungary Empire, Rip's resolve was strengthened to revive his pre-war reputation as an artist in the top galleries of Europe and America.

The Vicomtess's salon was a place where 'everyone' congregated and everyone included the novelist André Malraux who had been appointed Minister of Information by President Charles de Gaulle. In a letter to Sulzberger after the party Malraux described Rip as 'a democratic patrician, displaying courage in several countries while serving a single cause. He emanated a contagious likeableness and willingness to help, his courage inseparable from good humour. If this is not the greatest praise one can give an artist-fighter, it is at least one of the rarest, and perhaps the most moving'. The democratic patrician celebrated the survival of everyone present by drinking lots of champagne and performing a party trick he had learned as a teenager in the circus. To uproarious applause, he crunched his glass with a terrible grinding noise and swallowed it. When Kenneth Downs, a journalist from *Collier's* magazine, cornered him in a Paris bar a few days later Rip confided his intention to settle in the USA and get back to painting in his New Canaan studio. Downs asked him to repeat the feat he'd performed with his glass at the Vicomtess's party, and he recalled that 'the chills ran up and down our spines until he had ground it up and washed it down with Veuve Cliquot'

Someone arrived at the Vicomtess's party whom Rip was relieved yet discomfited to see. Often, he must have pondered her fate whilst he himself had been freezing in a dugout in Italy waiting for the next German offensive. Would Mopsa survive the horrors of Ravensbrück concentration camp? In wartime each new day had been a gift, a temporary stay of execution for everyone in danger on the battlefields and in the death camps. Now, here she was, safe and sound, a heroine of the war, and although she was thin and waif-like, her spirit remained undiminished. After the Gestapo arrested and tortured her, despite having to endure eighteen months under horrific conditions, Mopsa had succeeded in saving many lives and she made heart-rending, evocative line drawings of distressing scenes she witnessed at the camp. In her capacity as a clerk she succeeded in removing many names from lists of women destined to be sent on the notorious 'Black Transports' to extermination camps. Later, as head of a barrack reserved for typhoid cases, so terrible German officers refused to enter it, she hid endangered women who went on to survive the war.

But Rip no longer felt tied emotionally to his wife. For him, the chapter of his life with Mopsa had ended seven years earlier when he left for America and their reunion was his opportunity to ask for a divorce. Their meeting in Paris must have unleashed complex emotions and memories of the past they had shared before the war. So many years, so much life lived fighting for this freedom that had come at last. They had come through so much, it would be impossible to take up their lives together as if nothing had happened, Rip might have said in a plea for their amicable divorce. Divorce would be a mere formality for him, but Sulzberger records that Mopsa reacted hysterically 'as usual', claiming that despite infidelities with other men, including the poet, Gottfried Benn, after the seventeen years since their marriage she still loved the Baron. Rip held his ground and their marriage was annulled the following November.

Everyone was determined to put the war behind them, yet those who had seen action at the front or struggled for survival from day to day in the death camps found it impossible to step back into civilian life as if nothing had happened. How surreal, how technicoloured life now seemed on the bright side of the moon. Now came the peace, but what would that mean for Rudolph von Ripper, who had proved time and time again, in Morocco, Germany, Spain and Italy, his need for intense active engagement in just wars to create his art? For him, art and resistance had become inseparable. Death had been a constant presence in wartime. Life had been urgent and precious and each new day a blessing. Now that they could count on peace, most Europeans – infused by the tiredness, tension, distress and distorted values of the past five years – welcomed it with flag-waving processions and jubilant street parties. Paradoxically, the years of war had been a fertile gift not only for Rudolph von Ripper, but also for many writers and artists. 'One doesn't feel one will have much energy for peace,' Graham Greene wrote at the end of the London Blitz, which inspired him to write two novels.

Before he returned to America a visit to his mother and sister was top of Rip's agenda. Ever since the Nazis had seized the Ripper lands in Austria, Mutti and her unmarried daughter, Valerie, had been reduced to living in a small flat in Salzburg. Their Aryan blood had protected them from the fate of the estimated sixty thousand Viennese Jews who perished in the concentration camps. Rip arrived in Vienna, now under the occupation of the Four Powers – France, Britain, the United States and the Soviet Union – a metaphor, some said, for the ruins of Europe. In February 1946, an edition of *Écraser l'Infâme* was exhibited at the Austrian-American Club as Rudolph von Ripper's tribute to those who gave their lives in two world wars.

That summer Kenneth Downs lost no time in tracking down the fascinating character he had met in the Paris bar and who bore some resemblance to P. G. Wodehouse's character, Bertie Wooster. At this stage of his life Rip was given to wearing a monocle over his weak right eye and favoured English tailored shirts in striped cotton. When Downs pulled up outside the New Canaan studio-barn on Smith Ridge Road, he could already hear Rip at work. 'A friend from the BBC gave him a radio and record player with a gigantic amplifier,' Downs wrote. 'He keeps a pile of disks – everything from Fats Waller to Bach – going at full volume, and bellows an off-key accompaniment. He wears only sandals and shorts at work and occasionally, when the right music comes on, he drops his brushes and pirouettes and leaps about the barn in mad Nijinsky bounds.'

Downs encouraged Rip to talk about his past, from the moment he fled his homeland for Germany as a teenager to his torture at the hands of the Gestapo and his arrival in America after the Spanish Civil War when the Gestapo was still hounding him. In the resulting in-depth article 'Soldier with an Easel', Rip put into his own words episodes from his 'turbulent existence with many painful, but few dull moments'. When it appeared in *Collier's* in November 1946, the article made startling reading for Americans eager to claim military heroes, and this one stood out – amazingly enough this soldier dude was also an artist. A graphic illustration by a *Collier's* artist marries Rip's artist and soldier selves in a striking portrait. Steely and determined, he holds up a drawing, a cigarette juts from his mouth. He gazes beyond the frame and in the background American soldiers march towards Nazi-held Monte Cassino, a scene Rip sketched during the Italian Campaign.

Rip had put on a good show for Kenneth Downs at the New Canaan studio but the truth was that, despite the upbeat accompaniment of Bach and Fats Waller and all the reasons he had to celebrate his success in America both as an artist and a soldier, he was struggling to produce the new work that would revive his artistic reputation. For him the risky business of avenging the Third Reich had been addictive, and now where was the edginess to life he needed for inspiration? He was suffering, like so many others in the aftermath of war, from another visitation of post-traumatic stress. Thousands of displaced Europeans who had fled to the Americas to escape the Holocaust were having a tough time, too. Living in a place that was not their own, many had had to endure news of the torture and deaths of loved ones in the extermination camps. Added to that, most had arrived penniless as well as stateless in their adopted lands. For many exiles the struggle to integrate and learn a new language proved beyond them. In 1942, Stefan Zweig and his wife had committed suicide in Brazil by swallowing large amounts of Veronal tablets. Depressed by the post-war rift between the USSR and America, Klaus Mann wrote, 'I'd like to see hundreds, thousands of intellectuals follow the example of Virginia Woolf, Ernst Toller, Stefan Zweig, Jan Masaryk. A suicide wave among the world's most distinguished minds.' Klaus would take his own life in 1949, but as Rudolph von Ripper had stated, suicide was an option only if he was threatened with torture a second time.

On the face of it Rip enjoyed many privileges others did not. His wartime buddy Fritz Molden was often in New York and they both belonged to the select club of 'The Upper Five Hundred' in Manhattan and fraternised with its influential members. Still, adjusting to peace was challenging and his drive to regain his artistic reputation intensely felt. A second Guggenheim Fellowship enabled him to show work at the M. Y. de Young Memorial Museum in San Francisco without actually having to travel there himself. As a distraction from his Connecticut studio Rip established the Quadrangle Press with the art collector Lee A. Ault. Their shared aim was to publish lavishly illustrated monographs about outstanding artists such as Miró and Tamayo, as well as artists' books including *Aesop's Fables* illustrated by Alexander Calder. Then with the new venture up and running, Rip crossed the Atlantic and drove from Paris to Austria via Switzerland in a car loaded with valuable paintings loaned from his gallery owning friends. It was an adventurous operation in post-war racketeering. The risk he took smuggling the paintings over each border gave him a high. Smugglers of art and jewellery faced severe penalties, but perhaps Rip felt invincible: this venture was small fry compared to smuggling copies of the Brown Book from Paris to Berlin or picking off Nazis in the Apennines. He told Kenneth Downs that his deception was fuelled by his passion to exhibit in his homeland works by Kandinsky, Brancusi, Giacometti and Jackson Pollock, artists virtually unknown in Europe.

True to form, Rudolph von Ripper had ulterior motives in undertaking his journey. Post-war dealing in contemporary art was one, and he also wanted to engage with an association of artists known as the Vienna Art Club, formed in 1946 to reinstate modern art suppressed as *entartete Kunst* (degenerate art) by the Nazis. Rip had suffered terribly as a result of that evil principle in the Columbia prison and at Oranienburg. He had avenged the Third Reich as a soldier. Now here was a chance to avenge it, albeit posthumously, as an artist and – as he would become in the early 1950s – an active promoter of the CIA backed Vienna Art Club.

The establishment of the Schloss Leopoldskron in Salzburg, known as a 'Marshall Plan of the Mind', further energised the post war Austrian art world, and, if Rudolph von Ripper did not engage with its inception, with

148

Catherwood Foundation/CIA funding he did go on to play a key role in its success from 1950. The palace belonged to the Jewish Reinhardt family and had been seized as a national treasure in 1939 when Jewish property had been seized throughout Austria. Hermann Göring immediately assigned the palace to Princess Stephanie von Hohenlohe (a spy for the Nazis) as a guesthouse for prominent artists of the Reich and for Hitler's receptions. After the war the palace was returned to the Reinhardt estate which loaned it to Clemens Heller, an Austrian graduate student at Harvard, who 'envisioned a cultural bridge spanning the Atlantic not only by introducing the demoralized Europeans to all sort of American cultural achievements, but also by stimulating a fruitful exchange between European national cultures and America'. Two other Harvard men backed Heller and the trio raised the majority of funds needed to kick-start the Salzburg Seminar. Rudolph von Ripper had several contacts at Harvard and is likely to have known Heller and his partners. Certainly, Heller's ideals chimed with his own. Both on a personal level and out of love for his native Austria and his adopted America, cultural bridge building inspired him. In the first 1947 summer school at Schloss Leopoldskron, prestigious international tutors, including the anthropologist Margaret Mead, ran courses on American history, art, literature and culture. Gerhard Habarta noted that the Americans encouraged the vigorous exchange of views and that a starving Austrian artist could eat enough food to last him a week at the Schloss.

Back in the USA Rudolph von Ripper's newly felt euphoria was related to a love affair with the art critic Evelyn ('Avi')

Leege, a San Franciscan corned beef heiress and society beauty of Austrian descent. His first encounter with Avi might well have reminded him of his meeting with René Crevel two decades earlier. Avi and René were both arrestingly beautiful, and despite her evident femininity, there was something boyish about his new lover. Her cropped hair emphasised the 'gamine' look being promoted by Hollywood stars such as Mary Pickford and Paulette Goddard. A photograph shows Avi at work, a pencil clenched firmly between perfect teeth, her long fingers hovering over the keys of her Remington typewriter. Rip was probably the photographer of the goddess he would valiantly attempt to make happy for the rest of his life.

Throughout Rip's infernal years fighting tyranny, like most Americans, Avi's wealthy San Franciscan family only half-heard the news from Europe. How could Avi, who was seventeen years younger than him, ever understand the inferno he had lived through? Europe was a long way off and the fascist threat had meant little to Americans like the Leeges. Where to invest profits from South American beef exploitation, land grabs and oil exploration, what cosmetics to buy and which health cures to take, what art to collect, these had been their concerns until the bombardment of Pearl Harbour shattered their illusions. Given their divergent backgrounds and the differences in their age and physical appearance, Rip and Avi made an odd match. Unlike her, he could never be said to have 'film-star looks'. The story of beauty and the beast springs to mind, since Avi must have sensed the princely qualities and animal magnetism underpinning her much older suitor's appearance.

After his Austrian escapade Rip was more than ready for paradise, and Cummins Catherwood was on hand to take him there in 1948. He had built the luxurious 100-foot schooner

Vigilant to his own specifications and planned an expedition to the West Indies sponsored by the Academy of Natural Sciences of Philadelphia. Rudolph von Ripper was appointed as the expedition's artist and its photographer was Charles Chaplin, Catherwood's brother-in-law, whose additional role was to collect fishes. The naturalists, James Bond and José Borrero, were there to study the bird life, and others in the party collected reptiles, amphibians, protozoan parasites, land snails, marine invertebrates and plants. They set sail from the Bahamas to the south coast of Cuba, then headed for the Cayman Islands and San Andrés Island off Nicaragua.

It has been claimed that character Milton Krest in Ian Fleming's novel *The Hildebrand Rarity* (later the James Bond film *For Your Eyes Only*) was modelled on Cummins Catherwood. Added to that, Catherwood's sister was a close friend of Ian Fleming's brother, Peter Fleming, an amateur ornithologist. Another of Ian Fleming's models for a fictional hero with a twist was the real-life Philadelphian, James Bond, a renowned ornithologist and friend of Catherwood, who was aboard the *Vigilant*. In this astute company, culturally and politically 'in the know', an offshoot of the embryo CIA was birthed. The Catherwood Foundation would soon become a Blue Blood benefactor and conduit for the CIA's web of intrigue that would extend behind the Iron Curtain, far into Russia. Indeed, Ian Fleming had already written the outline charter for a Central Intelligence Agency after a visit to Washington with his boss, Admiral Godfrey, Chief of British Naval Intelligence.

After the US Congress passed the National Security Act of 1947, President Truman's signature legalised the CIA. Its creation had been inspired by the wartime success of Donovan's OSS, dissolved in October 1945 when its functions had been transferred to the State and War Departments.

In 1944 the then President, Franklin D. Roosevelt, had accepted Donovan's proposal for a new peace-time organization 'which will procure intelligence both by overt and covert methods and will at the same time provide intelligence guidance, determine national intelligence objectives, and correlate the intelligence material collected by all government agencies'. Under Donovan's plan, a powerful, centralized civilian agency would coordinate all the intelligence services. Furthermore, the CIA would be divided into sections, one of which, the Counterintelligence Centre Analysis Group (CIC/AG), would identify, monitor and analyse transnational threats posed by foreign intelligence services and their activities.

In light of his actions shortly after the voyage, it seems that Catherwood and others aboard the *Vigilant* strengthened Rip's resolve to become a CIA/CIC agent in Europe. Fritz Molden was another influence who was now a diplomat working in the information service of the Austrian Consulate General in New York. That year of 1948 Molden married well. His wife, Joan Dulles, was the daughter of Allen Welsh Dulles who had been recruited to oversee the CIA's covert operations as Deputy Director for Plans, as well as the niece of the prominent Republican, John Foster Dulles, who would become US Secretary of State in 1953. Rudolph von Ripper was supremely well connected and had proved his worth through wartime service in the Intelligence Division of the OSS. He was the embodiment of sophisticated European culture and he was ardently seeking a new identity. He had discovered that the solitary life he had been living as an artist working from a New Canaan barn thwarted his craving to become a significant player on the post-war stage.

Thanks to his friends in high places Rip was one of the boys, a highly influential network of the USA's corporate establishment, intelligence personnel, political strategists, and, to a lesser extent, the old school ties of the Ivy League universities. This influential and disillusioned network was easy bait for the idea that the world needed a *pax Americana*: a cultural offensive aimed at inoculating the world against the contagion of communism and, at the same time, oiling the wheels of American foreign policy interests overseas, as Frances Stonor Saunders observes in *The CIA and the World of Arts and Letters*. Few writers, poets, artists, historians, scientists or critics in post-war Europe in the late 1940s were not in some way linked to the covert birthing of the CIA.

The British MI6 liaison with the CIA and the FBI in Washington after the war was 'Kim' Philby (the KGB double-agent) who recorded in his memoirs from Russia meetings he attended with Frank Wisner, head of CIA Policy Coordination and responsible for 'Covert Operations and Dirty Tricks'. According to Philby, Wisner preached the need to camouflage the source of secret funds that were being supplied to apparently 'respectable bodies' overseas in which the CIA was interested, and he quotes Wisner as saying, 'it is essential to secure the overt cooperation of people with conspicuous access to wealth in their own right'. Cummins Catherwood, the friend whom Rip now called 'Cummie', was one of those people, and his Catherwood Foundation was one of those apparently respectable bodies.

The voyage on the *Vigilant* and the new horizons it opened up, had the effect of lifting Rip's artistic ennui, and, added to that, somewhere along the route his beloved Avi stepped aboard. A photograph taken on deck shows Rip wearing a string vest and holding a palette prepared with oil paint. The energy of creation radiates from him. No longer compelled to record violence, war and destruction in black-and-white, he can revel in painting exotic, brilliantly coloured specimens and sketching picturesque islands seen from the deck of the ship. Surrounded by turquoise seas, palm trees and shell-strewn white beaches, he married Avi Leege. The prospect of living in Europe must have been a factor in Avi's decision to marry the man she called 'Ripsky'. Her sister, Gwen, was living happily in Switzerland with her European husband, Rudi Walti, and Avi, too, loved the idea of playing a contemporary version of one of Henry James's American heroines in Europe. She responded eagerly to Rip's old world charm, heroism and artistic brilliance, and felt glorified by her coveted new title: Baroness von Ripper.

Thus began one of the happiest and least turbulent times in Rudolph von Ripper's life. He had stepped aboard the *Vigilant* as a lonely, recovering war artist with 'painter's block', and by the end of the voyage in Providencia Island off Colombia, he had become a married man who had produced startlingly new work and was about to embrace a new identity that would involve subterfuge and disguise, a role he would pull off with aplomb. He resolved to put torture and tyranny behind him, forever and ever, Amen. The war was over. Life was to enjoy, Ave Maria. He had told his new wife so, with bunches of roses in his arms and a song in his heart. But once tortured, always tortured. And war wounds are hard to conceal, such as the punctured lung courtesy of the Druze, the ridge where his skull fractured under Nazi jackboots, the shrapnel fragments embedded in his legs since Spain, the missing finger joint. The injury to his lung forced him to walk bent to one side. The past was written all over his body.

CHAPTER ELEVEN
THE THIRD MAN

Rip returned home in 1948 and swiftly adapted to post-war Austrian cultural life as an exchange professor at the Vienna Academy of Fine Arts funded by the CIA/CIC via the Catherwood Foundation. Graham Greene was also in Vienna with a commission from the film producer Alex Korda (a known CIA operative) to write and research 'an original postwar continental story'. Von Ripper and Greene are likely to have met previously through mutual contacts in the London based German Resistance in the 1930s.

Half-deserted, *sui generis* Vienna captured Greene's imagination as nothing else had done since the end of the London Blitz. He recreated in his work Vienna's wet pavements shining under gaslights in empty streets, shadowy doorways, baroque cupids shooting arrows from the rooftops of crumbling neo-classical façades, Four Powers intelligence patrols and subterranean sewers. Korda's representative in Vienna, Elizabeth Montagu, showed Greene the sights of the badly bombed and impoverished city. She took him to see ruins, to restaurants and bars that had survived the bombing, and to the *Riesenrad* or Ferris wheel of the Prater Park that would become an iconic image in Greene's story. Greene met a zither player in one of the bars and heard what would become known as the 'Harry Lime Theme' in Korda's film of his book, *The Third Man*. Montagu introduced Greene to British military officials who explained the insidious workings of the black market and the tensions between senior officials of the Four Powers. He met the Austrian journalist, Peter Smolka, who guided him into the labyrinth of sewers under the city. Greene eventually came up with an idea for a character, an American called Harry Lime who is assumed to be dead, but like Vienna turns out to be living a shadowy half-life in its doorways and sewers.

In Vienna, Rudolph von Ripper soon became a prominent cultural figure allied to the American cultural network of the CIA. Surely Greene modelled a character in *The Third Man* – Crabbin – after Rudolph von Ripper? Apart from the fact that the fictional Crabbin was British, his role in the film was almost identical to Rip's in real life. Crabbin was a British cultural attaché responsible for arranging lectures by outstanding artists and academics visiting Vienna. In a comedic scene Harry Lime's friend, Holly Martins, a writer of third rate Westerns, finds himself on a podium fending off questions fired from Austrian intellectuals about topics including 'stream of consciousness' and James Joyce. Can it be mere coincidence that Rudolph von Ripper organized a James Joyce Symposium in the city shortly afterwards? When *The Third Man* was released in Britain in 1949 in was an immediate box office hit. Viennese filmgoers, who perceived the film as a tragedy about Austria's troubled relationship with its past were less enthusiastic, but the Viennese newspaper, *Arbeiter-Zeitung*, praised the film as a masterful depiction of a time out of joint in a city redolent with insecurity, poverty and post-war immorality.

Now living in relative poverty in Salzburg, Rip's mother was overjoyed to have her prodigal son home at last and she and Valerie welcomed the new Baroness into the family with open arms. The newlyweds were photographed relaxed and smiling on visits to the extended family, including Avi's sister, Gwen and her husband, Rudi Walti, who had become a partner of Cummins Catherwood in Zurich banking. Vienna was all very well and would have to do, but Avi aspired to join what she regarded as a far more sophisticated set in Paris, the city of choice for post-war artists, writers and musicians, many of them Americans. She had read all about it in *Vogue* and *Paris Match* and seen photographs of Henry Miller and Lawrence Durrell fraternising with Francoise Sagan, Jean-Paul Sartre and Simone de Beauvoir, and, on the society pages, images of rich Americans living glamourized versions of *la vie bohème.*

In fact, Vienna would do well enough for now since the Baroness soon found herself swept into the bosom of the Austro-German cultural elite on her husband's coat tails. During the *Anschluss* Rip and his family had lost their estates and associated income and, although Avi anticipated being the benefactress of an inheritance in America, for the time being the couple largely depended upon Rip's salary from his new paymaster, the CIA. Fired by his prestigious role at the Vienna Academy and by his belief in the, more or less, hidden agenda of his CIC assignment, Rudolph von Ripper had become one of the leading men in a tight network of CIA/CIC agents now operating in West Germany and Austria, as Gerhard Habarta relates in *Kunst in Wien nach '45* ('Arts in Vienna from '45').

The Vienna School of Fantastic Realism had been founded in 1946 to embrace the work of students of the Academy's Professor Gütersloh, including the artists Ernst Fuchs and Fritz Janschka. Gütersloh's advocacy of the techniques of the Old Masters was designed to ground his students in realism and the use of religious and esoteric symbolism. In 2011, an extraordinary museum opened its doors to the public in Vienna's Palais Palffy, the brainchild of Ernst Fuchs and Gerhard Habarta. Named the Phantastenmuseum, it aims to demonstrate the evolution of fantastic, surreal and visionary art from the postwar period to the twenty-first century. Examples of the work of 'the CIA agent' Rudolph von Ripper are archived under 'Contemporaries', a section of the Museum devoted to artists who survived the Third Reich.

Habarta is regarded as an authority on the Vienna School of Fantastic Realism, and one of few historians to shed light on the CIA's involvement in Viennese cultural life during reconstruction under the Marshall Plan, and especially in the influential Vienna Art Club. Habarta has researched Rudolph von Ripper's pioneering cultural and political influence in Austria that resulted, among other things, in the first major international exhibition since the Vienna Secession (1950) and in his support, through the CIA, of the Art Club. The Vienna Art Club provided a lively platform for young painters, sculptors, authors and musicians to exhibit jointly and meet in each other's studios and favourite city cafés. Surrealism and Abstraction were 'in' and in the late 1950s the Art Club promoted Fantastic Realism.

Rudolph von Ripper headed the Catherwood Foundation in Austria and his funding was filtered through the European Research Institute for Contemporary Studies, according to Habarta whose older colleague and business partner in the Phantastenmuseum, Ernst Fuchs, worked closely with Rip at the Vienna Academy in the 1950s. Rip threw himself into the challenge of making the Vienna Academy a centre of excellence and an important node on the CIA network. Playing an active role in the life of the Art

Club, he established the Austrian College with backing from the Catherwood Foundation, whose assistance he acknowledged in the College prospectus, as Frank Tichy notes in his biography of the Austrian writer Friedrich Torberg. A remit of the College was to organise and supervise the important annual two-week conference of leading figures from the worlds of science, business, the arts and politics at Alpbach in the Tyrol whose nickname became 'The Village Of Thinkers'. There, Rudolph von Ripper gave a keynote lecture on the nature and content of abstract art.

The European public was slow to catch on to the Central Intelligence Agency's shadowy presence among them, yet from its inception the Soviets knew that a secret relationship existed between the CIA and the philanthropic American foundations. The Bear set about constructing its resistance and prepared to engage with its bitter enemy, the Eagle, in the Cold War. All over Europe, intellectuals and artists allied themselves to CIA networks, passionate to play a part in steering hearts and minds towards western culture and away from communism. One of the West's most effective focuses of intellectual resistance against Stalinism emerged as the Congress for Cultural Freedom. The American art critic, Hilton Kramer notes in *New Criterion* that in 1950 Soviet expansionism 'was understood to mean the spread of Communist rule by means of terror and the Gulag ... the rule of Soviet-style socialism had turned the societies upon which it was inflicted into despotisms of the most extreme and unrelieved cruelty ... for much of its seventeen year existence, the Congress for Cultural Freedom – and thus its principal publications and programmes – was covertly financed by the Central Intelligence Agency in Washington.' When the first public meeting of the Congress for Cultural Freedom was convened in Berlin in June 1950, 'almost all the participants were liberals or social democrats, critical of capitalism and opposed to colonialism, imperialism, nationalism, racism and dictatorship,' writes Peter Coleman in *The Liberal Conspiracy: The Congress for Cultural Freedom and the Struggle for the Mind of Postwar Europe.* 'They supported freedom and thought and the extension of the welfare state.' Its covert flagship publication became *Encounter* magazine.

The Congress swiftly became active in thirty-five countries worldwide, and that most liberal and democratic of patricians, Rudolph von Ripper, played a leading role in its development in Austria. He had close contact with everyone in the Art world, was knowledgeable about the Arts in America and elsewhere, and thus well placed to invite the West's cultural elite to Austria as well as to arrange extended study tours in America for Austrian artists.

The Baroness was soon to become a millionairess through inheritance and the von Rippers began to dream of renting a flat in Paris and owning a second home in Mallorca where she could 'swim, swim, swim' and 'Ripsky' could 'paint, paint, paint'. Cyrus Sulzberger had settled in Paris where he enjoyed long conversations with Rip on visits from Vienna. Accompanied by his sister, Valerie, in 1951 Rip and Avi drove by car from Vienna to Francoist Mallorca. Although the indigenous islanders suffered extreme hardship and austerity under Franco's dictatorship, it turned a blind eye to the excesses of foreigners and actively encouraged their arrival with much needed dollars to assist the revival of its depressed economy. The von Ripper party stayed at the recently built Hotel Majorica overlooking Palma harbour where they disembarked from the Barcelona ferry. During their stay,

Rip painted watercolour views of Palma and the Gothic Cathedral, which would be shown in an exhibition in the United States the following year. They took excursions to view properties, but none could match Ca'n Cueg, Rip's dream home, which was up for sale. The villa's setting between the Roman Bridge and the Moorish aqueduct, clean Bauhausian lines and elegant interior delighted Avi no less than her aristocratic aesthete husband. Rip's excitement increased when he noted a garage set apart from the house that could be converted into a painting studio. He gave Avi his word; she would have her dream. As soon as he had finished his work in Vienna they would rent a flat in Paris and buy Ca'n Cueg.

Soon after the travellers returned to Austria, Fritz and Joan Molden and her father, Allen Dulles, joined Rip and Avi at a rented neo-baroque chalet in Strobl on Lake Wolfgangsee. Joan was an artist studying with one of the great sculptors of the twentieth century, the Austrian Fritz Wotruba. Molden had become a CIA agent and his father-in-law Allen Dulles had been promoted to Deputy Director of the Central Intelligence Agency. Thus, Rudolph von Ripper found himself the third man in a CIA dream team. On sorties into the Salzkammergut Mountains, Rip was their knowledgeable guide and, relaxing at the chalet afterwards, he and Molden often reminisced about their wartime experiences. Molden was twenty years younger than Rudolph von Ripper whom, after his ambivalence during their first meeting in Italy, he had come to love and respect as 'a Lord of the old school' and an Austrian patriot. Molden had himself experienced the horror of imprisonment by the Nazis and had been awarded the American Medal of Freedom in 1947 for his work on behalf of the Allies during the war. He described his friend Rip as 'the most colourful and adventurous character I've met in my life.'

He was always ready to drop everything to go on a spree Fritz Molden recalled, and in 1948 'Ripsky telephoned and said he had heard that I was a Hemingway fan. I said yes, and he told me that Hemingway wanted him [Rip] to come to Venice and join him in a trip to the battlefields of Anzio.' Molden went along, driving with Rip in 'his huge old American Cabriolet' from Vienna to Venice where they met Hemingway for 'long, merry drinking nights' at Harry's Bar before they all set off for the battlefields. Since both Hemingway and Rip were enthusiastic drinkers, alcohol flowed freely while the old warhorse Hemingway spoke of his love for the sea, fishing and life on the Italian front during the First World War. Fritz Molden drank little and was content to remain in the background observing the performances of his two heroes. Rip relished provocative discussions during which he remained wholly dedicated to the ideals he believed in. He was a match for Hemingway, who would have agreed that art and politics are strange bedfellows, yet always closely linked.

Habarta devotes a chapter of his book on Viennese art to 'The Little Cold War' in which he relates 'the only known attempt to recruit an artist as a direct agent' of the CIA/ CIC. Whilst he was organising exhibitions for contemporary Austrian artists, Rudolph von Ripper befriended Rudolf Schwaiger, an artist from the Salzkammergut who had been a radio operator with the German Wehrmacht. According to Habarta, Rip and Molden and their wives were 'cozily installed in the pleasant atmosphere of a Salzburg villa' with the artist when Rip successfully appealed to Schwaiger's patriotism. Surely he didn't want his Alpine home to fall into the hands of the 'red hordes of world communism'? By the early fifties the CIA had started enlisting the exper-tise of former Nazis in the *pax Americana* and Rip needed

Schwaiger's skills as a key operator in the CIC's Radio Free Europe network of more than 2,000 radio stations throughout Europe.

That autumn, there were few opportunities to paint between his duties at the Vienna Academy, his CIC missions and support of Congress for Cultural Freedom programmes. Yet Rudolph von Ripper kept his resolve to reinstate his reputation as an artist and seized every opportunity to escape to his Böcklinstrasse studio on the edge of the Prater Park. Fritz Molden wrote that he loved meeting Rip there, or at Heroes' Square in front of the Albertina and at Salzburg Cathedral Square. In this Viennese period, Rudolph von Ripper painted *Salzkammergut-Landschaft* (oil on canvas, 1951), a celebration of the geopoetry of his homeland in a style reminiscent of Hundertwasser, a fellow member of the Vienna Academy of Arts. The painting is a celebration of the risks and triumphs afforded by these beloved, jagged mountains of home during his service with the Austrian Resistance less than four years earlier.

Yaddo Artists 1939: Rudolph von Ripper back row right of statue with
Hermann Broch, Richard Berman and Martin Gumpert on his left

Rudolph von Ripper's American benefactor
billionaire Cummins Catherwood

War Art 1943–4: Self-portrait in dugout, Italy

War Art 1943–4: US Army Marching towards Monte Cassino

War Art 1943–4: Murdered Rape Victims in Caiazzo Woods

War Art 1943-4: Waiting for Spring, Looking North to the Po Valley

Captain Ripper in Uniform of the American 34th Division
(The Red Bulls) Italy c.1944

Illustration 'Soldier with an Easel'. *Collier's* November 1946

Baron and Baroness von Ripper with CIA agents Allen Dulles (far left)
and Fritz Molden (right) in Austria, 1951

Baron von Ripper (right) with composer
Benjamin Britten (left) Austria 1952

PARADISO
1952–1960

CHAPTER TWELVE
THE HOUSE OF THE FROGS

P rior to the discovery of the blue file in the swimming
pool pavilion at Ca'n Cueg very little was known about
Rudolph von Ripper's life in Mallorca. It is thanks to the
letters he wrote to Avi between 1952–9, other letters from
family and friends and the photographs contained in the
file that this era of his life can be reconstructed for the first
time. In his own words, written in his copperplate handwriting on tissue thin airmail paper, Rip springs vividly to
life. Remarkably, Avi von Ripper not only kept the letters
her husband sent to her in Paris, Switzerland and America,
but also brought them back to Mallorca for safekeeping in
her blue file, as if she imagined that some future biographer
might find them interesting.

The story begins with the Baroness leaving Vienna to cross
the Atlantic in February 1952, bound for San Francisco
to visit her mother, Annelise Stein ('Mups'), and deal
with her financial affairs. En route she stopped over in
Philadelphia and New York where she acted as an emissary
for her husband with the aim of securing exhibitions for
the following autumn as well as commissions from wealthy
contacts. Rip wrote frequently, directing her efforts on his

behalf. Every letter to Avi (whom he variously addressed as Angel pie, Darling, Schnooks, Scnucki-Putzi, Wooks and My Angel) ends with a declaration of love. He lists people to talk to in New York and Philadelphia. 'Show Carlen [of the Robert Carlen Gallery] photos,' he prompted. 'Talk about an exhibition. See Marcus Neiman [owner of the New York department store] about the Vienna tapestries.' Increasingly frustrated that his many responsibilities at the Vienna Academy left little time for painting yet, ever inventive, he had hit on the idea of producing tapestries that could be woven in Vienna from swiftly drawn cartoons. He asked Avi to visit Charles Chaplin with a view to securing a commission for a tapestry with aquatic images, inspired by their voyage on the *Vigilant.*

Rip was not entirely well and willing to try anything to improve his health. 'Send the liver stuff. It sounds fantastic … I am very good and try to eat as little as possible,' he wrote. During the time Avi was in America, the list lengthened of the things he needed: four packs of ten Valet razor blades, a Chevrolet convertible to be shipped over to Europe, two books by the Swiss architectural historian, Sigfried Giedion (*Space, Time and Architecture* and *Mechanization Takes Command*) and another by his wife, Carola, to help him prepare for a forthcoming lecture tour by the Giedions.

When Avi arrived on the West Coast, Rip pictured his wife strolling in San Francisco, a city he had never visited. Aware that her six-week stay with the redoubtable Mups, would be fraught with tension, 'Don't fight with your mother,' he pleaded, 'you're a big girl now.' He urged Avi to consider the pros and cons of selling her stocks and shares to release the capital they needed to buy Ca'n Cueg: ' … don't forget the US will build bases in Spain; prices, especially the cost of labour, will go up!' Ca'n Cueg was to cost thirteen thousand dollars, plus extra funds for furnishings and refurbishment and the construction of his studio.

When Avi's capital came through Rip embarked on a journey to Mallorca to sign Ca'n Cueg's title deeds on her behalf. The villa was to be in Avi's name, the von Rippers' second home, but the Paris apartment would have to be postponed until Rip secured a CIA/CIC transfer there. He took a detour to attend a wedding in 'one of the most beautiful small churches of Rome, Santa Maria, a Romanesque church with lovely frescoes from the 12th century around the altar … Everybody missed you terribly, but most of all me … Spring is in the air,' he wrote; 'the flower stands on the Spanish stairs are covered with roses and lilacs and I have been walking like a drunk through the streets all morning. At the Sistine Chapel I was again overwhelmed with this work. It's the color – it's this wonderful integration of color and lightning that get's me … When I sit in the sun and listen to the murmur of the fountains on the Piazza Navona – this most Roman of all Roman squares – I remember when you were sitting next to me with your bright, hungry eyes that are trying to take everything in at once, to be sure to miss nothing!'

Three days later, Rip was in Madrid dining with a German industrialist and Willy Messerschmidt and his wife; 'They are not my cup of tea,' he wrote, adding that the industrialist sparked off a political discussion that lasted until four in the morning. Messerschmidt's presence in Madrid in 1952 is unsurprising. His firm had designed the Hispano HA-200 jet for Hispano Aviación and the deal went through that year. Many former Nazis had moved into Spain and established industries with headquarters in the Spanish capital. Former SS *Obersturmbannführer* Otto Skorzeny was one, declared *entnazifiziert* (denazified) in absentia that year by a

West German government arbitration board. Free to travel with a Nansen passport (issued by the League of Nations to stateless refugees) he set up a small scale engineering works in Madrid. Rudolph von Ripper would have given his bête-noir a wide berth in the Spanish capital unaware that Skorzeny was also bound for Mallorca.

For now he had other things on his mind. Hungry to see great paintings, Rip went straight to the Museo del Prado, 'God, what a place ... the first thing we have to do when we go to Mallorca is to take a week off for Madrid and spend the whole time there. It's just incredible, and instead of crushing me, it gives me the desire of giving up everything [to] just paint and paint and paint. There are some of the most incredible pictures in the world here (Bosch – *Les delices*, the black paintings of Goya's from his house (*La casa del sordo*) – some phantastic Titians; the other Goyas, the Grecos, etc.) – one can spend days and days there ... I'm going to try to do as much painting as possible this spring – but God knows if I get around to it.'

With that thought spurring him on he drove south to Barcelona and took the ferry to Mallorca, his 'haven of peace and beauty' where he had created the preparatory drawings for his own masterwork, *Écraser l'Infâme*. On 14 February Rip wrote to Avi from Hotel Miramar in the port of Pollensa. The rickety *hostal* Rip had known in the 1930s had been transformed into an upmarket hotel catering for the post-war increase in island tourism. A long wide patio set with tables and white umbrellas flanked the revolving doors leading into the impressively tiled entrance hall. Here, the reception area was furnished with comfortable sofas and tables. A grandfather clocked ticked away the hours under chandeliers and recherché oil paintings hung on the wall. The comings and goings of the effete Austro-American

academician must have intrigued the casually dressed holi-
daymaking guests, since Rip would have kept a low profile,
dressed in a hand-tailored suit and wearing his monocle
perhaps, ready to do business and secure Ca'n Cueg. 'This
hotel is full of middle-class English tourists – a race by itself.
Sad!' Rip observed.

The Registers of Property in Pollensa reveal that a
German named Horst Werner Seygarth and a local builder,
Martín Amengual, had bought the land, with two *casetas*
(cottages) dating back to 1896 and known as La Sort
(Fortunate Place), from a Mallorcan couple. Seygarth might
well have been the industrialist whom Rudolph von Ripper
had met in Madrid with the Messerschmidts. Centuries
earlier, the Moorish population of the island had flattened
the land of the *possessio* to construct the aqueduct between
Pollensa and the nearby town of Alcudía and the unusually
level land had been commandeered as the town's football
pitch before Seygarth and Amengual bought it and built
Ca'n Cueg. Messerschmidt's role in the sale of Ca'n Cueg to
Baroness von Ripper is obscure, but the appearance of the
names of Seygarth and Amengual on the title deeds might
have been a front to conceal his involvement.

The inherent irony in buying a house associated with
the designer of the Luftwaffe's favourite Bf109 bomber
must have sat uneasily on Rip's conscience, a considera-
tion only outweighed by his love for the property. In 1948
Messerschmidt had been tried by a denazification court for
using slave labour (mostly Jewish) in his manufactories, and
convicted of being a fellow traveller with the Nazis. He spent
two years in prison but later resumed his position as head
of the Messerschmidt firm. The company was barred from
manufacturing aircraft and turned instead to producing
automobiles and innovative prefabricated homes, sold as

'self-building kits' to which the unusual design of Ca'n Cueg might be linked.

Willy Messerschmidt was no stranger to Modernist architecture having lived at one of Europe's greatest examples, Villa Tugendhat, designed by Mies van der Rohe in 1928. The Bauhaus architect had been commissioned by a wealthy young Jewish couple to design their dream home in the Czech city of Brno. They shared van der Rohe's vision of untrammelled living in expansive 'spiritual' spaces made of glass and steel, and the villa he created thrilled them. Soon after the Nazis invaded Austria the family feared Czechoslovakia would be next to fall and they were forced to abandon their beloved Villa Tugendhadt. In 1941 the Gestapo confiscated the villa and the Third Reich rented it to Messerschmidt. Safely beyond the reach of Allied air raids, Villa Tugendhadt contained the offices of the airplane works as well as an apartment set aside for Messerschmidt's own use before the Russian army liberated Brno in 1945. Clearly Messerschmidt appreciated Modernist architecture, and although the more modest Ca'n Cueg is constructed from solid materials (glass and steel being unsuited to a Mediterranean climate) it, too, is a white cuboid building. Ca'n Cueg might well have been one of Willy Messerschmidt's Spanish bases during his negotiations with Hispano Aviación. Certainly, he pulled off the deal in 1952, in perfect timing to sell the villa to Baroness von Ripper via Seygarth and Amengual.

During his brief visit to Pollensa, Rudolph von Ripper reaffirmed his love of the villa. He made a detailed plan of Ca'n Cueg and its ancillary buildings and noted alterations that would need to be made. He sent off a letter to Avi: 'Ca'n Cueg means 'the house of the frogs': don't you think the name is divine?' ('Ca'n' is a derivation of *Casa Na*: 'the house of'. 'Cueg' does not exist as a word in Catalan but mimics the sound frogs make.) Every spring, hundreds of frogs arrived from their mountain pools to the *torrente* skirting Ca'n Cueg's garden. There they croaked love songs under the full moon and spawned before returning north. Rip loved the frogs: 'I hope we'll keep [the name] and then I shall make a glass-relief with a frog to be set in the wall! ... So happy you understand and see why we need that house,' he wrote. 'I have given Amengual, on the former owner's recommendation, a power of administrator. I like that guy – he is OK. We have gone over the house carefully together. It's really lovely (Messerschmidt and Amengual say it's a terrific buy ... since we saw it last year prices have gone up 25%.)'

Rip decided to retain the two nineteenth century *casetas* still standing on the land, and to construct another as a tied cottage for servants. 'The gardener's cottage is absolutely necessary,' he wrote to Avi; 'a childless couple would live there, keep a few chickens and a pig. The man would work the garden and the land and get half the fruit – no pay [Rip's double underlining]. So the place would always be guarded and the woman would work in the house and cook when we are there – when she would get some pay.' He persuaded Avi that his studio took priority over a swimming pool if he was to augment their income by selling his work and he drew up designs for a studio with a garage attached.

Ca'n Cueg was supplied with water from the aqueduct courtesy of an agreement with neighbours. It was, and still is, common for island neighbours to share water supplies by allowing others to fill up their *estanques* on certain days of the week for a specified time. Swimming pools were all the rage with foreign owners, and, while Avi badly wanted one, Rip used the water issue to dissuade her, at least in the short term. 'The water for the swimming pool has to be bought from the farmer second to us (west),' he wrote. 'He has a spring and plenty of water. The water situation is not as good as I thought; the rivers dry out in May or June and the water is too polluted to use even for a [swimming] pool ... At present we are getting water for the house from the public aqueduct (silent arrangement with the *Alcalde* [Mayor]); but we need to build a reservoir and I told Amengual to go ahead ... he has planted a lot of grapes along the fence. The studio will cost eight hundred dollars to build and we should not wait with that – prices are going up – whereas the swimming pool we better talk over.'

He reported that some good and some bad furniture had been left behind in the house as well as mattresses that needed replacing. 'You can get wonderful skins [sheepskins] for about three dollars! and rugs can be made in a local factory ... you could have, for instance, a lemon-coloured rug with Mexican pink chairs! Oh, darling, the place will be heavenly.'

Rudolph von Ripper's fellow Austrian aristocrat, Archduke Louis Salvador, had been an early founder of the Mallorcan Chamber of Tourism (*Fomento de Turismo*) that in the 1950s seized its opportunity to revive the island's economy. Before the Spanish Civil War Mallorca had been famous as a winter resort where doctors sent wealthy patients suffering from tuberculosis and other ailments for a rest cure in the sun. The most famous of these was Frederic Chopin who arrived in 1839 with the writer Georges Sand. But after the discovery of penicillin and the outbreak of the Civil War visitors no longer came for health reasons and the island's economy plummeted. When the *Fomento* woke up to the fact that Mallorca offered all the attractions of the French and Italian Rivieras and that the island lay within easy reach of

Europe's capitals and their expanding airports, it devised an international advertising campaign with a flagship poster showing a full-colour montage of Palma Cathedral, a sprig of almond blossom and paradisiacal beaches. Mallorca, it declared, was *the* place of choice for honeymooners. Visitors soon arrived in droves to stay in newly built hotels, such as Pollensa's Hotel Miramar, whose prices were controlled by the Government to make sure the island remained an inexpensive destination.

Tourist complexes, *urbanizaciones*, chalets and hotels sprung up and speculation became rife in Mallorca and along the coastline of the Spanish mainland. Planning permission in supposedly protected areas was readily available if substantial bribes fell into the right pockets; the protection of unspoiled coastal areas was low on the agenda of the controllers of the booming economy. Hard currency brought in by tourists and changed at Spanish banks was flown by the planeload to Madrid to pay for imported steel works, cement factories and the new car-assembly plants. The island experienced a domestic property boom, too. Mallorcans welcomed new owners such as the von Rippers as *etrangers* rather than *turistas*, and they began to sell off their homes, second homes and parcels of land to foreigners attracted by the island's beauty and by the opportunity to buy a place in the sun where the living was cheap and easy. Most of the incomers wanted properties near the sea and coastal land everywhere was snapped up. It had been traditional for Mallorcans to bequeath fertile land in the countryside to their sons and coastal land to their daughters. Many impoverished island women now became wealthier than their brothers as new hotels, bars, restaurants, shops and streets sprung up on their previously unproductive plots. Like other coastal towns, Pollensa and its port expanded almost beyond recognition during the 1950s. When he first encountered the von Rippers, Mallorca's exponential touristic development meant Martín Amengual's construction company was flourishing and he was well on his way to becoming wealthy.

The Baron radiated joy at the prospect of eventually settling down as an artist in their wonderful house on his paradise island, but, in an ironic twist of fate, even as he was planning improvements to Ca'n Cueg, Otto Skorzeny was in the process of buying a house between Pollensa and the neighbouring town of Alcudía.

After leaving Amengual in charge of works at Ca'n Cueg, Rudolph von Ripper took the night ferry to Barcelona through a 'terrific storm', and sent a photograph of the villa to Avi from Vienna. He had thought through the interior decoration in great detail and had already bought silver cutlery: 'six spoons, knives, forks and small spoons in old Vienna silver'. '*Je t'aime tellement, mon petit,*' he wrote, but the next letter reveals that he had forgotten Avi's birthday. She was rankled and told him so. 'Please forgive me; it's hopeless with me, I always forget such dates,' was his rather inadequate reply. Where was the promise of a belated birthday gift, jewellery perhaps, to make up for her disappointment the Baroness might have wondered?

The Baron was photographed deep in conversation with Benjamin Britten who had arrived in Salzburg to perform his 'Michelangelo Sonnets' in February 1952. Avi had been successful in persuading Charles Chaplin to commission two tapestries and Rip set to work on cartoons for the work, inspired by coloured prints of fishes in *National Geographic* magazine. He supervised the programme of visiting luminaries he had set up at the Vienna Academy. Carola Giedion arrived from the USA to give an illustrated lecture on James Joyce. Her husband, Sigfried Giedion joined in a discussion with other architects about the CIA's role in the education of young architects. Carola was Swiss-American who had been well known for creating a circle of vanguardist artists when the couple lived in Zurich in 1925. Their home had been a meeting place for Modernist artists including Hans Arp, Kurt Schwitters, Paul Klee, Max Ernst and James Joyce. When the Nazi threat had intensified in 1938, the Giedions emigrated to America, the same year as Rudolph von Ripper. Sigfried Giedion had taught at Harvard University's Graduate School of Design and was now an influential teacher at the Massachusetts Institute of Technology. Luring the Giedions to Vienna had been something of a coup for Rip and the CIA was a hot topic for discussion. They were all in it together.

Rip sent a paper to Washington and sought an appointment with the 'top guys' of the CIA in Europe about his transfer to Paris. He then drew up a proposal for the CIA/Catherwood Foundation and presented it to an agent named Laugh. 'Laugh was here and we discussed business,' he wrote to Avi. 'He thinks Paris is in the bag and that I shall get an official invitation soon ... It's a very simple job, mostly a question of the right psychological approach – that's what they want me for. Laugh says that the general situation has changed a lot since last fall – as far as this job is concerned – so it is not 100% sure if it still is interesting. No news from Washington about my paper [proposal] yet.' Rip's letters reveal that he doesn't relish the prospect of another CIA posting. Time and again, he expresses his passionate desire to devote the next phase of his life to art. 'On the whole I'd rather tell them all to go to hell and just paint. We'll be quite poor – it's the end of the fleshpots – but I'm not afraid ... we'll be much happier.'

He had reached a stage in his life when the untrammelled life of an artist was all he craved, but he was up against
a wife with different ideas. Intent on living life to the full in
her role as a European Baroness, Avi had no intention of
giving up 'the fleshpots'. When she wrote that she planned
to buy a mink coat, *de rigeur* for a socialite of the fifties, Rip
reminded her that she already had a fifteen hundred dollar
share in her mother's mink. 'Wouldn't another mink be
extravagant when there's so much to buy for Can Cueg?'
he asked. His worries about Avi's profligate ways made him
tetchy: 'I'm really not someone who likes to pull in the reins
all the time and yell at you – but you must admit you are too
extravagant and you become the slave of your belongings!'

Rip was close to treating his extremely beautiful younger
wife like a child, an attitude the fickle yet sophisticated Avi
must have resented. He was desperately in love with her,
and his attempts to control her were driven by his fear of
losing her. During the three months of their separation, Avi
was seldom out of his mind. Rumours that she had been
seen in the company of a 'butch looking woman' in San
Francisco did little to allay his fears. Yet, had not he, in his
youth, explored the many facets of love, particularly in the
ménage-à-trois with René Crevel and Mopsa? The truth was
that he found himself bestriding an ever-widening gorge.
On one side stood the artist with a burning need to develop
his art, and, on the other, the aristocratic householder and
academician with an aspiring wife to maintain. To make up
for forgetting her birthday perhaps, he wrote that he had
bought 'heavenly material for a cocktail suit in black and red
brocade for my Schnucki'. But he was living on a restricted
income and found it necessary to ask Avi for a loan of five
thousand dollars in advance of the next CIA appointment.
The Vienna Academy big shots wanted him to stay on, he

told her, and, in anticipation of an annual salary of around ten thousand dollars from the Catherwood Foundation, he predicted quitting Vienna by the spring of 1953 when Avi's dream of living in Paris as well as Mallorca would become reality. 'Please don't talk about it [the Foundation],' he wrote, and added, 'The house is so important, you know why.' Did he view the prospect of a new life in Mallorca as his liberation from the CIA?

If not now, then somewhere down the line of his life, Ca'n Cueg would be just the place to fulfil his blistering need to create. He could hardly wait. Meanwhile he was forced to accommodate in his plans Avi's need for glamour: parties beside the swimming pool (still vetoed by Rip), dinners in fancy restaurants by the sea, tailor made clothes from Gaby Couture in Palma, the low-cost servants that were hard-to-come-by in Vienna or Paris, the stunning villa to impress friends. Their dream was still on hold, and negotiations with the Catherwood Foundation were beginning to worry him: 'All the emphasis is on sociological work and hardly any artistic work is planned ... Well, we will see about that ... The ungratefulness!' He planned to participate in 'Frankfurt conversations' later in March, when he hoped to sort out the snags.

Rip sent a letter describing the influenza epidemic that had led to overcrowding the hospitals of Vienna, and he came down with it himself. One night, he 'ran round the city for three hours' until he managed to secure a bed for a friend suffering from pneumonia. He recovered in time to travel to Frankfurt for conversations with the CIA: 'nothing much has resulted from them. These people are just too vague ... We have worked out and I have dictated an exposé for the Catherwood Foundation. So we'll see what will happen.' Someone named 'Attie' then jumps into Rip's letters. 'Attie says that Cummie [Catherwood] had told him he would set aside $10,000 if we would present them with a project that would stress Austro-American – or European-American problems and relations.'

With Easter approaching, Rudolph von Ripper's longing for his wife intensified and he anticipated their reunion in a few weeks' time. 'A second honeymoon,' he wrote, the very thought sending him into rhapsodies over their lovemaking. In fact, he was so impatient to be with Avi that he offered to fly to the States right away if she would wire him an advance. En route from Frankfurt he took a detour to Paris where he relished 'little spring buds on the trees' and admitted, 'this trip is a little extravagant, but I did want to talk to some people here and since it cost only $40 to make this detour, I decided to blow myself to a weekend in Paris … Meanwhile, I'm glad you're having such fun with your fur coat … but aren't you a little extravagant? Of course I'm extravagant too, but only to the tune of a little something around $150, for which I bought two Chinese pieces.'

When Easter arrived with no sign of cash from Avi, Rip drove with Valerie to spend Easter Sunday with their mother in Salzburg. Times continued to be tough. In addition to his separation from Avi, tests being carried out at the Army Hospital may have been associated with the angina pectoris he would suffer for the rest of his life, and it must have seemed to him that his condition had been precipitated by the mock execution at the SS Columbia prison, when *an agonizing spasm seemed to rend my heart.* He was frustrated, too, when Charles Chaplin sent a message to say he wanted only one tapestry from the original commission of two, and a smaller size at that, to replace a mirror in his house. 'So I just wrote to him and said, never mind – I would send him the cartons [cartoons] to look at and then he can send them back. But to make tapestries the size of an average painting or mirror I will not do – it never looks right – I just went to the studio, because it didn't leave me in peace. It's a pity, because [my] designs are very good and he would never have them made at that price anywhere else.'

To add to his frustration, Rip was annoyed with the 'damned [Austrian] College people and God knows what will happen', he wrote to Avi, who was now in Philadelphia. He never revealed details of 'the exposé' he had written for the Catherwood Foundation, but its title suggests that it contained information about the Vienna Academy of Art from his insider perspective and its future role in the CIA. To his relief, the funds that would enable him to continue in Vienna for another year were approved in April.

Meanwhile the worldwide Congress for Cultural Freedom had been evolving rapidly. Nicolas Nabokov, the Russian-born composer (and cousin of the novelist) who became an American citizen in 1939, was Secretary-General to the Congress. During the war he worked as a translator for the government in Washington and afterwards was posted to the US Military Government in Berlin (where he had grown up after fleeing the Bolsheviks with his family). Nabokov also worked for Voice of America after it started broadcasting to Soviet citizens in Russian in 1947 with the aim of countering anti-American Soviet propaganda. Nabokov believed that the Congress's obligation to foster the artistic life of the West was a vital alternative to the Soviet cultural model, and towards this end in May 1952 he organized a massive arts festival at the Congress for Cultural Freedom's European headquarters – the Festival of Paris – that lasted for thirty days.

Rudolph von Ripper headed for Paris to join the cultural elite of Europe and America and deliver a keynote speech on the evolution of abstract art. In *Legacy of Ashes*, Peter

Coleman describes the extraordinary event that springtime in Paris: there were 'one hundred symphonies, concertos, operas, and ballets by about seventy twentieth-century composers. Paris had its first productions of Alban Berg's *Wozzeck* (by the Vienna Opera), of Benjamin Britten's *Billy Budd* (by Covent Garden), of Gertrude Stein's and Virgil Thomson's *Four Saints in Three Acts* (with Alice B. Toklas attending), and of Arnold Schoenberg's *Die Erwartung.* Igor Stravinsky conducted *Oedipus Rex* for which Jean Cocteau designed the set and directed the choreography. There were performances by the Boston Symphony Orchestra and the New York City Ballet. William Faulkner, Katherine Anne Porter and Allen Tate came from the United States for literary debates. There was an exhibition of 150 modern paintings and sculptures. As well as celebrating the cultural freedom of the West, the Festival also made its anti-Soviet point indirectly, by performing works by Sergei Prokofiev and Dmitri Shostakovich that were banned in the Soviet Union, and directly, by arranging church services for the victims of totalitarianism oppression.'

Back in Vienna, an exhibition of *Écraser l'Infâme* opened at the Vienna Academy of Arts supported by a scholarly catalogue written by the Munich art historian, Franz Roh, and the completed Vienna tapestry *Atlantis* went on display in a window of the information centre. Gerhard Habarta comments that Rudolph von Ripper's public commitment to abstraction contradicted his own Surreal etchings in *Écraser l'Infâme* and he quotes Rip's written justification for exhibiting his anti-fascist art: 'I do it to show how sadly history repeats itself ... Instead of the fascist danger, today we face the red menace of Russian-Asian communism. Another ideology tries by every means to ensnare individuals and cast a spell. Man dies again in Buchenwald.'

He was on the quay at Le Havre to meet Avi's passenger liner, the *New Amsterdam*. They flew directly to Mallorca to discuss the works at Ca'n Cueg with Martín Amengual.

CHAPTER THIRTEEN
THE NEIGHBOUR
FROM HELL

Rip and Avi were together at Ca'n Cueg and in Paris and Vienna between May and October 1952. In his Böcklinstrasse studio that year, Rudolph von Ripper painted *Die Schwarze Sonne* (The Black Sun) in the style of the Nouvelle École of Paris. The female nudes he had portrayed in *Weibliche Form Mit Spiegelbild* (Female Figure with Mirror, 1949) and Through the Mirror (1950) reappeared in the painting. Were these representations of the two women in his life: Mopsa and Avi? They diverge from each other on a geometric background of triangles and circles through which other diminutive figures wander. Everything is in action, a ship sails on the horizon, and above it all hangs a crescent moon and an eerie black sun. Rudolph von Ripper is desperate to develop his life as an artist, but his current anxieties and the shadow of his past suffering haunt the very title of this work, *Die Schwarze Sonne*.

In the autumn it was Rip's turn to visit the USA to see 'the top boys' who would sort out his CIA/CIC Paris appointment. With a friend called Howie he reviewed the 'whole situation and connected problems ... [Howie's] absolutely on my side. But he has not seen any of the boys for nearly a year and is not quite sure who to talk to best.' He sent Avi a letter from New York: 'Great excitement all round,' he wrote, even as he fell into the arms of old friends who had lined up welcome lunches and parties.

Avi's efforts of the previous spring to secure exhibitions and commissions had borne fruit. Rip based himself at Sumatanga, courtesy of Cummins Catherwood, to prepare the exhibition at the Robert Carlen Gallery. 'Cummie and I are making big plans for next summer,' he enthused. 'The basic idea is that we would meet them and go shooting chamois at the Brandhof and then they would come to Ca'n Cueg (7 persons! Hooray!).' Socially, Rip was having a ball; a never ending round of parties entertained him. He toured the galleries of New York and Philadelphia, attended a matinee of 'South Pacific' whose songs were on everyone's lips and sat up all night watching Eisenhower's campaign on TV. 'I did not like the latest phases of his campaign ... Apparently Washington is in a turmoil and all the Government small fry are packing their bags waiting to be fired. Everybody is predicting a depression and God knows what.'

It was the McCarthy era when Cold War tension between the United States and the Soviet Union had become intensified by paranoid fears of Communism and the presence of Soviet agents in the US. The expansion of the Congress for Cultural Freedom and the *pax Americana* was of vital interest to the US Government and, with friends in high places, Rudolph von Ripper must have felt confident about achieving his transfer to Paris. Washington turned out to be 'very interesting' and Rip's aim looked achievable: '... long discussions with Allan D. [Allen Dulles], [Frank] Wisner etc. – the top people OK – but God damned the bloody bureaucrats. Anyway, the decision is to work out a definite program for fall 1953, with the idea to run it from Paris – provided the Paris office agrees. The cover would be Research Director for Europe of the Catherwood Foundation; the activities intensification of visual propaganda on the one hand and support of student groups and young intellectuals on the other hand – could be fascinating work. I have to work out a whole project and that means a lot of thinking and then putting it down very clearly and convincingly. Then you can have your dream and we shall live in Paris for at least two years.'

He organised a trip to New England. At New Canaan he visited old friends from the 1940s and lamented the death of his close friend Hermann Broch in New Haven the previous year. Broch, who had been nominated for the Nobel Prize for Literature, had written a moving tribute to Rudolph von Ripper in 1945: 'You have realized in very young years that [the] neighborhood of death is also the neighborhood of life, and with all the errors you made – and living a dynamic life your errors too were more dynamic than those of the average man – you managed pretty well to bring yourself always onto the straight path again, which, in fact, is the path of reality.'

Now Rip's challenge was to shape his reality as a player in a very different field. He took his CIA/CIC role seriously but viewed it as a stepping-stone to the simple life of an artist, a dream that would have to be postponed until his financial affairs were stabilised. 'I'm trying to spend as little as possible because here money gets out of one's pockets fast,' he wrote to Avi, but never mind, he could deduct the cost of his entire trip from taxes. Avi had been unwell with a temperature when Rip left Europe, and when she wrote to tell him that she planned to spend time in Mallorca he replied, 'Enjoy yourself, relax in the sun, but watch your health.' Clearly, their relationship had been strained before he left for America. 'What a funny girl you are that you always need to be away from me to realize what we mean to each other … I'm dying to hear from you about the house,' he wrote. 'How I wish I were there to go with you to the house, our house.' But it was not *his* house, and surely that fact increased Rip's apprehensions. He was well aware that in his role as Ca'n Cueg's factor Martín Amengual, swarthy and insouciant in his black beret, needed no invitation to the villa where he would become Avi's frequent visitor.

El Borne, where a river once ran down to the sea, is a graceful tree-lined boulevard in the heart of Old Palma. In her husband's absence, Baroness von Ripper lost no time in getting to know Mallorca's capital city. The river had been drained in medieval times to become the jousting field of the Conquistadorial knights of Provence whose palace, La Almudaina, soars above the gardens at the southern end of El Borne. In the 19th century four sphinxes had been erected, two at either end of El Borne, and a fountain topped by an obelisk held aloft on the backs of tortoises. It had become a tree-shaded *paseo*, a promenade, a place to see who was out and about, and to be seen. In the 1950s the city still lurked in the doldrums, a poverty-stricken backwater held in the grip of Franco's regime, its architectural treasure trove of Renaissance and Baroque palaces and townhouses shuttered up or abandoned by wealthy owners who had retreated to mainland Spain and South America. Wooden tramcars clanked through the city, horse-drawn carriages conveyed tourists to the sights. There were few private cars but many noisy motorcycles. The island boasted some light industry and the production of jewellery and leather goods – gloves, shoes and jackets – was a mainstay. Dusty downtown *tiendas* sold woven baskets, espadrilles and straw sunhats.

Photographs of Avi leave no doubt: she was elegant down to her fingertips, and a woman of her standing, unable to find the fashionable clothes her lifestyle required, was forced to secure the services of a dressmaker. Around the time Baroness von Ripper arrived on the island, Robert Graves, Mallorca's most famous expatriate, was photographed at Bar Bosch, shouldering his ubiquitous woven basket. Bar Bosch, at the head of El Borne, had been a favourite haunt of the cognoscenti ever since Mallorca began to attract a foreign community and Avi is sure to have been seen sipping coffee there, her beauty turning heads before she slipped up an alleyway beside it to be measured for her latest costumes. Invoices sent to Avi at Ca'n Cueg from Gaby Couture, 6–8 Calle Jovellanos, reveal that Gaby was Avi's dressmaker of choice.

Nowadays, El Borne is Palma's most elegant thorough-fare, a consumers' honeypot with the emphasis on fashion, ringed with traffic and flanked by boutiques and chain stores including Zara and H&M. Calle Jovellanos has under-gone a similar transformation. While door number 6 with its smart green paint and handsome brass knocker has hardly changed since Gaby's day, number 8, has become an open-plan block selling T-shirts and jeans, its ground plan altered beyond recognition. It is possible, though, to imagine how Palma's salons operated in the 1950s from a twenty-first century survival a few streets away. The late Doña Altimira Pino de Monserrat, a ceramicist and couturier, once catered for foreign women like Baroness von Ripper and well-to-do

Palmesanas (who disdained Catalan, spoke Castilian only when necessary, and adopted French as their language of choice like the Russian elite described in the stories of Tolstoy and Dostoievsky.) Roughly one-third of the extensive *planta noble* that had been Señora Pino de Monserrat's home in the old quarter is a time capsule of those salon days. Her private museum is laid out as it always has been with ensembles of feminine sofas, conversation chairs and Louis XV-style bergéres, each grouping in shades of pink, blue or gold. And high above each island of comfort and delight, Murano-style waterfall chandeliers made by Mallorcan glassmakers hang in brilliant hues. Here Señora Pino once reigned over each season's collection, displayed by models (known as 'mannequins') who catwalked among sofas and chairs occupied by wealthy women eager to choose their favourite designs. Clients of the salons could also select costumes they admired from magazines such as *Vogue* and have copies run up by their dressmaker. A random selection of Avi's tailor-made clothing is detailed on Gaby's invoices, including a silk cocktail dress, dress and jacket in 'pink sari', beige hat, black georgette dress and a suit of striped flannel. Dressmakers served their clients in other ways, too. The salon was a place to unwind with a coffee, make contacts and influence people. A long distance telephone call and 'airmail postage packages' sent to Paris and Zurich are noted on the invoices.

After the end of food rationing in Spain in the early 'fifties, the unprecedented demand for luxury goods spurred on the traditional island practice of smuggling. Mallorca became a de facto free port for a highly lucrative trade financed by businessmen who utilised *secretos* along the coastline, either by enlarging suitably hidden caves or by excavating new ones into the steep cliffs. Private houses in Palma sold on contraband goods such as cameras, film, radios, contraceptives, cigarettes, cigars, Zippo lighters, Gillette razor blades and perfume. Like other expatriates, no doubt the von Rippers made regular trips to Palma to pick up items that were otherwise unavailable on the island in the 1950s. Robert and Beryl Graves travelled there once a week by taxi from their mountain home in Deìa, and spent the morning on business calls, at the post office and in specialist shops, such as a well-supplied delicatessen selling cheeses and meats, as William Graves relates in *Wild Olive*. He remembers, too, that his father always went to the *Tabac* to buy cigars for himself and mentholated cigarettes for his wife, Beryl.

In America, Rudolph von Ripper's Private View took place at the Robert Carlen Gallery on 14 November 1952. Like a shooting star he had seared the American art scene with *Écraser l'Infâme* and other works between 1939 and 1942, and this was his longed-for opportunity to make a comeback. The *Time* coup, born of that extraordinary era, was such a hard act to follow he would be content to regain a modest reputation in America and Europe.

'The show is hung,' he wrote to Avi, 'and looks very beautiful. Two paintings have sold already ('le 14 juillet: la nuit' and 'fly, little bird, fly').' An entrepreneur offered him a show in Hollywood the following year and, thus encouraged, he immediately planned 'a circuit for next spring: Dallas – San Francisco – Hollywood and New York.' Charles Chaplin softened his earlier blow by purchasing the two cartoons Rip had made for the aborted tapestries. A college professor wanted to buy a painting titled 'The Kites'. 'Arthur Pew has commissioned 2 tapestry cartoons [gouaches] like Charlie's for $1500,' he wrote. 'That means I shall have made so far about $2000. Not bad but also not much for 3 years work (although only part-time).' In December Rip wrote that Ellen Catherwood wanted to buy 'Spring after the War' as an anniversary gift for her husband, Cummie, 'Which pleases me very much, because that would give them one of my major paintings.' In the same letter, Rip advised Avi that Cummins Catherwood had come up with a scheme for her to invest in an oil development with 'enormous capital increase possibilities'.

Avi was suffering from haemorrhoids when she wrote from Ca'n Cueg. 'Glad you feel [the house is] a success!' he replied. 'I'm only sorry you had such lousy weather and felt so badly ... what a disagreeable thing to have – but it really is nothing and will go away! I do hope you are all right – but really all right now! I shall get all the combs and all the nylons you need.' As for the other things Avi has requested – rubber-mattresses, 'Liquid Veil' make-up, fabrics and a record player – he'll get them next time he is in New York. 'I have never loved anyone so intensively. Pollensa and Ca'n Cueg sound really wonderful,' he wrote. Yet by the end of November he was picking up distress signals: 'I pray that you really will get over all your defensiveness and give yourself to me without reservations, without self-assertion – wholly ... we belong together – even with all the shortcomings we have, which make us fight each other.' He longed to spend Christmas alone with Avi at Pollensa: 'to hell with the ever *beleidigte* family' (their respective relatives in Salzburg and Zurich). But Avi wanted to join him in the USA. 'Too extravagant,' Rip replied, 'think of Mallorca and all the things we need, and the Paris deal. Besides, if you come here, it'll be the same old circus – and I've really had my fill of it ... In the meantime – please be good and send all the European

Christmas cards – if you want to send any. I'll take care of the American ones.' Again, thoughts of their reunion awakened his longing for Avi. 'It is incredible how these months of absence – this absolute faithfulness to you – has built up not only the desire for you, but has deepened my love.'

Rip lunched with the Austrian Ambassador in New York then returned to Washington for meetings. 'It looks good – you shall have your dream,' he wrote to Avi. He attended a trustees meeting of the Catherwood Foundation, a lunch hosted by the Tysons [billionaire tycoons] whose Cézannes 'are really magnificent', and visited Tini Matisse. Then, his mission accomplished, Rip flew out of New York on 23 December 1952. 'Wait till you see what I got for Pollensa! Whoa! … And your Christmas present!' The couple planned to spend Christmas in Paris then fly to Marrakesh. Why to Morocco, not to Can Cueg, 'our house'? Had Avi and Martín Amengual embarked on an affair?

Despite the fact that Rudolph von Ripper's Paris appointment did not materialise (in 1953 he became a CIA/CIC agent working under the cover of the Catherwood Foundation based in Madrid) thanks to Avi's inheritance they were able to rent a flat in Paris. Together they made a short trip to the USA to select furniture and furnishings and shipped them back to Mallorca. Catherwood's son, also named Cummins, remembers, 'Ripper was a great friend of my parents, and I often saw him and his wife Avi at our home near Philadelphia and a number of other places. I even talked him into illustrating a scrapbook that, as a young child, I was preparing for a school project. He was a very charming person.'

Martín Amengual's firm had begun the construction work at Ca'n Cueg, and, despite the palpable attraction between

Avi and the Mallorcan, Rip formed a bond of *amiguismo* with him. Together they built the studio in the form of a modest 'Roman tower'. At the same time, Rip busied himself with painting a mural on the wall behind the cocktail bar that was planned for the second floor balcony of the villa. He designed a frog motif for a wrought iron garden gate that he also incorporated into letterheaded notepaper. He created two ceramic reliefs, one for each side of the entrance gate: a mottled brown frog, and a turquoise and gold frog worthy of the tomb of Tutankhamen. The frog sculptures flanking the gate were the first things visitors to Ca'n Cueg saw, and they might well have wondered if the ordinary frog was intended to represent Rip and the exotic frog Avi.

The interior of the villa was painted and perfected and the five upstairs bedrooms and ancillary bathrooms made ready for guests. A large Westinghouse refrigerator was installed in the kitchen to cater for parties, the cool underground wine cellar was supplied with fine vintages, the living room shelves were filled with coffee table books on art and culture, and objets d'art including a bronze bust of Avi, provenance unknown. Two leather poufes the von Rippers had purchased on their Moroccan trip were positioned on the black-and-white tiled floor beside a sofa covered in fabric of a Mallorcan design. A local couple was hired to live in the cottage and their teenaged son was on hand as *camerero*, serving meals and drinks when they had guests. The man also looked after Rip's dog in his absence. Its breed is not recorded but Rip would have loved hunting dogs and pointers, the dogs of choice for Mallorcan landowners, were readily available on the island.

Otto Skorzeny was settling into his villa, too, when his busy schedule allowed. Just as Rudolph von Ripper's Catherwood

Foundation appointment (ironically, also based in Madrid) veiled his CIA involvement, Skorzeny's engineering business was a convenient front for his role as Spanish coordinator of the ODESSA network (Organisation of former SS members), as well as a player in the international arms smuggling trade. Under the cover of invented names, he set up a secret organization, *Die Spinne* (The Spider), through which he assisted several hundred former SS men to escape through rat lines to Spain, Argentina, Paraguay, Chile, Bolivia, and other countries. The extensive shoreline fronting his Mallorcan property was said to be a ratline through which he smuggled former Nazis into and out of Spain and on to South America and elsewhere. Skorzeny and the former Nazi general and senior intelligence officer, Reinhard Gehlen, would eventually set up a network of collaborators which gained enormous influence in Europe and Latin America. Skorzeny travelled frequently between Franco's Spain and Argentina, where he encouraged the establishment of a 'Fourth Reich' in Latin America, and acted as an advisor to President Juan Perón and as Eva Perón's bodyguard.

In 1952 Egypt became another destination on Skorzeny's itinerary. That year, the country was taken over by General Mohammed Naguib in the *coup d'état* that ousted King Farouk. Reinhard Gehlen, now recruited to the CIA, sent Skorzeny to Egypt the following year to act as President Naguib's military advisor. Skorzeny harnessed prominent ex-SS officers to train the Egyptian army and Arab volunteers in commando tactics that could be used, if necessary, against British troops stationed in the Suez Canal zone. Palestinian refugees also received commando training, and Skorzeny planned their initial strikes into Israel via the Gaza Strip in 1953–1954. One of these Palestinians was

Yasser Arafat who would eventually serve as an adviser to the Egyptian President Gamal Abdel Nasser.

Otto Skorzeny, the former SS *Obersturmbannführer* whom Captain Ripper had arrested in the Alps in 1945 was the neighbour from Hell, a force to be reckoned with in the murky waters that were seeping into Rip's paradise island.

CHAPTER FOURTEEN
PARADISE, IF YOU CAN
STAND IT

True to his word, Cummins Catherwood brought his entourage to Ca'n Cueg during his Mediterranean voyage of 1953. Prominent among the guests was Reeves Wetherill, the Philadelphian socialite with film-star looks who, like his fellow American Gertrude Stein, made it his business to know everyone who counted. It was quite a party, as the photographs Rip took from the second floor balcony reveal. Gwen and Rudi Walti arrived from Switzerland to join the close-knit group. Dressed to the nines, the men slick in dinner suits, the women wearing fur stoles and glamorous full-skirted dresses of the era, the group photograph resembles a still from a Hollywood movie. No doubt Cummie held long private discussions with Rip and Rudi Walti about the Catherwood Foundation's continuing support of the CIA.

The Foundation's beneficiaries now included the Russian Orthodox Church, and its activities extended far beyond the Iron Curtain where a main focus of the CIA was to turn Communist agents and recruit new operatives. Rip sat on the Foundation's Madrid based panel of judges charged with selecting Spanish painters to study in the USA.

He took his task seriously; after all, he had been the grateful first recipient of the award in 1938. The Catherwood Foundation had become a big player in the Cultural Cold War, promoting the *pax Americana* by fair means and foul, and one of von Ripper's tasks would have been to identify Communist agents who might be turned. Seeking out agents, double agents and former Nazis was tricky since many were now 'clean' like the denazified Skorzeny, and others, such as Reinhard Gehlen, were protected CIA plants. If the arrival of Otto Skorzeny in Mallorca had rattled the phlegmatic Rudolph von Ripper, the news that a friend of both Skorzeny and Rudolph Diels was also hiding out in the Pollensa area was potentially even more threatening. Prominent among ex-Nazis, this man calling himself 'Schmidt' had been involved in Nazi espionage in Catalonia during the Second World War.

In all probability the Catherwood party visited the nearby, now legendary Hotel Formentor. After air travel took off in the fifties Hotel Formentor had become an upmarket holiday destination and favourite haunt of millionaires, stars of stage and screen and artists and intellectuals. The hotel's guest book would have delighted Reeves Wetherill with its signatures of international celebrities including Charlie Chaplin (the movie star), Winston Churchill, Gary Cooper, John Wayne, Audrey Hepburn, Ava Gardner (who befriended Robert Graves) and Sir Laurence Olivier. The underworld, too, was attracted to the luxury venue. During the Second World War and into the Cold War, spies and counter-spies, agents and double agents mingled with Hotel Formentor's wealthy guests. It was one of Rip's favourite haunts.

The Catherwood group's visit to Mallorca was a huge success. That year Cummins Catherwood had commissioned

Salvador Dalí to design a collection of Surreal Objects known as the Dalí Jewels, which included the fabulous 'Royal Heart'. Dalí s domain at Port Lligat was a mere eighty miles over the Mediterranean, and surely the billionaire seaman sailed over with his party to view the results of his commission. According to Cummins Catherwood, Jr., 'It is highly likely that my parents did indeed visit Dalí, as they were good friends during that time period. My father's foundation did purchase Dalí's jewellery collection at some point during that time. It was owned by the foundation for several years, and was displayed widely in the US, Europe and (I believe) parts of South America. Subsequently the collection was sold to the Owen Cheatham foundation.'

Joan Pujol García, alias 'Garbo', the most successful double-agent of the Second World War, had rendezvoused with his MI5 case intelligence officer and artist, Tómas 'Tommy' Harris (1908–1964), at Hotel Formentor for the last time in 1948. Passionately pro-British, Garbo's mission had been to supply the Abwehr with false information, most significantly about the Normandy Landings. Harris also supervised another spy for the British, Dusko Popov alias 'Tricycle' (from his penchant for ménages-à-trois) who had also bought property in Pollensa. Popov had collaborated with Harris and Garbo, the masterminds behind Operation Fortitude, which deceived the Third Reich into believing that the Allies under General Patton intended to land at the Dover Strait rather than Dunkirk. After the war Garbo defected to South America under an assumed identity and remained incognito until the writer Nigel West tracked him down in Venezuela in 1984.

Tómas Harris's mother was Spanish and his English Jewish father's renowned Spanish Art Gallery in Mayfair specialised in works by Velázquez, Goya and El Greco. The El Greco School influenced Harris's early painting, and Goya later became his foremost inspiration. Given Rudolph von Ripper's love of these Spanish painters, it is likely that he had encountered the gallery – and the Harris family – during visit to the London Resistance in the 1930s by which time Tómas had joined the family firm. Tómas Harris and Rudolph von Ripper had a great deal in common. Harris was highly regarded by critics for his painting and etching and is likely to have seen Rip's exhibition 'Kaleidoscope' in London in 1935. Like Rip, Harris also worked in ceramics and tapestry. A description Garbo wrote of Harris could be applied to Rip: he 'was no unkempt bohemian but an extremely sensible and capable individual, who always dressed impeccably in an elegant sports jacket, which he wore with a most distinctive air'.

When the von Rippers arrived in Mallorca, Harris had already settled on the island and, again like Rip, he was re-inventing himself as the very good artist he had been before the war claimed most of his time and energy. In 1951 certain members of the British Intelligence community who had been involved in Harris's wartime operations were suspected of having worked as Soviet spies. Guy Burgess, Kim Philby and Anthony Blunt were all close friends of Harris, but an investigation concluded that he was an innocent acquaintance of all three. Now he was living with his wife, Hilda, at his luxurious Camp de Mar villa in southeast Mallorca. The von Rippers and the Harrises must have met socially. Mallorca was a small island; a place where rich and artistic expatriates partied with the specific intention of getting to know each other and like Rip and Avi, Tómas and Hilda Harris had a reputation for producing fine wines and gourmet meals for lavish gatherings. William Graves remembers boyhood trips with his parents Robert and Beryl to visit the Harrises at Camp de Mar. A card sent by Avi to Robert Graves on his seventieth birthday in 1965 indicates the von Rippers' familiarity with the Graveses.

Another prominent couple had arrived on the island in 1951 and were living a few miles from Baron and Baroness von Ripper. In a white stucco villa perched high above Hotel Formentor, dining was an extravaganza masterminded by the travel writer, Temple Fielding, and his wife, Nancy. When *Time* magazine correspondent Gavin Scott visited Villa Fielding in 1968 he felt he had 'just checked into one of the grand hotels of Europe'. The dining table was laden with imported delicacies including pheasant in Burgundy jelly, smoked swordfish, Scotch grouse pâté, Norwegian kippers, whole lychees and albacore tuna from Oregon. Fielding's bar was stocked with over one hundred varieties of liquor including Peruvian pisco, Greek ouzo, Indonesian arrack, Irish moonshine and Spanish absinthe. During the Second World War Temple Fielding had been an intelligence agent spreading anti-Nazi propaganda in Yugoslavia where he narrowly escaped capture and execution. From its first appearance in the late 1940s, *Fielding's Travel Guide to Europe* had been a sensational hit with American tourists such as the Catherwoods. It was updated regularly and Villa Fielding became 'a sort of secret services command post, a map of Europe replacing one of the rugs on the living room floor, Fielding, Nancy and the staff hunched over it planning how best to infiltrate hotels and restaurants, and report on them to readers.' In 1969 Temple Fielding shared with Rudolph von Ripper the distinction of being represented on the front cover of *Time* magazine, designated 'The Supertourist'.

The Harrises, the Graveses and the Fieldings were just the sort of people Baron and Baroness Rudolph von Ripper wanted to know. But renovations at Ca'n Cueg and the lavish lifestyle involved in socialising with the cream of the expatriate community drew heavily on their funds. To augment their income they embarked on a scheme to sell costume jewellery designed by Rip: precious and semi-precious stones set in gold, earrings, bracelets, necklaces and evening bags or *minaudières*. Avi would attend to the business side, and the second cottage on their land was converted into her office. Her task was to attract upmarket clients, keep the books and cajole her husband into action.

But Rip felt deeply frustrated that his desire to 'paint, paint, paint' was continually thwarted by distractions. In God-given moments when he was not travelling to Paris, Barcelona and Madrid on CIA business, partying with Avi or creating jewellery designs at Ca'n Cueg, he could be found in his studio, re-discovering the landscape and atmosphere of Mallorca. He experimented with different techniques and styles and revelled in colour and texture, and although he was a self-confessed 'lonely traveller' from time to time he fraternised with the Pollensa School artists, such as Tito Cittadini and others who lived in Ternelles, the *barrío* neighbouring Ca'n Cueg.

In 1954 the Baroness became pregnant and Ca'n Cueg was in full swing as the ideal base for the 'gracious living' she felt was her destiny. Letters arrived regularly at the *telegrafos* office in Pollensa from the couple's mothers, Mutti and Mups, and from Gwen Walti. The news arrived, and must have saddened Rip, that Mopsa Sternheim had died of cancer in Paris. Mutti's affectionate letters offered vignettes of her life in a small flat in post-war Salzburg. 'The house owner lives downstairs,' she writes, 'a 70 year old father and his energetic daughter … quite cultured people one can live with … I doubt the hope of a free Government flat will materialise.' From Switzerland, Gwen sent Avi amusing, affectionate letters describing the joys and tribulations of family life. While their mother Mups's letters reveal her as opinionated and all too ready to give her daughters advice – their success and wellbeing was paramount – she also looked upon life with shrewd amusement and to guide her through it she sought the advice of a fortune teller called Mrs Trost on her frequent visits to Vienna. Mups Stein's surname came from her second marriage to Herman Stein. She was of Austrian descent and had served during the First World War: 'I remember so well my time as an Austrian Armee Schwester [army nurse] in Knittelfeld … where we would hear the thunder of the shooting from the Italian Border. I still have a snapshot in my Austrian uniform, which looks very funny to me now, but was serious business at the time.'

Making his beloved Avi happy was not the least of the peacetime challenges Rudolph von Ripper faced. Gwen Walti and her family were frequent visitors to Ca'n Cueg, and her letters reveal that beneath the surface glamour of their lives the von Rippers' relationship was far from harmonious. She describes their frequent quarrels, criti-cism and ridicule of each other, in no small measure due to Avi's passion for Martín Amengual and her inability to resolve the situation. Had Avi and Amengual acted out their passion? Did Rip condone an affair? Rip was too sophisti-cated to blame Avi for falling in love with a man he, too, respected, yet the consequences for them both were dire. Avi was temperamental, and her inability to possess Amengual would have fuelled both her desire for the Mallorcan and her growing dissatisfaction with 'old Ripsky'. Perhaps Rip chose to believe that the upstanding Martín would never risk jeopardising his marriage to Catalina, a Mallorcan beauty, by becoming sexually involved with Avi. Family was sacrosanct to Mallorcans, and Martín and Catalina had two children. Rip trusted Martín and they had become friends. Surely he would not betray their *amiguismo*.

Another devastating blow to their marriage that year was Avi's miscarriage as a letter from a friend reveals: 'All you have to do is get the factory working again,' she wrote. In the circumstances her advice was cavalier. Rip was forty-four and the child he longed for might have cemented his relationship with Avi and grounded her capriciousness. The affection Rip had for his nephews, Gwen's sons, and the fun he devised for them during their visits, indicate that he had the makings of a devoted father. The loss of their baby must have fuelled the unhappiness that was creeping, stealthy as a thief, into their marriage. Yet, despite her moods and demands, Avi was the love of Rip's life. He went to great lengths to please her, incorporating shells into the beach jewellery he designed for her, wining and dining her at upmarket restaurants in Puerto Pollensa, graciously receiving their many visitors to Ca'n Cueg, and, overcoming his reservations, installing her swimming pool in the garden beside a cottage-style pavilion. Photographs show the first flow of water into its aquamarine tiled depths with Rip laughing and splashing about like a happy schoolboy. But the truth was that life for the von Rippers was becoming a living hell. As his friend, Gertrude Stein, had famously remarked: 'Mallorca is paradise, if you can stand it.'

Cyrus Sulzberger arrived to visit his old comrade and found Rip walking in Ca'n Cueg's colourful garden of flowers and palm trees, seemingly content with his new life of 'glamour, parties, yachts and the frivolous women of nearby Formentor'. Like Rip, Sulzberger was a CIA agent, though as chief foreign correspondent of *The New York Times* he was so undercover that his involvement was not open to discussion. Sulzberger was fascinated by Avi, a beauty almost beyond compare, 'very slim and athletic', who always had a flawless hair-do and wore shoes with high heels when going out, even although without them she was still a good bit taller than her husband. Perhaps his fascination with Avi's good looks blinded the newspaperman to the fact that Rip's capricious second wife bore remarkable similarities to Mopsa, whom Sulzberger himself had described as 'hysterical and erratic'.

The expatriate community continued to make hay in the sunshine, worlds apart from the reality of leftist Mallorcans. Eager to improve the economy of the island, the regime actively encouraged foreign residents and tourists and turned a blind eye to their drinking, drugs use and previously forbidden behaviour, such as wearing bikinis on the beaches. But its tolerance did not extend to the island's indigenous population. Even before the dictator's rise to power, Mallorca had been a predominantly right-wing island. Under Franco it became uncompromisingly fascist. Francoist agents were posted in every town and village, priests and nuns fell into the grip of the regime, neighbours spied and reported on neighbours and the forbidden Mallorcan language went underground. Rudolph von Ripper had seen it all before, in Europe under the Nazis and in Spain during the Civil War. Now, on his paradise island, Mallorcan 'misfits' were brutally removed to a Palma prison for interrogation. Hundreds of people disappeared. Valldemossa and Puerto Soller on the north coast where high forbidding cliffs drop sheer to the sea, were locations favoured by Franco's henchmen for pitching their victims to horrific deaths. For all his privileges, Rip must have suffered acutely from the knowledge that tyranny he could do nothing about was being enacted daily on the shadow side of Mallorcan life.

Eighty miles across the Mediterranean Sea at Port Lligat, Salvador Dalí was plotting a spree involving Rudolph von Ripper. Dalí had become rich and famous and, urged on by Gala, ran to keep up with the demands of wealthy collectors for his art. Gluttony disguised as art, might have been Rip's judgment, first advertised to the world in the 1942 New York exhibition of Dalí's Surrealist Objects that had sensationally displayed 'Mae West's Mouth' (rubies and diamonds). The 'Royal Heart', one of his latest Objects, had a mechanical beat and was set with gold, rubies, sapphires, emeralds, aquamarines, peridots, garnets, amethysts, diamonds and pearls. This staggeringly valuable object was to be exhibited at the Pallazzo Pallavicini-Rospigliosi in Rome, and Dalí persuaded his aristocratic *amigos*, Fulco, Duke of Verdura, and Baron von Ripper, to accompany him as top-drawer bodyguards. The flamboyant former British Army captain, John Peter Moore, who happened to be working in Rome with Alexander Korda of London Films, joined the colourful entourage and immediately hit it off with Dalí. Moore had had a distinguished military career and claimed to have been a secret agent working on behalf of Winston Churchill during the Second World War.

In Dalí's view, people were there to do his bidding and if they happened to be aristocrats so much the better. During the Rome exhibition Dalí was the centre of attention, the knight in shining armour flanked by his henchmen. Rip's special designation was 'Keeper of the Dalí Jewels', and especially of the 'Royal Heart'. If Dalí's sycophantic posturing was profoundly irritating, Rip nevertheless threw himself into the glittering occasion and played it to his advantage by drumming up contacts for his own jewellery business.

He returned to Mallorca stimulated by the experience, and during the next few years he and Avi regularly travelled to Madrid, Barcelona and Paris. In contrast to the rancour that afflicted their daily life at Ca'n Cueg, their shared interest in achieving certain aims when they were on the move meant they worked well as a team. In Madrid, Rip had CIA business to attend to as well as trips to the Prado that nourished him as an artist. In Barcelona they supervised the execution of Rip's costume jewellery designs at a goldsmith's studio. In Paris they visited friends and secured orders for jewellery; to supply the House of Chanel was the height of Avi's aspirations. They crossed European borders as if they had diplomatic immunity, frequently defying customs regulations by smuggling goods in and out of the various countries they visited. In the 1950s, European governments strictly controlled contraband, including watches, jewellery and art works, but the von Rippers were sophisticated travellers, and Rip relished the risks he took in the knowledge that a nod, a wink and a roll of dollars would buy him out of tricky situations.

Well aware of the power of media coverage to promote themselves and their jewellery in northern Europe and America, they commissioned a Palma studio to take professional photographs at Ca'n Cueg. Dressed with casual elegance, Baron and Baroness von Ripper posed at the entrance to the villa. They were also photographed behind the bar with its soda syphon, array of liquors required to create the perfect cocktail and Rip's Modernist mural in the background. Avi, looking stunning in profile, wears an off-the-shoulder dress that highlights fashionable earrings, presumably designed by her husband. It's a revealing shot: Rip looks strained and crumpled as he gazes appealingly at his rather disdainful goddess of a wife. They posed in the salon, too, where Rip resumes his groomed and authoritative look as he points out something to Avi in a book. Anyone familiar with their backstory can discern in these shots of a glamorous and successful couple, the torments that plagued their existence.

Soon the von Rippers were supplying markets in Europe and the USA and their distinctive jewellery attracted articles in USA publications including the *New York Herald Tribune*. In 1955 Rudolph von Ripper had a one man show followed by a group show with the Pollensa School artists at the Rotary Club in Pollensa's main square. But his ambition vaulted far beyond Mallorca. He had worked hard to create a series of paintings and aspired to exhibit them internationally, starting with London's Redfern Gallery. He was also in contact with Madrid's Museo del Arte Moderno with a view to exhibiting '*pinturas, dibujos, aguafuertes, tapices, alfombras, joyas*' [paintings, drawings, watercolours, tapestries, rugs, jewels]. The tapestries were woven at the Manufacture des Gobelins in Paris.

The Baron and Baroness left Mallorca for a tour of northern Italy in October 1956. During their visits to see the art treasures of Venice and Milan, Rudolph von Ripper heard radio reports of the spontaneous and unexpected popular revolution in Hungary against the Communist government and its Soviet-imposed policies. A student demonstration in the Hungarian capital Budapest on 23 October had triggered one of the tensest periods of the Cold War. As the day progressed tens of thousands of people poured onto the streets and the initial uprising turned into a full-scale revolt against the regime and its Soviet masters.

For a few heady days they seemed to have succeeded. Then on 4 November the CIA controlled station Radio Free Europe broadcast news of the Soviet invasion of Hungary. Soviet tanks entered Budapest and crushed the revolution. The city endured days of heavy shelling and street battles, and thousands of citizens fled to neighbouring Austria. The Hungarian uprising and subsequent Soviet suppression took the United States Government and the CIA by surprise. The Suez Crisis and other international predicaments had heightened tension between America and Russia and President Eisenhower decided to maintain a policy of non-intervention in Hungary. Thus the USA's feeble response was reliant on the CIA to effect change by means of Radio Free Europe and its covert agents. Rip and Avi immediately left Italy and drove to Austria. Notwithstanding the fact that CIA agents failed to locate any of the US weapon caches hidden across Europe, there was a massive increase in Radio Free Europe broadcasts supporting the revolutionaries and encouraging violent resistance against the occupying Soviet troops. The agency's sources of information were lamentable: local newspapers and the only CIA operative in Budapest, a State Department employee called Geza Katona.

In Vienna Rudolph von Ripper packed a large brown suitcase with pistols, ammunition and hand grenades and arrived at Fritz Molden's door. He hoped his friend would join him, but Molden had been detailed by the Red Cross to deliver medicines to crisis regions. A United Nations High Commission report recorded that during the weekend of 4 November alone, around 10,000 Hungarians entered Austria. Students, teachers, doctors, famous athletes and footballers, farmers, architects, labourers, housewives, children and the elderly all streamed into Austria across the loosely guarded border. This was the first major crisis to appear on television and cinema newsreels. A shocked world gawped at the heart-rending scenes from Budapest and the snow-covered border.

Within days of the exodus an extraordinary operation sprang up in Austria, not only to care for the refugees but also to move them out of the country as fast as they arrived. In Vienna, a committee was immediately set up comprising the Austrian Interior Minister Oskar Helmer and his staff, the United Nation's High Commission for Refugees (UNHCR), the Intergovernmental Committee for European Migration (ICEM), and the League of Red Cross Societies (LRCS), as well as a number of local and international NGOs. The UNHCR dealt with the over-arching legal and protection issues, as well as the integration of refugees remaining in Austria. The LRCS, to which Fritz Molden was affiliated, was the prime mover on the assistance front and backed up the ICEM whose task was to register, document and transport the refugees out of Austria. Rudolph von Ripper's specific role as an Austrian citizen and a covert CIA agent is not documented, but he is likely to have assisted the ICEM.

The von Rippers set about raising money from wealthy friends to support the refugees. 'It is wonderful that you and Rip were able to collect so much money for the good cause,' Mups wrote in January 1957. 200,000 refugees had crossed the Austria-Hungary borders before they were sealed that winter. Eventually 180,000 people were resettled from Austria and Yugoslavia to thirty-seven countries, including the United Kingdom, the USA and Canada.

At home once more, Rip engaged in a short period of intense artistic activity at his Ca'n Cueg studio. The continuing crises in his private life found expression in *Landschaft Mit Schwarzem Himmel* ('Landscape with Black Heaven'): the landscape of Mallorca with its textures and colours – orange, gold, ochre and brown – depicted under the dramatic contrast of a black heaven. The black sun of his 1952 painting has become a black heaven. According to Rudolph von Ripper's great nephew, Stephan Koja, his exhibition came off at Madrid's Museo de Arte Contemporaneo in June 1957. It was a retrospective exhibition including oil paintings and gouaches (1953–1958), seven drawings (1943–1957), twelve prints from *Écraser l'Infâme*, 'The Soul and Body of John Brown', two tapestries titled 'Little Night Music' and 'Atlantis', ten pieces of jewellery and three carpets woven in Mallorca.

Winter ushered in a very different mood for the artist. Mallorca is often grey, chilling and damp in winter when an atmosphere of desolation permeates the country towns. In November 1957 Avi had gone to a Zurich clinic to 'get the works' and Rip found himself alone at Ca'n Cueg. Increasingly suffering from angina attacks and struggling to recover from influenza, the housebound lonely traveller cheered up a little when Martín Amengual arrived to go over the accounts. With only his dog for company, Rip felt so disconnected he was unable to paint. His letters to Avi convey the extent of his suffering, 'The weather changed suddenly ... today the most brilliant sunshine, although brisk and cool. There is snow on the Puig Tomir ... I want a bit of happiness and [to] live in harmony with you – and not this wrangling, this never being satisfied and contented – we are holding our happiness in our own hands.' Two days later, he wrote again: 'Heavy grey clouds cover the sky. That makes this place feel even lonelier and somewhat desolate.' Then, in an effort to be cheerful he went on to share the local gossip, 'which you so enjoy', gleaned from trips to his favourite haunts, Puerto Pollensa and the Hotel Formentor.

'Martín came for dinner and after dinner we went over all the accounts. Martín has stuck to his estimates ... with additional things you ordered – like the bar. In all, the rebuilding and all the purchases come to what I had figured prudently: about 550.000 pesetas or $10,000. Martín [is] very appreciative of the way I've handled the payments. He and Catalina are giving me dinner in the *Puerto* tonight ... The birds are noisy, the dog full of play. The only thing that is not so good is me; I feel listless, tired ... That *gripe* [influenza] has done something to me. No mail at all; how I hate that when I'm alone here. When there is mail, one feels connected. Like this, the isolation is heavy and feeling as I do I have to force myself to work. And the results are not satisfactory.' A few days later, Avi received another letter, 'It is in the days of isolation that one looks into oneself; into the things that make one's life worth living. The joy of the presence of a beloved person! I must get away from here now – I have worked well this year – but I'm getting stale. Something new is brewing in my mind; something has to take shape and form. Having never been part of a group or a movement, but always a lonely traveller, I'm so much more vulnerable and dependent on the person most directly concerned.' That person was, of course, Avi who was increasingly distant.

Despite his depression, he succeeded in getting himself to Paris – 'grey, grey and cold ... And I've been working like a beaver.' But he and Avi quarrelled during a telephone call. 'Really, why do you have to be so disagreeable even on the phone!' he wrote afterwards. 'I fully understand your impatience and annoyance – but don't let it out on me! Please do finish what you've begun and cheer up, old girl!'

He had chosen the upmarket Hôtel de France & Choiseul on the Rue St Honoré as a venue to display and sell his jewellery and evening bags. The arrangement was that his contact at the hotel, 'Annemarie', would phone him or leave a message with the concierge of his apartment to alert him to potential clients. Rip would meet them for viewings over tea or cocktails between the hours of four and seven o'clock. He sold a bracelet to a Madame Lefevre. 'Everybody who has seen the *minaudière* just goes "Oh" – especially the females,' Rip reported to Avi. Another customer was a trustee of the Henry Clews Foundation, owner of the Chateau de la Napoule near Cannes, 'where they give concerts and have exhibitions of American artists. They are coming to see the jewels, and since I just got the photos and clippings back from Redfern [London Gallery] (without even one single line! the bastards!) I can show that too.' Rip's anger and disappointment over the Redfern Gallery's ill-mannered rejection was somewhat mollified by the offer of an exhibition at the Chateau de la Napoule.

Gwen and Rudi Walti arrived at Ca'n Cueg with their young sons, Peter and Chris, in August 1958. This time the Waltis departed on the Palma to Barcelona night ferry with heavy hearts. Gwen's letter of thanks for the holiday reveals the extent of the deterioration of the von Ripper's marriage.

'I can't tell you how I wept over that steamer's railing, for you both and my infinite concern about your relationship. I and Rudi could only in standing by show you or try to show you our full sympathy for your problems,' (the underlining is Gwen's). She emphasised that Rip and Avi must solve their problems 'alone, on the basis of deeper understanding and reciprocal tolerance of each other's individual needs – in short, a reaffirmation of respect for each other, banning the infernal daily criticism of each partner's moves, banning threats and the too easily uttered ridicule of one partner before third persons.

'Now that we are gone and the Catherwood schedule and annoyance have been removed, you have more peace of mind and less hectic activity to reconsider your relationship.' Gwen's reference to the Catherwood Foundation suggests that it did not meet over the summer since, given Rip's CIA activity in Vienna the following year, he is unlikely to have released his appointment. At the height of the Cold War, quitting the CIA was a risky process.

Gwen begged her sister, 'and heaven forgive me if this sounds too much like Sunday's sermon – you must take time to help each other out of this deadly day to day self-destruction by reciprocal torment … It meant a great deal to be with you again in spite of the tension and fear of oncoming tension present in your lovely place.' Gwen referred to 'violent emotional reactions set off on all sides' during the last 'gourmet lunch' at Can Cueg, yet, through it all 'the fundamental ever-present deep affection and love binding us each to the other regardless of the issues involved.'

She concluded by saying how marvellous the vacation had been for her son Peter 'who keeps referring to the wonders and joys of his stay at Avi's and Rip's. He will never forget all his privileges of sailing, staying up until dinnertime with us, the glory of the pool and the companionship of local boys.' Peter, she wrote, 'beamed affectionately' over Rip's greetings of 'one sailor to another' in his last letter. 'A thousand thanks, for giving that boy such a divine time.' Evidently, Gwen breathed not a word to Mups about Avi's and Rip's 'living hell' since Mups wrote to Avi later that month, 'Gwen told me what a wonderful time they had with you and Rip.'

Mups and Hermann Stein visited Ca'n Cueg the following summer when she delivered a prediction from Mrs Trost that her son-in-law would soon face a great crisis. Undeterred, Rudolph von Ripper set off for Vienna where he joined Fritz Molden, the Austrian Foreign Minister, Bruno Kreisky, the German artist, Georg Furstenberg, and the Austrian lawyer and Social Democrat Party politician, Christian Broda, to organise a CIA-backed counter-event to the Communist Youth Festival. They were curious to observe at first hand the Soviets' staging of an event for 20,000 participants. Rip and his colleagues teamed up with other non-Communist Americans who perceived the event as an opportunity to win the hearts and minds of uncommitted individuals to whom they could present the *pax Americana*, thus countering the Communist party line with their own opposing propaganda. Before he left Austria, Rip joined his mother and Valerie on a visit to Hellbrunn Palace near Salzburg. The last known photograph of Rudolph von Ripper freezes a moment of that day. He is fifty-four years old and his dark hair has turned to silver.

Later that year, the von Rippers were planning a more glamorous journey that would alleviate Rip's tribulations, at least in the short term. In all probability the scheme had been seeded six years earlier, during Cummins Catherwood's visit to Ca'n Cueg, and had gathered momentum during Rip's escapade as 'Keeper of the Dalí Jewels'. After the Rome exhibition, the wily John Moore had installed himself at Cap de Creus as Dalí's right hand man and secretary and stealthily assumed control of the artist's activities. He accompanied Dalí on world tours as a pivotal figure in his entourage. No doubt Moore as well as Cummins Catherwood had a hand in plotting Rip's next journey, which would benefit everyone concerned. Whilst Dalí and the von Rippers needed a supply of precious and semi-precious stones for their respective jewellery enterprises, such an epic journey would have been beyond their means. The von Rippers were practically broke.

CHAPTER FIFTEEN
GEMSTONES AND A PARROT

In January 1960 Avi and Rip closed up their home in Mallorca and Martín Amengual drove them to the port of Palma. Their wardrobe trunks had gone before them, splattered with Pacific & Orient Line stickers and labelled 'Baron and Baroness Rudolph von Ripper, Palma de Mallorca to Shanghai'. They left the liner to explore Athens and Alexandria before sailing on through the Suez Canal, the Red Sea, and out into the Indian Ocean. Somewhere near the Equator, on the twenty-ninth of January they celebrated Rip's fifty-fifth birthday with magnums of champagne and the captain at their table.

Thailand and Cambodia were ravishingly decked with spring blossom when Rip and Avi disembarked to tour the sites. Rudolph von Ripper, the 'third man' of his Vienna period, in Southeast Asia takes on some of the colouring of the 'quiet American'. Graham Greene's novel of that name (1955) depicts one of his central characters as an American CIA agent named Alden Pyle. Pyle works under cover for the Agency and supports the theory that neither Communism nor colonialism can provide solutions to Western threats from the Far East. Given his vast trove of wartime experience, his disillusionment with Communism and his frustrations with the CIA backed Congress for Cultural Freedom, Rip is likely to have supported Pyle's albeit fictitious view. There is no record to suggest that Rudolph von Ripper was active as a CIA agent on the trip to the Orient, but espionage was his blood as an intelligence officer/solider. Certainly he would have had access to CIA agents wherever he went and to foreign diplomats sympathetic to the *pax Americana*.

The knowledgeable Baron and his wife revelled in Oriental art. Letters in the blue file reveal that they purchased red lacquer furniture to send home to Mallorca. Whilst Rip haggled for unpolished gemstones in souks and mines all the way to China, Avi looked on, elegant in linen dresses, in her element. They filled velvet pouches with unpolished gemstones: black and white pearls, rubies, sapphires, opals and uncut diamonds, sufficient for themselves and their 'amigo' Salvador Dalí. Magnanimously, Rip offered Avi his savoir-faire. She had fallen for another man, but he intended to win her back now that Martín Amengual was far away, his feet firmly planted in the concrete of Mallorca's building boom.

Rip showed Avi the sights of Shanghai and must have reminisced about his adventures in the city in 1926. Perhaps he imagined the skeleton of his American boss still lying in the hovel in the Pudong district where he had been assassinated, the flesh eaten by vermin down to the bones, since who would have bothered to clear away the remains of a Western capitalist? Slum dwellers in all probability, since the smell of the American's rotting corpse would have become unbearable. And, although the hovel could have housed a family of ten the way some Chinese had to live, not even the most destitute souls would have squatted in a place haunted by a foreigner's ghost.

The Shanghai episode and most of Rudolph von Rippers' other narratives were closed books to his wife. Chapters of his life before he met his wife, set in the elite salons and artists' studios of Paris and Berlin, in the battlefields of Europe and North Africa, in the Nazi concentration camp and the Spanish Civil War. In the Orient three decades earlier, he had felt truly free for the first time in his young life. Freed from stultifying Viennese society and his aristocratic inheritance; liberated from the chaos and disorder bred by the First World War. The shots fired in Sarajevo in 1914 from Gavrilo Prinzip's revolver when he had been a kid of nine signalled far more to him than the end of the Austria-Hungary Empire. Perhaps he remembered a tableau vivant captured in a black and white photograph of his childhood: himself as a boy, squinting into sharp sunlight, beside his father and sisters on the eve of the Great War. He knew it must be somewhere among the jumble of letters and photographs Avi kept in a blue file back home in Mallorca.

Rip's friend, Captain Peter Payne, who had also undergone parachute training in 1944, met them when they disembarked at Athens in May. 'You struck me both of you – maybe because I was very low at the time – with your extremely happy faces,' he wrote to them later. 'Rip looked an image of health and gaiety.' They travelled by train to Paris where Rip's red Chevrolet and Avi's black Mercedes were parked in the garage of their apartment. After three months in the Orient, Rip was raring to get back to painting in his studio in Mallorca. He set off sometime in June and it is highly probable that he took the Paris-Costa Brava route in order to drop off Dalí's share of the gemstones at Port Lligat, close to the French-Spanish border. He knew the route from Paris to Barcelona well from previous journeys.

Accounts of his journey south differ; there is a suggestion that Avi accompanied Rip, another that he was alone, but the narrative that follows adheres to the version of events that suggests Avi followed Rip in her Mercedes a day or two later. Rip's subsequent arrest and imprisonment in Barcelona and the story of the parrot is confirmed by several sources. Taking all the evidence into account, and, in particular, a remark made by Mutti in a letter to her daughter-in-law, that 'he thoughtfully sent you back to Paris', I conclude that Rip did send Avi away before or at the border checkpoint. What follows is an imaginative reconstruction, based on known facts about Rudolph von Ripper's last journey.

He felt fitter than he'd done in a long time, and they had returned in high spirits from the Far East. Certainly, their odyssey had fulfilled one of Avi's dreams and brought them closer. Their mission had been accomplished and surely even Salvador's gargantuan appetite for glamour, and Gala Dalí's taste for filthy lucre, would be satiated by the stash of unpolished stones in the boot of his tomato red Chevy? The hot Midi embraced him, and in a market somewhere south of Carcassonne a parrot caught his eye: a talking parrot, an African Grey. The bird would be company the rest of the way and Avi would love it, so he bought it and wedged the cage between the back and front seats of the car. At Perpignan, he paid his respects to the statue of King Jaume I, the conqueror of Mallorca in the thirteenth century who had repressed the Jewish and Moorish population. Gazing at the stony-faced king atop his splendid horse, Rudolph von Ripper might well have pondered the endless fluid passage of humanity through endless time. Never-ending wars and suffering, and to what end? Surely his mind swirled with remembrance when he approached the French-Spanish border town of Cerbère? The area had been known as *La Retirada*, the Retreat, after refugees fleeing from Franco's

Spain, and later from the Nazis, had swarmed to safety over the mountains at Col-des-Balitres. Perhaps the very hotel Rip might have checked into at Cerbère was where Walter Benjamin had committed suicide in the company of Paul Klee's painting *Angelus Novus*.

Cerbère would have been a convenient rendezvous point for the couple, and I imagine Avi arriving there in her Mercedes, glamorous in a wide brimmed sunhat and sunshades. She knew the score: it was unlikely to happen, but if there was any sign of trouble at the checkpoint, at a signal from her husband she was to drive away pronto. The Chevrolet and the Mercedes stood out among a tailback of dusty black SEATs waiting to cross the border. On they drove then waited again, repeating this action several times before Rip reached the barrier. The official cast emotionless eyes over the car and Rip's passport, and just when he thought he'd get the go-ahead, the parrot squawked. After that everything turned to slow motion: the guy pulling the cloth off the cage, seeing the parrot, beckoning to a colleague, exchanging jokes in Catalan then demanding of Rip in Castilian, did he have a license to take the bird out of France? They took the car keys, scorned the wad of notes Rip offered from his wallet, and when they went to open the boot he gave Avi the signal. She engineered a tight three-point turn, her wheels screeching and raising a cloud of dust before she drove away.

For decades Rudolph von Ripper had crossed and re-crossed borders with contraband and seldom had to resort to bribery. The only time he had been (illegally) arrested had been for smuggling 'shipments of cement' into Switzerland in 1933. These days it was common knowledge among expats living in the Mediterranean that you could buy off customs officials with a wad of dollars, *ningun problema.* The moment his bribe was refused, Rip knew that he must have been set up and that no amount of money would buy him out of this mess.

Inside the checkpoint, unpolished rubies, sapphires, diamonds, opals and pearls spilled from their velvet bags at the instruction of the *Guardia* detective. Some accounts suggest drugs were also found in the cache, and given Rip's addiction this is more than likely. Before he was handcuffed and driven from the checkpoint to Barcelona jail the detective confirmed Rip's supposition that he had been betrayed. They had been looking out for him at the checkpoint, he said, because 'a friend' had denounced him for smuggling. Cyrus Sulzberger later corroborated the fact that Rudolph von Ripper had been set up by the fascist calling himself Schmidt.

Would his attempts at bribery this time tell against him if, God forbid, he was brought to trial for smuggling? Rip must have wondered. The situation was so dire he must have felt the optimism of the past weeks draining out of him, just as it had done when he first set eyes on Otto Skorzeny striding around Pollensa as if he owned the place in 1952. The cliché Nazi: a beefy hunter-gatherer, with emotionless eyes, blue and deep-set under a protruding forehead – and that scar. Ears like slabs of veal under the SS headgear he had replaced with a sailor's cap and the legend 'Club Nautica'. When he heard that Skorzeny had actually bought a house near Pollensa, Rip must have known despair before he rallied. After all, the war was over. Bonhomie with your former enemies was the way to go. Skorzeny never spoke about the war but loved to boast about his recent purchase of a second estate in Ireland.

Had Rip occasionally sat in a bar with Skorzeny, filled with a sense of life's ironies? Rule number one: *don't mention*

Scarface's surrender to you in Austria in 1945. Then one day at the Hotel Formentor, had he glimpsed Skorzeny's henchman, Schmidt? Did that sighting trigger in Rip's mind the words he had spoken the day he arrested Skorzeny: *what a satisfaction it is for me to take you, the top Nazi, in my home town, back to Salzburg as my prisoner and throw you into jail?* Fifteen years after the event, was the predicament he found himself in now Skorzeny's revenge?

In the Barcelona jail, Rip might well have remembered that in 1778, the year of his death, his hero Voltaire returned from exile to Paris and was met at the frontier by a customs official who questioned him closely. Was there contraband in his carriage? Did he have anything to declare?

Voltaire replied, 'Nothing but myself.'

Several days later, Rudolph von Ripper was discharged without his passport, Chevrolet, gemstones or parrot and escorted to the Trans-Mediterranean ferry. Amengual, prosperous looking in navy blazer, slacks and Panama hat, is likely to have been waiting beside his SEAT 1400A for Rip to disembark at the port of Palma. The sight of Martín would have spelled home to Rip, regardless of the extent of his involvement with Avi. 'In love' was different from an affair, of course, and nobody could ever be blamed for falling in love. In all probability, Rip had resolved to turn a blind eye to Avi's adventures so long as he believed she would not leave him. She had been a good companion on their trip to the Far East, but how would she handle the stress of the smuggling charges and the court appearances they faced? When they were tethered up at Ca'n Cueg, would life once more be a living hell?

On the two-hour journey from Palma, driving along curving dusty roads, through almond orchards and somnolent towns – Santa Maria, Binissalem, Lloseta and Campos – Martín would have heard about Avi's retreat to Paris, the confiscation of the gemstones, the parrot and the car, the denunciation by 'a friend' and the likelihood that the set up was linked to Skorzeny. When they drove into the Pollensa Valley, Rip said he planned to send the servants away until Avi's return since he needed time alone to process the drama that had ensued on the French-Spanish border.

Rudolph von Ripper rose in the translucent dawn and left a note for the servants on the kitchen table: he would be working all morning in the studio and must not be disturbed. He would not come to say goodbye, they were simply to leave as soon as they were ready. The dog stirred in the kennel and he blessed the fact that it didn't bark when he slipped through the gates of Ca'n Cueg. The first cockerel would crow in the *barrío* of Ternelles soon enough. Silence was what he craved in the half-dark, crossing the tarmac road to his studio. How slowly he walked, hunched like a freak in a child's storybook, he thought, struggling towards its endgame.

The road from Pollensa divided their land and, after a few kilometres, climbed sheer to the mountain stronghold of Lluch Monastery: *El Monasterío de Lluch*. Centuries earlier, the unearthing of a statue of the Black Virgin with her crown of thirteen stars had led to the monastery's foundation. Now it was a place of pilgrimage. Aloof in its vale of cypress trees whose geometry reminded Rip of tears, Lluch held out the promise that there, in that mountain wilderness, prayers might be answered. Rip knew better. The history and architecture of the monastery interested him, but he had discarded Catholicism a while back in favour of Art. Art was his spiritual practice and the studio his sacred space.

After the trauma of the past days he felt frantic to open its door and seal it behind him. Here was his refuge in times of suffering, like now when the stress of recent events had intensified the pain in his arms and chest and the frequency of his angina attacks.

He had designed the simple stone structure to resemble a tower: the studio above a garage large enough to house the Chevrolet and Avi's Mercedes. Stiffly, he climbed the stairs to the door that had remained closed ever since they had set out for Indochina six months earlier. He had been relieved to shut up the studio last January, since Mediterranean winters filled him with an almost unbearable melancholy. He fumbled with the key, stiff in its lock before it yielded, and the hinges rasped when he thrust open the door. The relief of arrival was so overpowering and the pain in his left side so severe, he searched like a blind man in the half-dark for his daybed.

As soon as he lay down, the musty smell of the blankets took him to Syria, to North Africa, to Anzio ... and the faint mingled odour of turpentine, paint and the fires he had lit in the stove all those months ago reminded him of incense. Beyond the studio window the dark mass of the Sierra reared against the lightening sky. Venus suspended; a sparkling diamond not even Dalí had the power to set. Later, when the rising sun shafted the studio with light, he hauled himself up to sit on the edge of the bed. This is what life had reduced him to. The edge of a bed, longing for another – the bed he had shared with Avi in a Shanghai hotel less than two months ago. They were used to 'doing their own thing' – a strategy that had saved their marriage – but now that he had come home alone under a cloud so black it defied reason or resolution – his longing for Avi was tinged with desperation.

Colour seeped into the studio even as he sat dazed on the bed. Like an exhausted animal in a trap laid by a cunning gamekeeper, he thought. Colour seeped into the landscape beyond the studio window: ochre, gold and various shades of terracotta, punctuated by cypress trees and date palms. Patches of lime green in the fields had been parched to dust by summer heat at the same time as the orchards of the Pollensa valley hung voluptuous with bee-droned fruits. Startled, he recalled painting the scene under a black heaven a year or two back. It had been an accomplished painting. How daring, said the artists of the Pollensa School. How surprising that black goes so well with the colours of the Mallorcan landscape. But he could not fool himself. Black had been the colour of his soul at the time and all the courage he had mustered could not alter that fact.

On the worktable the off-white page of his sketchpad confronted him when he shifted his gaze, but he was in no mood to design jewellery. How could he when he must endure this continuing dark night of the soul, when nothing less than alchemical inspiration could save him. *No one who has been tortured can endure it a second time.* He ran the tap at the stone sink in the far corner of the room, opened his pillbox and swallowed the drugs for his angina with a glass of water. After that, his hands fumbled on shelves ordered with paint tubes, brush jars and boxes of crayons until he found just the colour he needed: alizarin – the colour of blood. He attacked the blank page with an enraged wavering line, and there it was, the redbrick wall of KV Oranienburg, sealed in his memory forever. The place where his young heart had shattered. With a black pen he printed 'INFERNO 1933–34' and, in the copperplate handwriting he had learned from the Jesuits, '*En el mezzo del camin de mi vida ...*'

He stood rigid for a few moments, then ripped out the page and scrunched it into a ball. The unholy alliance of Diels, Skorzeny and Schmidt, the horrifyingly long arm, more CIA than Gestapo these days, had set him up on the Spanish border. Why had he not seen it coming?

The room flooded with sunlight and became unbearably hot. His hands shook, carrying the blue file to the table, opening it up to the mess inside. Photographs, jumbled up memories of his life. Here was his father, Baron Eduard; there was his nineteenth-century grandfather in uniform in Japan. And there he was, not so long ago, with Mutti and Valerie in a Salzburg park, and there were he and Avi, lunching at Ca'n Cueg with Gwen and Rudi. Here was one of his nephew young Peter, peeking over the top of a canvas he'd painted during the Waltis' last visit. And there it was, himself when young, at Lemberg, or had it been Goerz, or another of their residences in the Crown lands? A boy squints into sunshine so sharp it almost blinds him ... where it all began: the tumultuous journey to this end.

Suddenly, the chug of the generator starting up over at the house distracted him and he went to look out of the side window. The servants, husband and wife, stood tête-à-tête in the olive grove beside their tied cottage. His beloved pointer strained against the man's leash. If he'd had the energy to exercise the animal he would have kept the dog beside him for company. When he saw the woman gesturing in the direction of the studio he knew they must have been discussing his unexpected arrival last night with Martín Amengual, without the Chevrolet, without *la Baronessa*. He guessed the simple souls felt uneasy about leaving without a formal goodbye. Yet he prayed they would so he wouldn't have to struggle back to the house and shoo them off the premises.

On a whim, he opened the window, called out and waved, *Hasta luego! Adios!* Not his usual Baron-like behaviour, but hopefully it would do the trick and they would just go. He sat in the wickerwork chair and heard the gate squeaking as it opened then closed, then the clip-clop of the horse's hooves as the servants' cart set off up the road to Lluch. He sat on until the sound became faint as a heartbeat rising towards the mountains.

Ich bin gestorben dem Weltgetümmel
und ruh' in einem stillen Gebiet.
Ich leb' allein in meinem Himmel,
in meinem Lieben, in meinem Lied.

I am dead to the turmoil of the world
and rest in a quiet region.
I live alone in my heaven,
in my love, in my song.

Rudolph von Ripper died during the night of 9 July 1960. Avi flew immediately to Mallorca and her brother-in-law, Rudi Walti, arrived with young Peter to support her. Gwen was about to give birth to her third child and was unable to travel. Mutti wrote as soon as she heard the news, 'My poor child, my thoughts are with you and my poor boy who has left us forever. Did he suffer a distressing death? He liked living and so thoughtfully sent you Avi, his Avi, back home [to Paris]. Your life with him wasn't always easy. He had so many difficult times that he often lost his patience, making him angry, but the depth of his heart was just goodness and love.'

On 14 July an obituary notice appeared in *The New York Times*: 'Rudolf von Ripper, Artist, Dies; War Hero Served

With OSS.' The obituary refers to the 1935 London exhibition of drawings from *Écraser l'Infâme*, which 'created a sensation in the art world'. 'Mr von Ripper was a courageous and colourful person who had justifiable reason to conduct an almost one-man campaign against the Germans ... It was with the Thirty-fourth [Division] that Mr von Ripper served heroically ... The end of the war found him tracking down SS generals, Nazi officials and Gestapo agents in various disguises and hideouts.'

The Cold War was a hair's breadth from becoming fiery when Rudolph von Ripper died, a CIA agent during Franco's dictatorship and an enemy of ex-Nazis living in Spain. The week of his death the Mallorcan Press Association put on a bullfight at Palma's Plaza de Toros; *The King and I* starring Yul Brynner and Deborah Kerr played at the Sala Regina cinema; Ex-King Farouk of Egypt's yacht slipped into Palma Harbour; the United Nations asked Belgium to remove its forces from the Congo; Kruschev invited Fidel Castro to visit Russia; Winston Churchill met Tito in Yugoslavia; Russia accused the USA of 'criminal action and piracy' after its RB-47 airplane strayed into Russian territory; John Kennedy was tipped to be the next US President.

Avi received letters of condolence at Ca'n Cueg. Captain Payne, whom they had seen so recently in Athens, wrote 'the disappearance of Rip must mean the amputation of life itself.' Cyrus Sulzberger noted that Rip 'had learned the meaning of political terror and enlisted in a life-long fight against it that never ended, even with his death.' Sulzberger referred to Rip's continual persecution by the Nazis ever since his arrest in 1933, and their ongoing attempts to malign him. When he heard that Schmidt, one of Rip's 'final vestige fascists', had issued a statement alleging that von Ripper had taken his own life with poison pills, a furious

Sulzberger summed up the 'ghastly paradox' of Schmidt's cowardly action as 'dead Fascism desecrating the system's own dead enemy'. Sulzberger and his wife offered Avi the use of their Paris apartment if she should need a bolt hole.

Rip's friends and family – even the servants – scorchingly denied Schmidt's allegation of suicide and claimed that the Baron had died of a heart attack in the garage underneath his studio. Yet certain references suggest that their claim might have been a cover up for crime. Some weeks after her husband's death, Avi received a letter (signature page missing): 'After many more or less fantastic variations, I finally hear the authentic story ... Poor girl you must have had a hard time! If you need a good shot to feed that bastard some lead, don't forget me!' Which 'bastard': the one who killed Rudolph von Ripper?

History has shrouded the 'authentic story', leaving only hints and guesses about the true circumstances of Rudolph von Ripper's death. My contact who discovered the blue file had mentioned the fact that, soon afterwards, she 'asked around' for information about him. Someone who had known Ca'n Cueg in the 1960s claimed that Rip had drowned in the swimming pool and that Martín Amengual had discovered his body. Several years earlier, Avi had photographed a jubilant Rip from the poolside on the day her swimming pool was inaugurated. But another grainy black and white photograph in Avi's blue file captures a very different atmosphere in the same location. It is a chilling image of the far end of the swimming pool and the wood beyond. Was its presence in the file intended to focus the viewer's attention on the spot where Rudolph von Ripper drowned? After all, an assailant had open access to Ca'n Cueg's garden by crossing *torrente* and slipping through the wood. Did an assassin, aware that Avi and the servants were away, confront Rip at Ca'n Cueg on the night he died? It is as if Avi slipped the photograph into the file as a clue to a truth that could not be openly told.

The supposition that Rip drowned in the swimming pool gains credence from Gwen's remark in a letter to Avi: 'Rudi said you went swimming and I am glad you did … it will help you if you can get up the willpower to do it.' Another letter from Countess von Salis-Samaden to Avi mentions the death of an acquaintance in Austria, 'it was a crime, not an accident.' Was Mutti speculating that her son's death, too, had been a crime?

Rudolph von Ripper died in Franco's Spain at the height of the Cold War between Russia and the USA. Against that grim backdrop people did die or disappear. Still today, anyone driving the Deìa-Soller road who looks down over the sheer sea-cliffs can see the rusty wreck of a car lying among the desolate rocks and fallen pine-trees. The car is said to have belonged to the former British agent, Thomas Harris, who shortly before his death in 1964 had refused to continue working as an MI5 agent. Oral tradition along this coastline implies that Harris' death was not an accident.

Whatever the true manner of Rudolph von Ripper's death, no 'final vestige fascist' had the power to obliterate his friends' beloved memory of him. 'It cannot be true – he must be alive. For me who first met him parachuting through the belly of an aircraft way back in 1944 in Italy it means the disappearance of one of the most loving, kind and extraordinary men I have ever met,' Captain Payne wrote to Avi.

'When I recall the great variety of subjects which he knew, from painting and art to sports cars, from the chamois to the US stock market, everything he touched was done with intelligence. And lastly, the wonderful house you both built, he loved it so much and was so proud of it. You must feel him everywhere – in every little corner and every stone. Yet Rip, apart from his mind, had life's bigger asset – his big heart in his hand – how kind and true he was in his friend-ships – He was always there – always out to start a discussion with a story on everything, and always ready to help … I will always remember the great and loving friend who has gone. He was truly a remarkable man, a rare phenomenon of kindness personified and *la joie de vivre*. I kiss you with all the love authorised by an old friendship – Pete.'

CHAPTER SIXTEEN
THE JEWEL CASE

The Palma to Puerto Pollensa motorway skirts the Sports Centre before a side road humps over a narrow bridge and curves between almond and fig orchards to a long, low neo-classical building: the archetypical Mediterranean Cemetery punctuated by tall cypresses. Beside the arched entrance, a rosemary bush is smothered in flowers so blue they beg to be admired. Baroness von Ripper, elegantly dressed in black with her face veiled, enters with a small group of mourners including Rudi and young Peter Walti. The priest leads them to a burial site outside the walls reserved for foreigners and Protestants. Years later, when the outré lives of expatriates had become more acceptable to the Catholic clergy and the indigenous townsfolk, a section for foreign residents was created within Pollensa Cemetery's walls where Rudolph von Ripper's remains were transferred.

The central area of the cemetery is laid out like a Moorish garden with cruciform paths enclosing, not orange trees, but monolithic grey family tombs surmounted with angels, monumental crucifixes and colour photographs of the deceased. The search for Rip's memorial ends up a ramp into an area at the very edge of the cemetery where tombs are set into a high wall, like drawers in a vast cabinet. Carved slabs bearing the names of former English residents surround memorial number 47, the resting place of Rudolph von Ripper. A finely carved rose coloured stone shows a knight on a charger, a sword aloft in his right hand, and the legend: *And there shall be no night there.* Paradoxically, in this quiet region of the cemetery the hero who tilted at the windmills of his times springs vividly to life. The headstone looks so fresh it might have been carved yesterday. A daub of bright blue paint, not household paint, but Prussian blue paint from an artist's colour box, stands out on the stone. Was the person who made that mark disappointed that the words carved on the stone failed to honour Rip's achievement as an artist? It is through his art that Rudolph von Ripper lives on.

The 'Jewel Case', due to be heard in the Baroness's presence at the court in Gerona that September, was postponed. Mups wrote to Avi, 'I am so relieved ... October is ever so much better for you Trost told me.' Mups reminded Avi, 'Trost DID predict last year the great crisis for Rip, and I did tell you at the time (God I hated to do it) as I was so worried and panicky during our stay [at Ca'n Cueg].' When Avi wrote of her concern that the outcome of the trial would be a penalty so large she would lose Ca'n Cueg, Mrs Trost replied via Mups that, although Avi would have to pay for 'the mistakes in reasonable measure', Ca'n Cueg would be safe and that the house must not be sold under any circumstances.

Mups then waded in with advice: 'Your very best weapon for this fight [the trial] is that you do NOT confide in ANYBODY about the case, the circumstances, the past etc. etc. to even the most intimate friends or people you know because there is always the possibility of a leak and you have

no chance to trace the leak, or defend yourself against it ...
you must outsmart them by living quietly and completely
without suspicion day by day until this nightmare is over ...
Darling, stay away from people like 'Gaby' [the dressmaker]
... and everyone who was ever part or connected with you
in the PAST when all these scandals and gossips were circulating on the island. PLEASE, no matter what they think,
just do not get near them ever.'

Where officials were concerned Mups advised, 'use only
charm and friendliness as well as diplomacy ... in connec-
tion with the jewel case ... You must conform to the customs
and feelings of the country and people there – no more
revolutionary gestures of any kind, *Achtung Kurve, Vorsicht*
... handle every official with *Glacé-Handschuehen* – no matter
how you feel inwardly – and don't irritate and annoy them
with gay-colored clothes, or wearing jewels when you deal
with them. The customs of a country and their people are
very important and serious to them. The Americans are
great offenders in that respect when they travel in other
countries.'

In March 1961, Avi and Gwen travelled to New York
together. Mups wrote to Avi on her return to Pollensa, 'Gwen
hasn't stopped telling us about all your wonderful friends ...
the unbelievable hospitality you received. True friends are
the most precious gift in life. Family you have for life, but
friends you have to deserve, otherwise you lose them. Gwen
told us how wonderful Cummie was, really a true friend.'

Baroness von Ripper informed her mother that she
intended to visit Allen Dulles and Chip Bohlen, both 'top
guys' in the CIA (Bohlen was American Ambassador in
Russia (1953–57) and in France from 1963). It is likely
that Avi was seeking a war widow's pension, given Rip's
outstanding service as an O.S.S. officer. Mups got on her

high horse to warn her daughter to seek the advice of Rip's good friends, Lee Ault and Cummins Catherwood. 'So far,' Mups replied, 'they both [Dulles and Bohlen] have the fondest and most respectful memory of Rip, knowing the magnificent things Rip did during the War, and his brilliant mind and individuality as a person – why would you want to put a shadow on his memory by telling them of [the] unfortunate mistakes of the whole jewel business (without a license?) and the smuggling in of the stones??? You would be terribly embarrassed if they would tell you, that in this case, they could not help you, so why not forget the whole thing and not mention it anymore … I have a definite intuition that talking this whole thing over with men of their standing is a grave mistake and would only lower Rip and you in their estimation. God knows, you may one day want to live in New York, or Washington, in the same circles and society, and there again you need above all an unblemished reputation.'

By November 1961 the first stage of the Gerona trial had taken place and the case was transferred to a court of appeals in Madrid. Avi wrote to Sherburn Becker (her 'broker and friend'), 'Briefly, I lost the appeal case – gaining only slightly in a reduction of one third of the total fine imposed, but having to pay additionally nonetheless $6,250 US.' She adds that the Madrid court ruled that Rip's car should be returned to his heirs: 'only the Gerona Tribunal cannot decide who the heirs are.' Avi maintained that this was 'just another stall' in the absence of New York State surrogate court papers proving that she was the heiress. Eventually the car was returned to the Baroness.

Avi von Ripper successfully applied for an administrative post at the Guggenheim Museum in New York in 1962, but she was reluctant to leave Mallorca. Mups wrote immediately, 'for once please use your head and not only your heart ... please snap out of the Mallorcan lethargy and get going again before it is too late ... get yourself out of the dopey atmosphere of the island ... Martín can be trusted to rent out Ca'n Cueg ... I would advise you most of all, knowing your love for this man, again and again, presents a terrible situation and problem. I don't criticize your falling in love with him, one cannot help these things – but he is married and worse has two children, and if his wife does not want to divorce him, you must stay away from him in the future, or you will be drawn into another scandal, if the wife should find out and name you in her case. So there is really no use to even think about keeping up an affair with a man in such a position. It is dynamite no matter how you look at it.' Mups added a customary sting, 'I should think you have had enough trouble to last you a lifetime?? Trost predicted a man for you, (younger than you, but not much) and a happy marriage ... The time element on these predictions is always variable but not too much.'

Although there was nothing to hinder her affairs with Amengual and others, the Baroness concluded that there was no future for her on the island without 'Ripsky'. That September, she placed an advertisement in *The New Yorker*, hoping to attract a rich tenant to Ca'n Cueg. She was successful and wrote to the tenants giving her Paris address as care of Cyrus Sulzberger on Avenue de Segur. She wrote to Mups that she was utterly exhausted, with a bad cold and confined to bed. 'The servants are acting up just when I need them most ... they are discontented and holding out and making more demands when they know perfectly well they have me on a spot.' But by October her letters to Gwen are upbeat despite the ulcer she is being treated for, 'feeling so much better than I have in years ... except that a wild monkey bit me in the leg ... and in order to avoid gangrene am having to have penicillin shots. I am not kidding.' After paying out fines and lawyers' fees relating to the trial, she was struggling financially. 'The only immediate solution I can see,' she joked to Gwen, 'is to marry Harry Guggenheim and his horses and cause an early heart attack, and you too can use my horses and sleep in my Museum.' She added that she was distressed that before going to New York she wouldn't be able to see her mother-in-law Claire 'who writes rather sad letters'.

The Jewel Case dragged on. Then Avi told Gwen that a 'famous Air Force Colonel' had managed to do 'something unique even in Spanish history – to get the Ministry in Madrid to order the Gerona Court to have the jewels auctioned.' The auctions, set for mid-October, were publicized in all the newspapers of Spain. 'This, heretonow, has been unheard of, even by experts in fraud.'

Ca'n Cueg found an American tenant and the Baroness left to join the staff of the Guggenheim Museum. Annelise Stein had been seriously ill but showed signs of improving before she died suddenly in 1963. Avi von Ripper returned to Ca'n Cueg in 1968 with the intention of reinventing herself as a journalist and travel writer with an ambitious journey in mind. She submitted an article about Mallorca entitled 'Visa' to Passport magazine. 'If you do go to Japan and India, keep us in mind,' the editor replied. It was a brave hope. The truth was that Avi was falling apart and would soon leave Mallorca forever.

One of the four sisters who now own Ca'n Cueg takes up the story. 'The Baroness drank all the time and had affairs, and when she became ill it was my mother she turned to. I remember, when I was a child, she came to our house one night in a terrible state and my mother comforted her. They became very close. My mother nursed and cared for the Baroness who sold Ca'n Cueg to her around 1968 before she returned to America for good. My mother died in 1975 and the Baroness died in America from cancer of her reproductive organs around six months later.'

On hearing this, I envisage Avi clearing Ca'n Cueg before taking leave of Mallorca forever. With the help of a removal firm she packs the goods she has chosen to save into crates and boxes for shipment to America. Then she carries her gowns and Ripsky's dinner suits to the swimming pool pavilion and hangs them there before she returns for another load containing books and the blue file. Why didn't she pack the clothes, the books and file with the shipment to America? My hunch is that she wanted the contents of the pavilion to be shipped to Gwen Walti and left instructions to that effect, which were never carried out.

On what the Spanish call *un dia precioso*, eighteen degrees and sunny, a light wind carrying the faint scent of blossoming trees and the promise of spring, Ca'n Cueg is an earthly paradise. I had hoped to visit Rudolph von Ripper's studio, but it was demolished years ago to make space for a new house on the other side of the Lluch road.

The sisters have decided to sell the villa and one of them is waiting at the old gate of Ca'n Cueg to show me round. This gate, still flanked by the ceramic frogs Rip lovingly created, is now the side entrance of the villa, the Señora explains. The first room to the right was 'their bedroom', the master bedroom with an en-suite bathroom and French doors opening onto the garden. Their king sized bed still stands here, where Baron and Baroness von Ripper must have known a version of paradise before the deterioration of their marriage. As we wander from room to room – empty but for a dusty chest of drawers here, beds there, a sofa in the main reception room, debris from the exit of the summer art school tenants swept into corners – I am struck by the remarkable elegance of the interior. I can picture Avi and Rip here. Its proportions seem ideally conceived to facilitate lives aspiring to *la dolce vita*. Every wall is a shade of white or beige. Fluidly, one room leads into another, or to a passageway, a stairway, and, upstairs, five spacious bedrooms with adjoining bathrooms.

A door at this level opens onto the balcony with impressive views over the garden and beyond the Moorish aqueduct to Puig Tomir, patched now with winter snow. The Señora explains that the aqueduct brought spring water from the mountains to Alcudía, Pollensa's neighbouring town that had no water of its own. The balcony with its built-in bar was where the von Rippers enjoyed sundowners at the end of the day's work. Here they had chosen to be photographed for some of their promotional shots. Rip's mural has been painted over and the playful carved wooden monkeys that once hung on the edge of the bar have disappeared. A metal cockerel (symbol of the town of Pollensa) designed by Rip and eerily reminiscent of the cockerel in his print *Merry-Go-Round* (1938) still stands on a plinth above the bar, one of the few reminders of his residency.

As we stand looking out over the garden, the aqueduct and the mountains beyond, the Señora reminisces, 'I was a child when the von Rippers were here, and I remember them well. The Baroness was tall, elegant, beautiful – but *caprichosa!* – and the Baron was smaller than his wife, with prominent teeth, and bent over to one side from a war wound.' When she bends over to the right and sticks out her upper jaw, mimicking her memory of Rip, my heart fills with compassion for the wounded man who was so heroic in war, resistance, art and love.

'We were the von Rippers' nearest neighbours,' the Señora said. 'We lived on the other side of the *torrente* and there was a bridge in those days so we children, there were four of us, were sometimes allowed to visit Ca'n Cueg. And the von Rippers' servants came to us for eggs and milk from our cow. They employed a gardener and cook, husband and wife, and their teenage son served their meals, that sort of thing. The family lived in the cottage by the gate, and they employed a second *camarero* (waiter) for special parties and lunches, as well as cleaners and laundry maids. Cars were not so frequently seen in Pollensa in the 1950s, but I vividly recall the Baroness arriving back from her travels in her shiny black Mercedes, and huge American automobiles arriving for parties and parking nose-to-tail all the way to the curve of the Pollensa to Palma road. The parties caused a stir here in the *Huerta*. They were so noisy and fantastic! Mallorcans had never experienced people behaving like they did, and most of us hadn't seen Hollywood movies. Huge quantities of food and alcohol were consumed, and drugs taken; *fu otro mundo.*' Truly, it was another world.

We go down to the kitchen with its sizeable adjoining pantry. 'It is much as it was in the 1950s,' the Señora says 'We changed some of the fittings, but the layout is still the same.' The enormous Westinghouse refrigerator with six wooden doors that catered for the von Rippers' parties stands recessed into a wall. Beyond the kitchen door a hatch set into the floor conceals white curving walls covered with a filigree of growth and a flight of white steps leading down to the wine cellar such an establishment required

The cellar shelves that once boasted fine vintages have been cleared. In my imagination I stock them with the bottles of Chateau Margaux, Syrah, Créman de Limoux and Muscat de Frontignan Rip might have bought at the Languedoc-Roussillon vineyards on his last drive from Paris to Mallorca. There would have been a section for Mallorcan wines, too, from the notable vineyards of Binissalem.

Outside again, at the poolside on this precious day, I am keen to hear the Señora's version of the Baron's death.

The servants always maintained the Baron died in the garage after a heart attack, she says, and that he did not commit suicide.

Are the servants still alive?

No, they both died years ago. Even their son, *el camerero*, died very young of cancer.

The servants' version of Rip's death comes as no surprise. If foul play had led to his drowning in the swimming pool, the servants would have been bribed not to mention something that would have put off most potential clients from renting or buying Ca'n Cueg, should Avi decide to sell the house. Hence Avi's comment in a letter to her mother, 'the servants are acting up … they are discontented and holding out and making more demands when they know perfectly well they have me on a spot'. But I refrain from sharing these thoughts with the Señora as we walk towards the cottage-style pavilion beside the swimming pool.

I have been waiting a long time for the moment when she will open the brown louvered door, but she walks past it and opens another door adjoining the pavilion. This was Avi's office, she tells me, an elegant small apartment with a corner *chimenea* (fireplace), white lattice-work cupboards and an en-suite bathroom. The perfect venue for her affairs, I can't help thinking, even as the Señora says the Baronessa worked at their jewellery business here. 'The Baron was arrested at the Spanish border for attempting to smuggle gems into Mallorca without a license,' she adds. 'He was driving back from some place abroad with a parrot in his car. The bird started squawking, the way parrots do, and the noise drew the attention of the customs officials. When they searched the car they found a load of precious stones, arrested the Baron, impounded his car, and sent him to a Barcelona jail.'

'And of course,' she continued, 'the humiliation of the arrest, the scandal, was a factor that led to his death. And after his death, the Baronessa had to deal with lawyers and attend the trial in Gerona. She had the stress of all that.'

And what of Martín Amengual? The Señora says she never knew him and that he died many years ago. 'Even the frogs have gone, it's many years since the frogs came, and the bridge has collapsed over the *torrente.*'

When I ask to look inside the pavilion before I leave, the Señora opens the brown louvered door at last. Apart from a row of white pegs where Rudolph and Avi von Rippers' mouldering evening clothes had been hanging when my contact stepped inside, it is quite empty ... except in the imagination of anyone who has read this story.

Ca'n Cueg, 'The House of the Frogs', Mallorca 1952

Ceramic frog at Ca'n Cueg, designed by Rudolph von Ripper

Avi von Ripper at Ca'n Cueg in the 1950's

Hollywood-style party Ca'n Cueg 1953, photographed by Rudolph
von Ripper from the second floor balcony showing (clockwise) Avi
von Ripper (far left), Liddon Pennock, unknown, Sally Wetherill,
Rudi Walti, Ellen Catherwood, unknown, Alice Pennock, Cummins
Catherwood, Reeves Wetherill and Gwen Walti

The balcony bar at Ca'n Cueg: wall mural and metal
cockerel designed by Rudolph von Ripper

Rudolph von Ripper in his Ca'n Cueg studio

The last known photograph of Rudolph von Ripper with his mother
Countess Salis-Samaden at Hellbrunn Palace, Salzburg, September 1959

Avi von Ripper and Martín Amengual

The swimming pool at Ca'n Cueg and the wood beyond

SOURCES

1905-48

Rudolph von Ripper, *Écraser l'Infâme*, Portfolio of 17 Signed Prints; Winfried Meyer, *Rudolph Carl von Ripper: Écraser l'Infâme* (Jahrbuch des Vereins für die Geschichte Berlins 46, 1997); Gert Schiff, *Écraser l'Infâme* (Antologia di Belle Arti, Roma, June 1977); Stephan Koja and Christoph Tinzl, *Werk und Widerstand: Rudolph Charles von Ripper*. Exhibition Catalogue. (Der Salzburger Nachlass, 1989); *Rudolph von Ripper*: Memorial Exhibition, Sachsenhausen Concentration Camp, Germany; Archduke Louis Salvador, *Die Balearen* (Leipzig, 1869–1884); Juan March Cencillo, *El Archiduque* (Olañeta, Palma de Mallorca, 1991); Joseph Roth, *The Radetzky March* (Penguin, 2000); Stefan Zweig, *Fantastic Night and Other Stories* (Pushkin Press, 2004); Rotary Club Pollença, 25 *Artistes a Pollença 1900–1950* (Ajuntament de Pollença, 2006); *Time* magazine editorial and cover, 2 January 1939; *Interview with Robert Carlen, June 28 – July 16, 1985* (Oral History Archives of American Art, Smithsonian Institute); Ed. Micki McGee, *Yaddo: Making American Culture* (Columbia University Press, 2008); *A Century at Yaddo*, (Corporation of Yaddo, 2000); *Rudolph von Ripper*, Yaddo Podcast; The Yaddo Archive, New York Public Library; Archive of the Corporation of Yaddo, Saratoga Springs NY; Robert Hughes, *The Shock of the New* (Thames & Hudson,

1991); Ian Gibson, *The Shameful Life of Salvador Dalí* (Faber, 1997); Carlos Baker, *Ernest Hemingway: A Life Story* (Penguin, 1972); Christian W. Thomsen, *Leopoldskron* (Verlag Vorlander, 1983); *War Artist Rudolph von Ripper 1942-4* (American Military History Museum, Washington D.C.); Rudolph von Ripper, *Introduction to an Exhibition of his Work as a War Artist* (American Military History Museum); Charles Ryder, *Preface to Portfolio of Rudolph von Ripper's Work as a War Artist* (American Military History Museum); Maxie Parks, *A Royal Pain in the Axis.* Lecture delivered at the US Army's 34th Division's 109th Reunion (American Military History Museum); Fritz Molden, *Exploding Star* (William Morrow & Co. Inc., 1979); C.L. Sulzberger, *A Long Row of Candles* (The Macmillan Company, 1969); David Nichols, *Ernie's War: The Best of Ernie Pyle's World War II Dispatches* (Pocket Books, 1987); Alfred McCoy, *The Politics of Heroin: CIA Complicity In The Global Drug Trade* (Harper & Row, 1972); *Soldier with an Easel,* article by Kenneth T. Downs (*Collier's* magazine, 2 November 1946); Dietmar Horst, *Dei Tänzer auf den Wellen* (Berenkamp-Verlag, Berlin 2010); Patricia Corbett, *Verdura: The Life and Work of a Master Jeweler* (Thames & Hudson, 2002); Alan Balfour, *Berlin: The Politics of Order* (Rizzoli, 1990); Anna Funder, *All That I Am* (Penguin, 2011); Evelyn Juers, *House of Exile* (Allen Lane, 2008); Simon Mawer, *The Glass Room* (Little, Brown Publishing, 2009).

1948–1960

The Blue File, Rudolf Charles von Ripper Archive, Private Collection Stephan Koja, Vienna. Gerhard Habarta, *Kunst in Wien nach '45* (Verlag der Apfel, Vienna 1996); Frances Stonor Saunders, *The CIA and the World of Arts and Letters* (The New Press, 2000); Tim Weiner, *Legacy of Ashes: The History of the CIA* (Penguin Books, 2008); Peter Coleman,

The Liberal Conspiracy: The Congress for Cultural Freedom and the Struggle for the Mind of Postwar Europe (The Free Press, 1989); *What was the Congress for Cultural Freedom?* Article by Hilton Kramer, The New Criterion Volume 8, January 1990; Frank Tichy, *Friedrich Torberg: Ein Leben in Widerspruchen* (O. Muller, 1995); David Wise and Thomas Ross, *The Invisible Government: The CIA and US Intelligence* (Vintage Books, 1974); UNHCR News Stories, *Fiftieth Anniversary of the Hungarian Uprising and Refugee Crisis*, 23 October 2006; William Graves, *Wild Olives: Life in Majorca with Robert Graves* (Pimlico, 2001); Juan Pujol García and Nigel West, *Operation Garbo* (Biteback Publishing, 2011); Margalida Cànaves Campomar, *Von Ripper, Un Agent de La CIA a Pollença* (Punts i Informatiu, Pollença, 2010); Gaspar Sabater, *La Pintura Contemporanea en Mallorca Temo I* (Ediciones Cort Mallorca, 1972); Gaspar Sabater, *Robert Graves de Wimbledon a Deyà* (Conselleria d'Educació i Cultural Mallorca, 1986); Mary Stuart Boyd, *The Fortunate Isles* (Methuen Press, London 1911); Gordon West, *Jogging Round Mallorca* (Black Swan, London 1998); Gaston Vuillier, *The Forgotten Isles* (Hutchinson, London 1896); Charles W. Wood, *Letters from Majorca* (Richard Bentley & Son, London, 1885); Barry Byrne and Pablo Espinoza Gannon, article *Going by the Book* in Contemporary Baleares, July 2007.

Other influences include:
Dante Alighieri, *The Divine Comedy*: 3 Vols. (Penguin Classics, 1974); John Lowney, *History, Memory and the Literary Left: Modern American Poets 1935–1968* (University of Iowa Press, 2006); *The Third Man*, film directed by Carol Reed. Criterion Collection; Graham Greene, *The Quiet American* (Heinemann, London 1955); W.G. Sebald, The Emigrants (Vintage Press, London 2002); W.G. Sebald, *The Rings of Saturn* (Vintage Press, 2002); *Majorca's WWII Spy*. Majorca

Daily Bulletin: April 22 and 25, 2010; *La CIA Destrozó a Mi Madre*. Interview with Diego Gary, Diario de Mallorca, April 2010; Norman Lebrecht, *In Search of Gustav Mahler*. BBC Radio 3 Sunday Feature, 18 July 2010; Rainer Maria Rilke, *Sonnets to Orpheus*, Ed. Stephen Mitchell (Pan Books, 1987); Carson McCullers, *The Heart is a Lonely Hunter* (Houghton Mifflin Harcourt, 1984); Carson McCullers, *Illumination and Night Glare* (Wisconsin Studies, 2002).

Epigrams appearing in Chapters Two, Four, Five, Nine and Fifteen derive from these sources:

Arthur Rimbaud, 'Introduction' to *A Season in Hell*
Rainer Maria Rilke, *Sonnets to Orpheus*
Gustav Mahler, *Kindertotenlieder, No. 5*
Carson McCullers, *The Heart is a Lonely Hunter*
Poem by Friedrich Rückert set by Gustav Mahler in *Rückert-Lieder*

ILLUSTRATIONS

The illustrations in this book are reproduced thanks to the generosity of the copyright holder, Dr Stephan Koja, with the following exceptions: 'Yaddo Artists 1939' © Yaddo Archive, USA; 'Rudolph von Ripper War Art 1943–4' © American Military History Museum, Washington D.C. The illustrations in the section 'Paradiso 1952–1960' are from the blue file.

Author's Note

B aron Von Ripper spelled his Christian name as Rudolf before he became an American citizen in 1942 when he anglicised it to Rudolph, and I have adhered to this in the book. The *Time* editorial and several other American sources chose to use 'Rudolph' before he anglicised his name.

The author delivered the blue file to Rudolph von Ripper's great-nephew, Stephan Koja, at a book launch in Mallorca in November 2016. Dr Koja has placed it in the Rudolph von Ripper Archive, Vienna, which he maintains.

ACKNOWLEDGEMENTS

For their generous contributions to various aspects of this book, I offer my gratitude to my agent Andrew Lownie, and to Larissa Boehening, Suzanne Bradbury, Cummins Catherwood Jr., Eddy Coodee, Barbara Despard, Francoise Ducroz, William Graves, Laura Kincaid, Stephan Koja, Patrick Meadows, Winfried Meyer, the late Doña Altimira Pino de Monserrat, Maria Paijkull, Nicki Rose, Francisca Martí Rotger, Hildburg Schlenzka, Peter Seiche, Janet Siegl, Max and Ursula Über, Peter Walti and John Wragg. Geoff MacEwan was my stalwart companion for most of the journey, as were my family – Ariane Burgess gave me hospitality and photographic assistance in New York, Julita Mazurek Burgess her unwavering support and Steve Burgess the gift of a talisman when the going got tough.

To the late Gavin Wallace of the Scottish Arts Council (now Creative Scotland), that beloved champion of authors he believed in, posthumous gratitude for backing this book with a travel and research grant. Thanks also to the Fundacío Bartomeu March Library, Palma de Mallorca, Yaddo Artists' Retreat, USA, New York Public Library, and the American Military History Museum, Washington D.C. for making their collections available to me and additional gratitude to Yaddo for hosting me during the summer of 2010.